Psi, Spirits,

AND OTHER PARANORMAL PHENOMENA

Scott Quimby

4880 Lower Valley Road • Atglen, PA 19310

Library of Congress Control Number: 2025930100

Edited by Ian Robertson
Designed by Alexa Harris
Cover design by Alexa Harris
Type set in Fino Sans/Minion Pro

ISBN: 978-0-7643-6992-6
ePub: 978-1-5073-0601-7
Printed in India

10 9 8 7 6 5 4 3 2 1

Published by Schiffer Publishing, Ltd.
4880 Lower Valley Road
Atglen, PA 19310
Phone: (610) 593-1777; Fax: (610) 593-2002
Email: info@schifferbooks.com
Web: www.schifferbooks.com

For Sally

THANKS SO MUCH FOR ALL OF YOUR LOVE,
SUPPORT, AND ASSISTANCE.

CONTENTS

INTRODUCTION

In many respects, the world today, with its amazing abundance of riches delivered by science and technology, can be seen as the realization of hopes originating 300 years ago with the Age of Enlightenment, an intellectual movement whose goal was to establish human reason as the highest standard of knowledge as opposed to divine revelation of the Christian church. A wide range of human phenomena came under study with the intent to achieve a kind of science of man.

In many ways the promise of the Age of Enlightenment has been met and exceeded. We are much healthier, safer, live longer, and have more amenities and a vastly expanded world to enjoy and marvel at than people 300 years ago. The same can also be said in comparison with people living just 100 years ago.

Yet if Enlightenment thinkers were to visit our world today, they might be disappointed as well as amazed. Along with our successes, major problems and unanswered questions are readily apparent. We continue to hate and kill one another in the name of religion that purports to be all about loving one's fellow man. We have been polluting our planet and rapidly exhausting its resources, and we have not eliminated prejudice, racism, or poverty.

Our difficulty in coming to grips with these problems doesn't lie in some inherent flaw in science itself, but in limitations of vision among most scientists. Science, as defined by its practitioners, involves the study of the natural world, those material phenomena and processes we experience through our senses and their extension through instruments. Science tells us that this physical material realm works on the basis of certain natural laws that are pretty well established, but can be modified by compelling new discoveries and theorizing.

Because of its enormous success in making our world understood, science has increasingly tended to view its scope of concern as being synonymous with reality itself. Not only is it the natural world that science studies, but the real world as well. We readily accept this. When a question comes up about the reality of some new experience or phenomenon we consult science to tell us whether it is real or not. Although they are much too small to be seen with the most powerful microscopes, quarks and other subatomic particles are real because science says so.

There is another rich realm of potential experience outside the natural world that is enjoyed by scientists and nonscientists alike: that of the imagination or fantasy. Phenomena in this realm were at some point created in our minds, either deliberately made up, or resulting from some nonreality-based mental activity, such as dreaming or hallucinating. Careful objective analysis should enable us to tell the difference between the real and the imaginary, but sometimes we are fooled.

For the most part the phenomena that we will be discussing do not conform to the operations and rules that science has determined characterize the natural world. But they also do not seem to fit comfortably into the fantasy realm either. So we have a kind of neither world of phenomena, neither real nor imaginary, that we characterize by such terms as paranormal and supernatural.

The predominant theme in the discussion to follow is that these nonmaterial phenomena comprise a major aspect of reality itself. They are not just fascinating or thought provoking, or in some cases inspiring, but may well offer clues pointing to a greatly expanded view of ourselves and our possibilities. The basic difficulty is that those in positions of authority do not fully accept these possibilities, if in fact they are aware of them at all.

SECTION I

PSI (PSYCHIC PHENOMENA)

We are fascinated by stories of unusual things that we think of as supernatural or paranormal: ghosts, hauntings, contact with deceased loved ones, direct awareness of people's thoughts, glimpses of the future, and the like. Many of us who view ourselves as normal, thoughtful individuals have had unusual experiences of this kind that we can't explain. We like mysteries, but even more, we like to solve them. This is what science is all about. Television and the movies feature ghost hunters and paranormal investigators who study these things. Yet the impression we receive is that this is entertainment, science fiction, or not real science. College textbooks, even those in psychology, often don't mention any serious study of paranormal phenomena or, if they do, suggest that there have been such studies but they were seriously flawed. Even those accounts that do accept that some credible evidence has been generated maintain that, viewed in the most positive light, it is inconclusive.

The term commonly used for the serious study of paranormal or psychic phenomena (psi) is parapsychology. Parapsychology is the scientific, usually laboratory based, study of four types of psi, or psychic phenomena: telepathy, clairvoyance, precognition (collectively known as extrasensory perception or ESP), and psychokinesis (mind over matter). There is an older, broader term, psychical research, first used by early investigators who, while interested in ESP and psychokinesis (PK), were primarily interested in phenomena related to the possibility of surviving physical death, suggested by such things as communication from deceased individuals through mediums, hauntings, apparitions (ghosts), and poltergeists. The term "psychical research" is a better term for these phenomena than "parapsychology," which seems misleading and derogatory. *Para* implies *apart*, that the phenomena studied are not part of nature. Biologists wouldn't refer to their specialty as parabiology or a doctor's paramedicine.

Perhaps the most prominent feature of psi is that it doesn't operate within the framework that science has established for the way the world is supposed to work. Even the very unusual things that occur in the quantum realm of physics aren't as strange in many respects as some of the phenomena we'll encounter in the psychic arena. In our discussion we're not only going to look at psi as typically described, but also at closely related phenomena, such as spirits and visions. We will maintain a scholarly and objective stance considering various perspectives.

Belief in unusual events and phenomena that don't fit the way we expect the everyday world to work has been around as long as we as people have been able to report their experiences. Although science, over the last 400 years, has very carefully examined almost every conceivable aspect of what we think of as the natural world and has concluded these unusual phenomena do not exist as part of reality, large numbers of people continue to believe that they do. A 2005 Gallop poll found about three in four Americans profess at least one paranormal belief. The finding that degree of education doesn't separate nonbelievers from believers may surprise those who see the latter as naïve and gullible (Gallup, 2005). A 2018 survey by Chapman University found that 58% of people believe places can be haunted by spirits, 26% that some people can move objects with their minds, and 17% that psychics can foresee the future (Paranormal America 2018).

CHAPTER 1

PSYCHICAL RESEARCH

Investigations of paranormal phenomena are associated with parapsychology—basically a laboratory-based science. But before this work was moved into the laboratory with strict scientific protocols, earlier field investigations were carried out in what was known as psychical research.

One of the first references to psychical research in English can be found in writings of Sir Francis Bacon, one of the seminal figures in the development of modern science. In his 1627 writings Bacon proposed that "force of imagination" [mental intention] could be studied on such things as the motions of shuffling of cards or casting of dice. Bacon also suggested studies of the "binding of thoughts," [telepathy] and suggested that the use of tasks involving meaningful targets might be more effective than tasks involving simple playing cards. Not only were Bacon's ideas 300 years ahead of their time, but they indicated that testing psi was among the very first suggested uses of his new method of science (Radin, 2009).

Psychical research began as a formal field of investigation at the same time as psychology—the study of the mind—first emerging as a separate discipline in science some 130 years ago. From the outset, the early pioneers were faced by very strong criticism from those in the established sciences. This criticism was and remains rooted in the conviction that its subject matter, psychic phenomena or psi, are not real. Defining what is real is truly a thorny philosophical problem that we might easily get bogged down in, but some attempt at clarification will be helpful. Psychic phenomena belong to a broad class of nonmaterial events and experiences that also involves what are loosely referred to as spirit or spiritual. Although both are experienced by a large number of people, finding objective scientific evidence for them in the material world is difficult.

For the early pioneers in psychical research the most obvious examples of supernatural phenomena, particularly involving the possibility that the soul continues on after the death of the body, were those involving the activities of mediums and the religious movement known as Spiritualism.

MEDIUMS AND THE FOX SISTERS

Accounts of mediums facilitated communication with the deceased performed while in a trance can be found in many ancient cultures in Korea, Siberia, South America, England, China, and Japan, as well as among the ancient Egyptians and Greeks. While Plato warned against necromancy, the art of predicting the future by consulting with the dead, Pythagoras is said to have used a version of the Ouija board in séances to gain information from the spirit world. To put themselves in a state of consciousness receptive to spirit contact mediums used a variety of potions, herbs, hallucinogenic drugs, rituals, prayers, and mental and physical exercises.

With the rise of monotheism in the West contact with the spirit world popular in polytheistic cultures became discouraged, particularly if it contributed to unorthodox ideas about the afterlife. As a Christian, attempting to contact the spirits of deceased family and friends could be dangerous. If caught doing so one could be accused of communicating with the devil or evil spirits and the penalty could be death (Schmicker, 2000). However, mediumship survived, and following the Enlightenment gained a more favorable reputation, at least in some circles. There were accounts of contact with the recently deceased, as well as "elevated beings" in the illuminist movements of the eighteenth century.

Mediumship became popular in the nineteenth century with the activities of the young Fox sisters in Hydesville, New York. In 1948, Maggie and Kate told a neighbor that every night around bedtime they heard a series of raps on the walls and furniture that seemed to manifest some kind of strange otherworldly intelligence. The neighbor was skeptical and came to see for herself. While they huddled together on their bed their mother began a demonstration.

"Count five," she commanded, and five heavy thuds were heard. "Count fifteen," she commanded, and the mysterious presence obeyed. She then asked it to tell the neighbor's age, and thirty-three distinct raps followed. She followed this by asking that if it was an injured spirit to rap three times, and it did.

The Fox family deserted the house and sent Maggie and Kate to live with their older sister, Leah Fox Fish, in Rochester, New York. Community leaders Isaac and Amy Post invited the girls to a gathering at their home to see if they could communicate with spirits in another location. Isaac Post wrote that he was convinced something real happened and that there were very distinct thumps under the floor that were in response to several questions. He also became convinced that Leah Fox was a medium when she communicated with the Posts' recently deceased daughter. They rented a largest hall in Rochester and 400 people came to hear the mysterious noises. Following this, Amy Post accompanied the sisters to a private room, where they disrobed and were examined by a committee of skeptics, who found no evidence of a hoax.

By November 1849 the sisters were both giving public performances of their skills. The ability to communicate with spirits soon attracted the attention of others, who began reporting that they too were able to communicate with the deceased. Although mediums were best known for having the ability to facilitate communication between the spirits of deceased family and friends and those desiring to communicate with them, they also received information about the spirit world related to a broad array of metaphysical issues that became the basis of the highly publicized movements of Spiritualism in the United States, England, and several other countries.

As the fame of the Fox sisters spread the intense publicity around them was not without controversy. They were routinely attacked by skeptics who claimed they produced their phenomena in a number of ways, ranging from toe and ankle cracking, to ventriloquism, to assorted mechanical devices. Despite this, no faking was ever discovered. A number of committees were created to test the powers of the sisters. Despite the hostility they showed to the sisters, most were forced to admit that they were able to detect no fraud.

In the years to follow fame took its toll on the sisters. Maggie abandoned mediumship for a love affair with a famed arctic explorer who tragically died. She was left broken-hearted and almost penniless and had to take up mediumship again. She began drinking, and her health and mental state began to decline.

By 1885 interest in Spiritualism had declined and investigations of fraud began to increase. Maggie was called before a commission in New York to prove her skills, a test that she failed miserably. Three years later she booked the stage at the New York Academy of Music and announced that she and Kate had created the strange rappings heard in their Hydesville home by simply cracking their toes. Kate, who was present, appeared to silently agree. The critics were quick to say, "I told you so," while devoted Spiritualists denounced Margaret's confession as the ravings of a tired and sad drunk.

Kate also had begun drinking heavily, which often wreaked havoc on her performances. While she did not speak at the public appearance, she later stated that she did not agree with her sister and continued to perform as a medium.

In 1891 Margaret recanted her confession. Many said that the confession was a sham itself and that Maggie and Kate only renounced the movement to spite their sister Leah, whom they had grown to hate. Kate later drank herself to death in 1892 at age 56. Margaret died in March 1893, at age 59. At the time of her death she was penniless (*The Fox Sisters and the Rap on Spiritualism*).

Popular mediumistic communication typically occurred in a group séance. A small group of interested people, at least one of whom was hoping for a message from a deceased loved one, would gather in a darkened room, usually in the medium's house. The medium might or might not put themselves in a trance. They would then announce that they were in contact with the deceased, or perhaps a go-between spirit called a control. Often the prospective recipient of the communication asked for and was given some kind of sign from the deceased, proving that they were actually who they said they were. In addition to the spirit communication other phenomena often appeared, including the tilting of the table around which the attendees sat, odd noises, cold drafts, and sometimes the materialization of the deceased in the gloomy darkness.

Mediumship became a profitable venture as interest and demand skyrocketed. Mediums competed in being able to deliver convincing performances, sometimes incorporating elaborate and startling phenomena into their séances. Given the completely dark settings of the séances trickery could fairly easily be introduced. A number of mediums were exposed for such things as employing accomplices to produce paranormal- appearing phenomena and surreptitiously gathering information about prospective attendees that could be later relayed in a séance to appear as genuine information from the deceased. Nevertheless, a great deal of communication occurred that seemed clearly genuine to the attendees (*Best Evidence*, Michael Schmicker, pp. 206–209).

In the early days mediums followed the practice of the Fox sisters, traveling to different venues where they conducted their spirit communications on stage. Many of the spiritualists were itinerant lecturers and mediums who went from town to town, giving lectures on spirit and giving communications from spirits to people attending through séances. Gradually, as the movement developed into a religion, a set protocol outlining a standard practice for mediums began to be used. Gatherings involved message services, where a speaker gave a lecture resembling a sermon and readings provided by several mediums who related spirit messages to those attending. Spiritualist camps sprang up where mediums gave readings to the attendees.

Over time these camps developed training to (a) prepare aspiring mediums with procedures for testing their ability under controlled conditions and to (b) ordain those who were successful as spiritualist ministers. Today vibrant spiritualist camps continue to exist, as well as spiritualist churches in various pockets in the US. In 2004 there were an estimated 163,710 spiritualists in the US. As time went by associations were formed with a list of principles, ministers, churches, and camps that emphasized credentials and certification of mediums based on procedures that required them to prove that their mediumship was authentic through testing and evidential demonstrations (*Talking to the Other Side: A History of Modern Spiritualism and Mediumship*, xxii).

Membership in the spiritualist religion has not remained anywhere near as high as in its heyday in the early decades of the century. Bad press resulting from the exposure of fraudulent mediums, the increasing power of materialist science calling into question the reality of life after death, and the rising popularity of a psychological interpretation of spirit communication all contributed to its decline (Leonard, 2005).

SPIRITUALISM

Spiritualism attracted several well-known supporters, perhaps the most famous being Sir Arthur Conan Doyal, author of the Sherlock Holmes mystery stories, who worked diligently to prove its validity. He collected all of the material available, lectured on Spiritualism, participated in spiritualist-related organizations, and wrote a very detailed two-volume book, the *History of Spiritualism*.

Spiritualism teaches that the existence and personal identity of the individual continues after the change we call death. "Life here and life hereafter is all one life whose continuity of consciousness is unbroken by that mere change in form whose process we call death" (Leonard, 2005 p. 87). The ongoing unfolding of a person's mental, moral, and spiritual potentials continue on while in spirit. The difference between Spiritualism and traditional religions is that it emphasizes the belief that the dead survive their physical death as spirit entities that are able to communicate with us on the Earth plane through mediums who can make contact with and relate messages from them. Contact with the deceased through mediums and living on the basis of underlying universal spirit teachings received constitutes the heart of Spiritualism. Spiritualist beliefs are based in nine principles outlined by the National Spiritualist Association of Churches:

> We believe in Infinite Intelligence.
>
> We believe that the phenomena of nature, both physical and spiritual, are the expression of Infinite Intelligence.
>
> We affirm that a correct understanding of such expression and living in accordance there with constitute true religion.
>
> We affirm that the existence and personal identity of the individual continue after the change called death
>
> We affirm that communication with the so-called dead is a fact, scientifically proven by the phenomena of Spiritualism.
>
> We believe that the highest morality is contained in the Golden Rule: *Whatsoever ye would that others should do unto you, do ye also unto them.*

We affirm the moral responsibility of individuals, and that we make our own happiness or unhappiness as we obey or disobey Nature's physical and spiritual laws.

We affirm that the doorway to reformation is never closed against any human soul here or hereafter.

We affirm that the Precepts of Prophecy and Healing contained in all the sacred texts are divine attributes proven through mediumship (Leonard, 2004).

SPIRITISM

A second religious movement based on mediumship, known as Spiritism, owes its birth and popularity largely to the work of Allan Kardec, the pen name of French educator, translator, and author Hippolyte Léon Denizard Rivail (October 1804–1869). He was raised as a Roman Catholic, earned a bachelor of arts degree in science and a doctorate in medicine, and was fluent in German, English, Italian, and Spanish, in addition to his native French. During much of his life Rivail pursued interests in education, philosophy, and the sciences.

In his early fifties he became intrigued by reports of strange phenomena occurring during séances, a popular form of entertainment at the time in Europe. Believing that, if genuine, this could be of vast importance to science and religion, he began a careful investigation of psychic phenomena, mainly mediumship.

Rivail had a friend with two daughters who were mediums and engaged in this activity. He was impressed with the communications that they claimed came from spirit communicators and began to attend regular sittings or séances with them. Before accepting a spiritual or paranormal cause, Rivail believed it would be necessary first to discover if ordinary material causes could explain these communications, such as fraud, hallucination, or unconscious mental activity. One thing that impressed him was that although the lively girls were fond of society and dancing, and when "sitting" by themselves or with their friends typically received communications that were in keeping with their worldly disposition, when Rivail was present the messages transmitted through the girls became very grave and serious. He immediately observed that the young mediums were incapable of inventing or appreciating the profundity of the material that was coming through them, a fact that strongly ruled out naturalistic explanations for the phenomena. Upon inquiring of the invisible intelligences communicating through them as to why this change occurred, he was told that spirits of a much higher order came expressly for him and that they would continue to do so to enable him to fulfill an important religious mission.

Rivail proceeded to investigate the truthfulness of these spirits' assertion that they were a higher form of intelligence by formulating a series of questions in relation to the various problems of human life and the universe in general and submitting them to his unseen spirits. Answers were given through the two young mediums, who agreed to devote a couple evenings every week for this purpose.

Kardec went on to develop more than 1,000 questions concerning the nature and mechanisms of spirit communications, the reasons for human life on earth, and aspects of the spiritual realm. In addition to the two girls he'd begun his investigations with, he posed those questions to ten other mediums, all of whom were purportedly not known to each other. In addition to orally communicating messages received from the spirits, some mediums also employed what has come to be known as automatic writing. This involved holding a pencil but not focusing any awareness on it and simply allowing it to write, almost of its own accord. Sometimes this occurred with an almost feverish rapidity. Kardec documented all of the responses received. He became convinced that the mediums:

Provided accurate information unknown to themselves or others present (e.g., personal information about deceased individuals);

Demonstrated unlearned skills, such as writing by illiterate mediums, handwriting similar to the alleged communicating personality, and speaking or writing in a language unknown to the medium (xenoglossy and xenography);

Accurately portrayed a range of personality characteristics of deceased individuals. (Kardec, Wikipedia)

After nearly two years of his conversations with spirits (always through mediums) he remarked to his wife:

> It is a most curious thing! My conversations with the invisible intelligences have completely revolutionised my ideas and convictions. The instructions thus transmitted constitute an entirely new theory of human life, duty, and destiny, that appears to me to be perfectly rational and coherent, admirably lucid and consoling, and intensely interesting. I have a great mind to publish these conversations in a book; for it seems to me that what interests me so deeply might very likely prove interesting to others (Kardec, 2015, pp. Kindle Locations 276–281).

He submitted this idea to his unseen communicators, who said that they had suggested it to his mind and that their communications were for the express purpose of giving this material to the world. Furthermore they said:

> To the book in which you will embody our instructions ... you will give, as being our work rather than yours, the title of *Le Livre des Esprits* (*The Spirits' Book*); and you will publish it, not under your own name, but under the pseudonym of Allan Kardec. Keep your own name of Rivail for your own books already published; but take and keep the name we have now given you for the book you are about to publish by our order, and, in general, for all the work that you will have to do in the fulfillment of the mission which, as we have already told you, has been confided to you by Providence, and which will gradually open before you as you proceed in it under our guidance (Kardec, 2015, pp. Kindle Locations 287–294).

The book, when published, sold widely all over Europe. Kardec (Rivail) founded the Parisian Society of Psychologic Studies for the purpose of obtaining more material from spirits to elucidate the truth of the teaching. Similar associations were speedily formed all over the world, which transmitted the most remarkable of the spirit communications received by them to the Parisian Society. Kardec thus acquired an enormous amount of spirit teaching from all over the world which he studied, collated, and coordinated to form an enlarged "Revised Edition" of the *The Spirits' Book*, again under the direction of the spirits by whom it was originally dictated. Kardec also drew on this same material to compile four other works, *The Mediums' Book*, *The Gospel as Explained by Spirits*, *Heaven and Hell*, and *Genesis* (Kardec 2015).

Kardec called the teaching he received Spiritism, rather than Spiritualism, to distinguish its specific emphasis. A Spiritualist, he maintained, could be said to characterize anyone who believes that there is something more than matter in the world and themselves. They may not believe in the existence of spirits or their communication with the visible world.

We say, then, that the fundamental principle of the spiritist theory, or Spiritism, is the relation of the material world with spirits, or the beings of the invisible world, and we designate the adherents of the spirit theory as spiritists (pp. Kindle Locations 401–407).

An even more fundamental difference between Spiritism and Spiritualism is that the former teaches reincarnation or rebirth into human life after death, whereas the latter does not necessarily do so. Spiritism maintains that humans are essentially immortal spirits that temporarily inhabit physical bodies for many incarnations to attain moral and intellectual improvement. It also claims that spirits through mediumship may have beneficial or detrimental influence on the physical world.

Spiritism never gained the degree of popularity in the US and Britain as Spiritualism, but it spread rapidly in Europe and South America, among other areas. Today thirty-five countries are represented in the International Spiritist Council. It has influenced a social movement with healing centers, charity institutions, and hospitals, involving millions of people in dozens of countries, with the greatest number of followers in Brazil ("Spiritism," Wikipedia).

WALLACE AND CROOKES

One of the earliest psychical researchers was Alfred Russell Wallace, the co-developer with Darwin of the theory of evolution by natural selection. While for Wallace Christianity's approach to understanding the world was antiquated and unconvincing, it did seem to him that there was some kind of spiritual or moral force at work which has to do with that something we call the human soul. While his and Darwin's theory of natural selection could explain things of the physical world, perhaps the soul, guided by this spiritual force, develops along other lines. Whatever this as yet undiscovered spiritual power might be, Wallace became convinced that science had the responsibility to investigate it. Any evidence supporting this possibility could only be found by investigating the realms of the supernatural.

To investigate this possibility of spirit contact Wallace began attending séances with London mediums. What he soon discovered was nothing that approached the level of scientific proof, but was strange enough to suggest that something was going on. A sitting with Daniel Douglas Home was particularly impressive, leaving Wallace with what he described as a " solid basis of fact." "Surely," he said, "other intelligent men must be troubled, as he was, by mysteries that science ignored because it could not explain."

Darwin was furious, and warned Wallace that by giving unwarranted credibility to the belief in Spirit powers he appeared to be strengthening the position of those who opposed evolution. In this Darwin was wrong. Wallace, throughout his long life, promoted and worked to refine the theory of evolution while at the same time strongly and tirelessly supporting psi research (Blum, 2007).

One of the more acclaimed scientists who Wallace convinced to at least look into the phenomenon of mediumship of D. D. Home was William Crookes. Crookes was a gifted chemist who had recently discovered a new element that he named thallium. He initially wasn't overly impressed with Wallace's arguments and thought that, by scrutinizing a few so-called mediums, he could straighten out the misguided naturalist.

What resulted was far different. One of the first mediums he investigated conducted her séances with the aid of a planchette, a heart-shaped piece of wood mounted on small wheels that held a pencil pointing down. She shut her eyes and put her hand on the planchette while supposedly allowing the energy of the unseen Spirits to flow through her fingers. The pencil then scrawled what appeared to be written messages on paper beneath.

Crookes was, as he told it, prepared to be entertained. He asked if the invisible Spirit could see everything in the room, including things the psychic could not, whereupon the planchette wrote "yes." Noticing a newspaper lying on a table he asked if the Spirit could read it. Again the response was "yes." Standing with his back to the newspaper, he reached behind him, put his finger over a word, and asked what it was. The planchette spelled out "however." He turned around and discovered that this was accurate.

Armed with this new found interest, Crookes contacted D. D. Home, who was by far the best known medium of his day and who had produced a number of phenomena that astounded and mystified his audiences. Although Home had been strongly criticized by some for faking his achievements this had never been proven. With the urging of Wallace, Home consented to allow Crookes to conduct tests of his apparent psychic ability in Crookes's own laboratory.

For these tests Crookes designed sophisticated devices and procedures to rule out possible cheating. In some tests Home was given the task of attempting to move various objects with the apparent psychic force of his mind alone. To further ensure that he would not be able to manipulate them in some way his hands and feet were held. Home succeeded in these tests, prompting Crookes to conclude that some as yet unexplained psychic force existed and that among those people who could manifest it, Home was the most remarkable.

Crookes anticipated that his scientific colleagues might not fully accept his conclusions and might well criticize his test equipment, call for replication of his tests, or suggest better tests. But the response he received was more of an attack on his character, which made it clear that they believed investigating supernatural phenomena was off limits to scientists unless they could produce findings that proved that fraud was involved (Blum, 2007). Like Wallace, Crookes was not to be deterred and went on to conduct important work in psi research and to champion its cause.

BRITISH SOCIETY FOR PSYCHICAL RESEARCH

Three people, less well known today, made particularly important contributions to developing the science of psi research: Henry Sidgwick, Frederic Myers, and Edmund Gurney. Together, in 1882, the three friends founded the British Society for Psychical Research. Sidgwick was a respected member of the classics faculty at Trinity College, Cambridge, who in the following decade published a book, *Methods of Ethics*, which was hailed as a major work of moral philosophy in the tradition of John Stuart Mill and Immanuel Kant.

Sidgwick's cousin, Edward White Benson, later archbishop of Canterbury, first stimulated his interest in the paranormal and encouraged him to visit some local mediums and psychics. Characteristically, Sidgwick took a tough-minded approach and easily detected the use of mechanical devices and sleight of hand. He wrote to his sister, "I gained nothing but experience in the lower forms of human nature." However, he was intrigued by the idea that it might be possible to prove there is some kind of power beyond what is recognized in science and he persisted in his investigations, glimpsing on occasion a glimmering spark of something unexpected (Blum, 2007).

Frederic Myers was one of Sidgwick's students who struggled to hang on to some religious faith in light of what he saw as the lessons of history and science. However, it was not these issues that initially brought the two together, but rather a shared interest in the cause of women's education. Most of English society at the time, including the Anglican Church, as well as Queen Victoria herself, believed that God intended women to be subservient to men. Like most universities Cambridge barred women from obtaining degrees. Sidgwick took the unpopular position of arguing that women should be allowed the "immense educational influence" of training for a profession that he called a matter of "simple justice." Meyers surprised him by immediately supporting that view. As the two began discussing their ideas the conversations turned to Sedgwick's other unpopular cause: the investigation of supposed Spirit communication. Meyers was fascinated by Sedgwick's accounts of what occurred in séances, with their faint glimpses into what might be a realm beyond death. For Meyers those early investigations signaled the possibility of a larger quest still, "an endeavor to learn the actual truth as to the destiny of man" (Blum, 2007).

Edmund Gurney, the third of the founders of the psi research movement, met Sidgwick and Myers while studying law and philosophy at Cambridge, and they bonded around a shared love of philosophical arguments and poetry. Initially Gurney was resistant to involving himself in the paranormal interests of his two new friends, but Sidgwick kept sending him information, including Crookes's detailed accounts of his experiments with D. D. Home and a plea from Alfred Russel Wallace for his fellow scientists to investigate "those grand mysterious phenomena of the mind, the investigation of which can alone conduct us to a knowledge of what we really are" (Blum, 2007).

This struck a receptive chord. Gurney, two years earlier, had experienced the drowning death of three younger sisters. While as an educated person he could understand the arguments that we inhabit a purely indifferent and mechanical universe, such ideas seemed unbearable. If scientists could possibly be mistaken in their definitions of life as strictly limited by physical existence he wanted a chance to find out (Blum, 2007).

Early in 1875 the three conducted their first serious investigation involving claims that a pair of teenage mediums could outdo D. D. Home in terms of producing mystifying effects. Like many other mediums the girls followed a particular routine. They would retire to what was known as a cabinet—a curtained-off corner of the room—and recline on couches with their hands and feet tied. Those in attendance, the sitters, would gather outside the cabinet. The séance room would be darkened, with almost no illumination. These teenage mediums insisted on beginning each séance with singing that went on until something would apparently materialize from the cabinet. During one séance, after a long wait, gauze draped "Spirit children" drifted out of the cabinet and, approaching the handsome Gurney, kissed him with "materialized" lips.

The too obvious fact that the girl mediums were fakes didn't discourage Sidgwick. Once he told Meyers that he looked at Spirit phenomena much like he did religion, "I believe there is something in it; don't know what." He was determined to not let the "obvious humbug" prevent him from being open to the possibility that somewhere there might be something genuine. At the least the investigators had established, at least in their own minds, that they were capable of detecting fraud.

D. D. Home, who had been scrupulously investigated yet never detected doing anything shady, was bothered by the extent to which unscrupulous people were attempting to cash in on the huge popularity of mediumship. In his 1876 book *Lights and Shadows of Spiritualism* he took a strong stand against the practice of conducting séances in gloom so dark that the medium's activities could not be clearly seen and expose the conjuring tricks many used.

On February 20, 1882, the British Society for Psychical Research formally convened for the first time, named for a new science that would, as Meyers put it, "embrace a group of subjects that lie on or outside the boundaries of recognized science." The organization was necessary, Sidgwick said at this first meeting, because there were questions of humanity and immortality that demanded investigation. Conventional scientists had tried to block even the most modest of inquiries along those lines, an activity he called "a scandal to the enlightened age in which we live." William Crookes and Alfred Russel Wallace attended this first meeting along with physicist William Barrett, who had been investigating thought transference (mental telepathy).

Membership in the SPR (or ASPR) grew rapidly, and soon involved more than 200 people, including politicians, clergymen, painters, Spiritualists, and writers such as essayist and social critic John Ruskin, Alfred Lord Tennyson, and the American writer Samuel Clemens (Mark Twain).

The best known of all the early supporters of the newly established SPR was another American, William James. In fall 1882 James had come to London on a sabbatical from Harvard to focus on writing a new textbook in psychology. He had been teaching the newly developing field of psychology since 1875 and inventing the coursework along the way. Guerney, an acquaintance of James's brother, the author Henry, invited William to dine at a philosophers club with him. James enjoyed himself, and he and Guerney soon became friends (Blum, 2007).

Among Sidgwicks' most impressive abilities was talent for recruiting excellent people. Richard Hodgson, Australian born, a cheerful cynic, and another of his philosophy students, was one of the best. Sidgwick had a special project for him: to investigate Madame Blavatsky, founder of her own Theosophical Society and author of a 1877 book of her philosophy called *Isis Unveiled.* Although she had her headquarters in India, she spent a good deal of time in the US and Europe, spreading her philosophy. In summer 1884 Blavatsky attended a meeting of the SPR, where she charmed everyone.

Per her account she had once lived in Tibet, and claimed to have a mystical connection to what she described as godlike mahatmas of the Himalayas, who had the power to send their "astral bodies" anywhere in the universe while their physical bodies stayed where they were. According to her followers the mahatmas sometimes rose in a mist from her shoulders. Blavatsky could produce amazing physical effects, such as mentally causing shattered dishes to mend and materializing objects. Sealed letters bearing personal Spirit messages floated down from the ceiling of her apartment.

Hodgson's investigation was thorough. He interviewed witnesses to her séances, compared letters from the mahatmas with examples of her handwriting, and hired handwriting experts to analyze opened Spirit letters. He repeatedly and persistently asked to inspect her shrine and its miraculous cabinet. When permission was finally granted he searched until discovering that some of the drawers in its ornate walls were double-sided, opening into a chamber which turned out to be Madame Blavatsky's bedroom. When interviewed her servants confessed to passing letters through the panels into the drawers on the other side. No sooner had Hodgson left than the building mysteriously burned to the ground. His report to the SPR was straightforward and to the point:

> For our own part, we regard her as neither the mouthpiece of hidden seers nor as a mere vulgar adventuress; we think that she has achieved a title to permanent remembrance as one of the most accomplished and interesting imposters in history (Blum, 2007).

Hodgson's painstaking investigation and unmasking of Blavatsky was a clear refutation of those critics who persisted in claiming that the SPR was populated by gullible dupes.

WILLIAM JAMES

In 1885 William James and other less well-known individuals founded the American Society for Psychical Research (ASPR or SPR). To establish a reputation for credibility it was to use only trained researchers as investigators. As James put it, "Not that scientific men are necessarily better judges of all truth than others, but they tend to be better trained to gather evidence and thus be more believable as experts." ... "What we want is not only truth, but evidence" (Blum, 2007).

In July that same year James' one-year-old son Herman died of pneumonia. Although he had hoped that perhaps Henry might enjoy some "promise beyond life on earth," as he put it in a letter, James had no intention to consult a medium in hopes of gaining possible evidence of this. Yet in what he always considered a remarkable coincidence, this happened.

The medium that was to become involved was Lenora Piper, the 26-year-old wife of a middle-class Boston shopkeeper. From early childhood she had been able to tell people things about their lives that she couldn't have known. In fact, she even related family secrets that they didn't know themselves. Her family wanted nothing to do with this, fearing she might become a freak celebrated for psychic gifts like the notorious Fox sisters, and they raised her as an upright member of the Methodist Church.

In the years following her sixteenth birthday Lenora had been conscious of a dull ache across her midsection that grew stronger after the birth of her first child. Doctors could not diagnose the cause, so she ended up visiting a clairvoyant who claimed he contacted Spirits to aid in healing. When he touched her she grew dizzy and tumbled to the floor. Voices started ringing in her head. Responding to one she got up, went to a table, scribbled a note, and handed it to one of the men waiting to see the psychic. Upon reading the note the man, a Cambridge judge, announced that it was a remarkable message from his dead son.

Hearing of this, strangers started coming to the Pipers' home, asking Leonora to give them similar messages from the beyond. She only wanted to be a mother and respectable wife, not a medium. But she did wonder if this was a God-given gift and she was reluctant to turn the callers away. A friend talked her into doing a sitting with a Boston widow who turned out to be William James's mother-in-law, Eliza Gibbens. After attending the sitting and, in fact, conducting an investigation of her own, Mrs. Gibbens enthusiastically related to James that the names and facts Leonora Piper had provided about family members was incomprehensible without supernormal powers.

James considered himself something of an expert on psychic performances, as he and Reverend Minot Savage had been visiting the more notable Boston mediums for the ASP. What they had discovered through meticulous investigation was only examples of brazen fraud. Nevertheless, he remained intrigued by the possibility that there might be some kernel of truth somewhere and he decided to personally check out Mrs. Piper.

Accompanied by his wife Alice, James visited Mrs. Piper for a sitting. They did not give their names, and his mother-in-law on her earlier visit had not disclosed their identities. James had coached Alice to observe strict rules of psychic research by not providing any information about their family whatsoever; not asking or answering leading questions, but to merely listen politely.

After engaging in small talk Leonora fell into a trance, her voice deepened a bit, and she began repeating the names she had previously given Alice's mother. She then began fumbling for other names which seemed to come with difficulty. Alice's father's name of Gibbens she first pronounced as *Niblin*, then *Giblin*, before getting the right name, as if she couldn't initially pronounce the words or couldn't quite hear them right. She went on to add details to the names and then asked about a dead child. This wasn't too unusual, as many couples had lost children, but after saying it was a small boy she fumbled for a name, perhaps Herrin, before concluding that it sounded more like Herman. James, as he later wrote, became increasingly uneasy. Could she be making incredibly lucky guesses about the personal life of strangers and their relatives? Could it be, regardless of how scientifically impossible it seemed, that she was possessed of supernormal powers (Blum, 2007).

Concerned that he might be, in some unknown way, duped by the medium, James asked his partner, Reverend Savage, to also check her out. He visited Mrs. Piper anonymously, only telling her he'd heard about her séances and wanted to observe one. At the first sitting Mrs. Piper began talking about his father, who had died years before in Maine, saying that he called Savage by the name Judson, his middle name used by only his father and half-brother, also deceased. She then correctly named this half-brother, who had died in Michigan two years before and had never been in Boston, and described with painful accuracy in both words and pantomime the way he had died. It wasn't only the details Mrs. Piper was able to provide that was so unnerving, but also the way she talked and acted while in trance, as if these dead people were somehow there beside her.

Savage and James were still cautious. After all, trusting any medium was not to be done without eliminating all conceivable methods of deception. It might be that Mrs. Piper employed detectives, or in some other way came to learn about their extended family histories, as extremely unlikely as it seemed since she didn't know who either one was during the sittings.

Savage devised a procedure that even the best detective network would be hard pressed to beat. To eliminate any possibility that Mrs. Piper was in some way able to recognize the handwriting of the person writing for an appointment he had his daughter ask a friend to write a letter for an appointment for her—the daughter under an assumed name. He asked another friend to provide three locks of hair placed in various places in a book to keep them separate. His daughter didn't know where the locks had come from. This was to be a test for something psychic researchers called psychometry, the possibility that some people might be able to deduce from physical objects information about such things as who had handled them and under what circumstances. Savage's daughter saw this all as quite ridiculous and had little expectation that anything interesting would result.

Savage reported that after Mrs. Piper had gone into a trance these locks of hair were placed in her hand, one after another. She provided names of whom they belonged, the name of the friend who had asked her to bring them, and even asked why one person had cut the hair from the end, where it was lifeless, instead of nearer the head. His daughter, of course, did not know whether any of the names given or statements made were correct, but she made notes. It turned out that Mrs. Piper had been accurate in every particular.

In a formal report about this investigation for the ASP James and Savage acknowledged that they found Mrs. Piper inexplicable and urged the ASPR to invest serious time and money to investigate her. This, they wrote, was a rare opportunity to put "real" science to work, and they hoped it wouldn't be lost (Blum, 2007).

Meyers and Gurney were particularly interested in those apparently paranormal occurrences that happened in the lives of ordinary people—Spirits, hauntings, and unusual physical occurrences, as well as dreams and premonitions—and developed the idea that accounts of them could be treated as pieces of an elaborate jigsaw puzzle that needed to be assembled to provide an image of some kind of greater truth. The SPR ran newspaper ads soliciting personal stories of such encounters and soon collected a very large number of replies. Gurney spent hours each day going through them and replying to personal accounts. At one point he wrote some 1,600 letters in a two-month period, often asking the more promising for confirmation, such as witnesses and documents.

Gurney was particularly interested in accounts in which people reported experiencing a voice, or shape, or touch of someone close to the time that they later learned that individual had died. One such account involved an English merchant who, on October 6, 1867, was present in a crowded theater in Toronto. The man saw a figure in the pit below him whom he clearly recognized as his twin brother. The brother he thought was in China. When he rushed down to the pit no one resembling his brother was there. When he returned to England he learned that his brother had died in a hospital in Shanghai on October 6, 1867.

Another such account involved a woman whose young nephew rushed into her room, saying he had just seen his father walking around his bed. She told him he must be dreaming, that his father was in another country. The child wouldn't be comforted and refused to return to his own room. An hour or so later she saw her brother sitting in a chair by the fire. He called her name several times, then faded away. In the morning she told this to her mother, who advised her to make a note of it. She did so with the time and date 10 p.m., August 21, 1869. When the next mail arrived from China there was a letter informing her that her brother had died on August 21, 1869.

Gurney called what was experienced by these reporters "crisis apparitions," because they occurred close to the moment of extreme injury or death. He received thousands of such accounts, some 700 of which he saved for a book because they contained some tangible evidence, such as diary notations, newspaper reports, and letters of corroboration. With assistance he conducted personal interviews whenever feasible to gain as much information as possible, particularly calculating time differences between the place of death and the place of vision.

These accounts contained little of the colorful descriptions and dramatics of good ghost stories, but their similarities, repetitiveness, and consistency, supported by careful documentation and double-checks, allowed Gurney and Meyers to hope that these would impress the reader, and particularly their scientific colleagues.

When *Phantasms of the Living* was published in 1886, Meyers worried that in spite of the great effort that had gone into the research, it would not make people really see and seriously give thought to the real issues involved. He had for years found religion wanting in its blind adherence to mythological stories and dogma in the face of what he felt to be compelling evidence to the contrary. Scientific dogma, he had come to conclude, was worse, and he fought back against the efforts of traditional scientists to marginalize the efforts of the psychical researchers: "We conceive ourselves to be working (however imperfectly) in the main track of discovery." The SPR had been careful to dissociate itself from "the crazy wonder-mongers." Where they differed from their mainstream colleagues was in not defining reality and limiting their scope to the narrow boundaries the "ruthless hand of science" allowed. With this and all the other work they had and were accomplishing, they genuinely hoped to persuade these colleagues to join with them "to lay the foundation stone of a study which will loom large in the approaching age."

William James gave *Phantasms of the Living* the only endorsement to appear in a mainstream science journal, noting, "This is a most extraordinary work." He praised the intellect and dedication of the authors in collecting facts and assuring that those facts were accurate. The work contains "learning of the solidest sort."

With barely any exception all of the other responses by the research community were negative. In an article published by the ASPR Charles Peirce, a friend of James, declared that he found every case of crisis apparition unbelievable. Gurney pointed out in a rebuttal Pierce had both misquoted and misrepresented the cases cited. However, he recognized that Pierce had raised some legitimate points, most importantly that people tend to remember those hallucinations and dreams that seem to coincide with death and forget all the rest, thus inflating the statistics. Certainly the sample size was too small. But as he and James noted, this work was only the beginning.

Hopefully, James stated in his review, the authors, in their combination of careful research and penetrating analysis, had made an argument strong enough to finally gain the interest and involvement of the research community. As he put it:

> The next 25 years will then probably decide the question. ... Either a flood of confirmatory phenomena, caught in the act, will pour in, in consequence of their work, or it will not pour in—and then we shall legitimately enough explain the stories here preserved as mixtures of odd coincidence with fiction [130].

In spite of the hostile reaction to the book James believed as others began investigating the same phenomena they too would recognize its legitimacy.

> I feel that I ought to describe the total effect left at present by the book on my mind. It is a strong suspicion that its authors will prove to be on the winning side (Blum, 2007).

Guerney proposed expanding the collection of accounts of death day apparitions that had been featured in *Phantasms of the Living*. Before he could begin this undertaking, quite suddenly in 1889, at the young age of 41, Guerney died, perhaps by suicide.

Soon thereafter Sidgwick and Meyers decided to carry forward that proposal. What they had in mind was truly impressive. They recruited volunteers in a number of countries to pose the following question to a wide assortment of adults: "Have you ever, when believing yourself to be completely awake, had a vivid impression of seeing or being touched by a living being or inanimate object, or of hearing a voice; which impression, so far as you could discover, was not due to any external physical cause?" [p. 151]. Results poured in from six countries: England, France, Germany, Russia, Brazil, and the United States. In Britain some 17,000 people responded, and in the United States over 7,000.

Nora (Sidgwick's wife) assumed overall responsibility for the study, and it was she who devised a statistical strategy for analyzing the results. Using official British data, she determined that the odds of any one person dying on a given day were 1 in 19,000. The possibility that on that same day a single event, such as a recognizable "hallucination" of a certain person, would occur was also 1 in 19,000. Thus, for every 19,000 deaths there should have been only one such occurrence.

Among the 17,000 British respondents, 2,272 claimed to have experienced such an apparition near the time of death. These were carefully examined. All cases in which there was a chance that a death might have been previously expected, such as an elderly or ailing relative, were excluded, as were ghost stories that relied on only one person's claim. Incidents in which the apparition was seen more than 12 hours after the death were also removed, as were reports that involved dreams or possible delirium. Only 32 cases remained, but using Nora's statistics, that was an impressive number. Given a rate of 1 out of 19,000, for the 17,000 surveyed .0723 instances would have been expected. Thirty-two was 442.6 times the chance rate. The American survey data yielded responses exceeding chance by 487 times (Blum, 2007).

In 1887 the American Society for Psychical Research, just two years after its founding, appeared on the verge of self-destruction. It had indeed attracted scientifically trained people, but they were skeptics who harshly criticized the very work it and its sister organization in England were striving to promote. William James was working on his psychology book and didn't have time to keep it together.

Fortunately a wealthy American Spiritualist came to the rescue. He admired Richard Hodgson, who had so convincingly exposed Madame Blavatsky, and offered to pay his salary for a year if he would come to America and get the ASPR's research program back on track. Hodgson arrived to do that, but he had an underlying agenda: to expose the medium Leonora Piper.

She, like many other mediums, had a Spirit guide or control who functioned to relay messages from the deceased and to summon others who might want to communicate to the sitters. Mrs. Piper's control was a French man who called himself Dr. Phinuit and claimed to have lived from 1790 to 1860. In her séances, after going into trance, he would take over. Her voice would become deeper with a French accent, and her personality would change from gentle and eager to please to abrasive and forceful.

James and his associates in France had never been able to discover any evidence that such a person as Dr. Phinuit ever existed. James was quite fluent in French, and when he had attempted to speak French to Phinuit the doctor suddenly would become silent. James thought that he was some kind of creation of Mrs. Piper's subconscious that seemed to function as a kind of buffer between her ordinary and strange trance personalities. Hodgson thought the whole notion of Phinuit a silly complication and called him/it a "freak personality."

In a sitting with the medium, while in trance with Phinuit speaking, Hodgson interrupted, telling him he was an obvious fake. Phinuit immediately ended the session, saying he didn't want to talk to "this man" any more that day.

Hodgson was persistent, returning to further his effort to discredit Mrs. Piper. Phinuit was also ready with a message to Hodgson from his deceased cousin Fred, describing activities they had enjoyed together and the circumstances of his death. The control also described a close relationship Hodgson had enjoyed with a woman in Australia who died several years after he had moved to England. Everything Phinuit said was accurate, leaving Hodgson with a dilemma. Either Piper/Phinuit had in some mysterious fashion drawn information out of thin air, a conclusion he could not accept, or she had been spying on him, and probably her other sitters as well. Without informing anyone, including James, he hired a detective agency to follow her for the next month.

Following a month of surveillance the detectives following Mrs. Piper provided Hodgson with their report. They had discovered absolutely nothing—none of the practices that had been uncovered among the many fraudulent mediums who had been unmasked. Neither she nor her husband had been heard asking questions about the sitters. They hadn't made any unexpected trips or engaged in any questionable meetings, and they didn't check out past issues of newspapers or visit cemeteries. She didn't employ her own detectives to gather information for Phinuit to reveal in her séances.

Hodgson didn't end his investigation there. He went to great lengths to limit her family's access to information, paying newspapers to only deliver morning papers on days when no sittings were scheduled. He carefully watched their house even in the worst weather. Mrs. Piper's young son later recalled him shouting at a visitor who had left her wet umbrella in the downstairs stand, "You idiot! Haven't you more sense than to do a thing like that? Don't you know you might be accused of being in collusion with Mrs. Piper if you leave your umbrella there?" Apparently he had thought she could possibly have concealed a note in its folds that one of the daughters could have retrieved.

On March 6, 1889, in a sitting with Mrs. Piper, William James' wife Alice and his younger brother, Robertson, asked about the health of the brother's aunt, who had been sick. Phinuit replied, "She is poorly." Suddenly Mrs. Piper threw back her head and said in a startled way, "Why Aunt Kate's here. All around me I hear voices saying, Aunt Kate has come." Upon questioning Phinuit related that the aunt had died early that morning, maybe around 2 a.m. Robertson immediately went directly to Hodgson's office, where he found his brother William. Hodgson wrote a statement about what happened, which the three signed, indicating the date and time, and that no news had been received by any of them about the aunt's possible death. A few hours later, after James had returned to his home, he received a telegram from his cousin saying that his aunt had died early that morning, shortly after midnight.

In 1892 George Pellow, a 32 year-old philosophy student, writer, and friend of Dick Hodgson, died from a fall from his horse. Pellow had been an outspoken critic of psychical research but enjoyed debating with Hodgson the possibility of life after death. A few months before he died Pellow half-jokingly promised that if Hodgson was right and we do continue on after death, and if he, Pellow, died first, he would return and make himself so obvious that his friends wouldn't be able to deny him.

A few months after the death a new personality began to appear in Mrs. Piper's trances, declaring itself to be the same George Pellow. At first the GP personality, as Hodgson came to call it, manifested as a voice, but soon indicated a preference for communicating through automatic writing. A few rather strange sittings occurred in which Mrs. Piper's regular control, Phinuit, would answer one question verbally while at the same time Mrs. Piper's right hand wrote GP's answer to another question on a piece of paper. Gradually the GP personality completely replaced Phinuit.

Hodgson wasn't sure exactly what GP was, but when he claimed to know someone Hodgson also knew this offered the possibility of more tests. Hodgson would bring a large number of people to attend Mrs. Piper's séances. Most would be strangers to Pellow, but some would be his friends. No clues were given as to who they were or what their backgrounds were. Out of some 130 people GP effortlessly identified and greeted nineteen of the twenty friends by name. The remaining one, now 18, had been only 10 when Pellow had met her. She had changed, he said, and he asked if she still played the violin as badly as she had as a child.

A major alternative to the survival hypothesis to explain the communications Mrs. Piper received was that some kind of telepathy was operating between her and the sitters, allowing her to gain access to their thoughts. However, Hodgson couldn't see how all twenty of Pellow's friends could be gifted telepathic agents capable of sending information. Sometimes GP gave accurate information about friends not present at the sittings, making telepathy even less likely. Sometimes Mrs. Piper received messages from people who had taken their own lives, and these messages tended to be garbled and miserable. If she were reading the minds of those people's friends and acquaintances to form a mental picture of them, why would her actual communication to the sitters be less clear than that involving other deceased individuals?

Occasionally a sitting with Mrs. Piper involved communication that was so clear and so personal that anyone would have been hard pressed to deny that the Spirit of a deceased individual was actually present. One such case involved the parents of a five-year-old girl nicknamed Kakie who had died a few weeks earlier. At a sitting with no names revealed they presented a silver medal and a string of buttons that she had once played with. The transcription of the sitting reads as follows:

> Where is Papa? Want Papa. [The father takes from the table a silver medal and hands it to Mrs. Piper.] I want this—want to bite it. [She used to do this.] ... I want you to call Dodo [her name for her brother George]. Tell Dodo I am happy. [Puts hands to throat.] No sore throat any more. [She had pain and distress of the throat and tongue.] ... Papa, want to go wide [ride] horsey. [She pleaded this throughout her illness.] Every day I go to see horsey. I like that horsey ... Eleanor. I want Eleanor. [Her little sister. She called her much during her last illness.] I want my buttons. Where is Dinah? I want Dinah. [Dinah was an old rag doll, not with us]. I want Bagie [her name for her sister Margaret]. I want to go to Bagie ... I want Bagie ... . (Blum, 2007).

Based on these investigations of Mrs. Piper, the tough minded and skeptical Hodgson concluded in a 1897 report that communication from the dead was a reality:

> At the present time, I cannot profess to have any doubt but that the chief "communicators" to which I have referred in the foregoing pages are veritably the personages they claim to be, that they have survived the change we call death, and that they have directly communicated with us, whom we call living, through Mrs. Piper's organism. (Blum, 2007)

Sidgwick, badly as he wanted more definitive evidence on this subject, could not completely accept Hodgson's conclusion and rule out telepathy as the source of Mrs. Piper's communications. He was troubled by the fact that the GP personality, while being able to readily recognize his friends, seemed to have little knowledge of himself. Pellow had been an avid student of philosophy, yet the GP personality coming through Mrs. Piper seemed woefully ignorant in this regard. In one sitting a visitor asked about the philosopher Chauncey Wright, who had been an early defender of Darwinism and had written that scientific investigation could never disclose or support the idea that the universe has a purpose. Did, the sitter asked, GP's life after death shed light on Wright's views of natural laws. GP responded, "Yes, law is thought." The interaction continued. Sitter: "Do you now find that law is permanent?" G.P: "Cause is thought." Sitter: "That doesn't answer it." GP : "Ask it." The sitter then asked if GP agreed with Wright and was first told "most certainly" and then told, "He knows nothing, his theory is ludicrous." "Cause is thought."

Certainly Sidgwick concluded the living Pellow could have handled these questions about a philosopher with whom he was very well acquainted with more sophistication. It did not seem to make sense that once a person died his mind might survive, but as an empty container without the knowledge that once filled it.

Hodgson recognized that Sidgwick's criticism exemplified one of the most difficult issues in Spirit communication: the influence of the medium. He pointed out that Mrs. Piper had no knowledge of philosophy. She could receive communication, but she wasn't necessarily a good interpreter. Normal communication between living people is difficult enough. In this case conversation is being attempted involving someone speaking from another dimension through an entranced medium.

In 1898 James Hyslop, a philosophy professor at Columbia University, read Hodgson's account of his work with Mrs. Piper and was immediately intrigued, as he had been intrigued with the notion of survival since the death of his father. He wrote Hodgson to propose a challenge for Mrs. Piper. He would attend four sittings anonymously, with a black mask over his face. Furthermore, he would wait outside a window for Hodgson to signal that the medium was fully entranced before Hodgson would signal him to enter. He would be referred to with a code name, "four times friend." At the second sitting Mrs. Piper stated that a visitor had newly arrived in the room whose name was Robert Hyslop.

Following the four masked sittings Hyslop was determined to carefully scrutinize and verify or discard every statement that his "father," speaking through Mrs. Piper, had made. A main source of assistance in this regard was his mother, whom he questioned closely about things his father had said and done. Over the four sessions the Spirit of his father described 205 incidents. Hyslop determined that 152 were true, 16 were false, and 37 unverifiable. But it wasn't only the actual pieces of information that came through, impressive as they were, but the expressions used; the turning of a phrase was so much like the way his father talked. Hyslop was left with a bone-deep assurance that, "I talked with my discarnate father with as much ease as if I were talking with him, living, through the telephone."

Hodgson cautioned Hyslop about undue optimism based on experiences with just Mrs. Piper, suggesting that to get a more balanced perspective he visit some other local working mediums. After only a few such experiences Hyslop became thoroughly disgusted with the devious practices he encountered. These mediums asked the sitters to write questions on small blank pieces of paper that they then wadded up into small balls and placed in a bowl in plain sight on a table. The mediums barely touched them before selecting one to read and respond to. Through careful observation Hyslop detected that they actually were able to conceal a familiar ball in their hands that they pretended to retrieve from among others in the bowl. As a result of this brief investigation Hyslop agreed with Hodgson that the commercial medium business was indeed reprehensible. Mrs. Piper, on the other hand, was altogether a different entity.

Hyslop wrote an essay for *Harpers* in which he discussed his investigation with Mrs. Piper, pointing out that it offered strong evidence for communication with the dead. He had been unable to discover any evidence of fraud or duplicity, or even any evidence that she had herself visited, or sent detectives to visit the small town of Xenia, Ohio, where his parents lived. That left only two explanations for the information apparently coming from his deceased father, "omniscient telepathy and discarnate Spirits." Telepathy seemed too unwieldy. Many of the verifiable facts about his family he himself didn't know at the time of the sittings. She couldn't have read them out of his mind. His father's Spirit must have, in fact, been present in the sittings.

Certainly this seemed improbable, but Hyslop pointed out that science was constantly exploring the improbable, even "wasting enormous resources upon expeditions in search of the North Pole, or in deep sea dredging for a species of useless fish to gratify the propensities of evolutionists.... Why is it so noble and respectable to find whence man came, and so suspicious and dishonorable to ask and ascertain whither he goes?" (Blum, 2007).

William James noted that while Hyslop's article was "horribly written," it "makes a stronger case for spirit return than anything I've seen." Others in the academic community were not so favorably impressed. At Columbia, psychologist James Cattell, well known for his pioneering work in intelligence testing and a strong critic of psychic research, was outraged that his own university had become associated with Spiritualist nonsense. He openly demanded that the university president order Hyslop to abandon further work of this type and, according to rumor, privately demanded that Hyslop be censored and fired [pp. 244–248].

Meyers, as did other early psychical researchers, struggled to make sense of the information that was being discovered. His conclusions, which were considered in our discussion of the history of psychology, he presented in a book to be called *The Human Personality and Its Survival of Bodily Death*. Unfortunately Meyers died in 1901, before the book was actually finalized. Hodgson picked up the remaining work and saw it through publication in 1903.

William James, in one of the more positive assessments of the book, thought Meyers' "ill-defined relations of the subliminal with its 'cosmic' environment" undermined his case for immortality, but he did laud "his willingness to tackle such a difficult and controversial subject." "Frederic Myers will always be remembered in psychology," James later wrote, "as the pioneer who staked out a vast tract of mental wilderness and planted the flag of genuine science on it."

On a December evening in 1905 Mrs. Piper experienced a disturbing dream. She had been walking toward the entrance of a tunnel when she saw a man ahead of her who raised his hand to block her way. She was startled by the appearance of that hand, with its strong long fingers and callused palm. It looked remarkably like the hands of Richard Hodgson. In the morning she told her daughters what she saw and that she was certain the man was Hodgson. An hour later the morning's newspaper contained an account of Hodgson's death.

Three weeks later, while delivering a written message in a sitting, Mrs. Piper's hand began to shake so badly she initially dropped her pencil. She managed to write the word Hodgson. A few days later, in another sitting, the message came through: "I am Hodgson ... I heard your call ... Piper instrument. I am happy exceedingly difficult to come very. I understand why Myers came seldom. I must leave. I cannot stay. I cannot remain today."

Two weeks later, in a sitting with Mrs. Piper attended by William James's wife Alice and son Billy, the Hodgson personality again appeared. "Why, there's Billy! Is that Mrs. James and Billy? God bless you! I have found my way, I am here, have patience with me. All is well with me. Don't miss me. Where's William? Give him my best wishes."

As the Hodgson personality began to flicker in and out of Mrs. Piper's sittings, it became obvious that this presented another opportunity to attempt to prove that Spirits of the dead do return, much like the case of the GP that Hodgson himself investigated. Yet who possessed the necessary objectivity, precision, and restraint to do so? No one, James concluded, except himself.

In analyzing the messages coming through Mrs. Piper from the Hodgson personality, James recalled there were times during the sittings when it seemed that the Hodgson personality was so real he broke out in a chill. Yet there were tedious hours of what he described as appearing to be some "peculiar creation derived from Mrs. Piper's interpretation of the masculine personality." Yet James persisted in plowing through piles of transcripts from the sittings, hoping some more concrete and verifiable piece of information might emerge.

The Hodgson personality in one sitting asked a friend to destroy some letters he had written to a woman and hidden in his desk. James couldn't locate the letters and asked for more information about the woman. The response was: "There was a time when I greatly cared for her and I did not wish it known in the ears of others. I think she can corroborate this. I am getting hazy. I must leave." When he returned another detail was added. The last time he had seen her: "I proposed marriage to her, but she refused me."

James had never heard a word from Hodgson while he was alive about this woman and he doubted this claim, but he wrote to her nevertheless. Her reply was completely a surprise. "Regarding the utterances of Mrs. Piper, I have no difficulty in telling you the circumstances on which she may have founded her communications. Years ago, Mr. H asked me to marry him, and some letters were exchanged between us, which he may have kept."

James described himself as feeling a leap of euphoria. Here, in this very secret part of Hodgson's life, seemed to be the proof he was seeking of the "return of the Spirit." But being the very careful investigator he was, James recognized he needed to establish that this was really private knowledge unknown to anyone. He interviewed a dozen of Hodgson's friends who knew nothing about this relationship. But one person did say that Hodgson occasionally consulted with Mrs. Piper's control Rector about his private life. There was thus a very remote possibility that she knew about the hidden letters and the proposal. She hadn't shown any signs of such knowledge, but it might just be hidden away in a "trance memory." James didn't believe he could call this incident proof of spirit communication. Unfortunately, by such strict standards he concluded acceptable proof might never be found. James wrote to a friend, "It would be sad indeed if this undecided verdict will be all I can reach after so many years," [pp. 286–287]. However, he steadfastly maintained his conviction that: "In order to disprove the law that all crows are black, it is enough to find one white crow" (Blum, 2007).

William James died in 1910. He had been friends with and championed the efforts of the founders of psychical research and had himself taken part in their investigations in spite of severe criticism of some of his professional colleagues. Recalling that Guerney and Meyers had once estimated that perhaps five percent of the paranormal claims they had investigated were legitimate, he had steadfastly supported the particular importance of studying that small number.

"Either I or the scientist is of course a fool," James wrote in his last essay on psychical research, "with our opposite views of probability here.... I may be dooming myself to the pit in the eyes of better judging posterity; I may be raising myself to honor; I am willing to take the risk, for what I shall write is my truth, as I now see it ..."

Odd, occult, so-called supernatural phenomena he wrote occurred with remarkable frequency, in spite of scientific claims that they were "so rare as to be unworthy of attention." He believed, he went on to state, in "the presence, in the midst of all the humbug, of really supernormal knowledge, beyond the ordinary senses." But he also regretfully believed he and his colleagues had been "too precipitate in their hopes" that they had trusted too much in the ability of science to solve all mysteries. The answers, he suspected, would not come in his lifetime, and perhaps not in his children's lifetimes either (Blum, 2007).

For sixty or more years, following the death of the early psychical researchers and scientific interest in life after death, it practically came to a standstill. A few research programs have continued to investigate mediums and life after death issues. One such is the Windbridge Research Center.

JULIE BEISCHEL AND THE WINDBRIDGE RESEARCH CENTER

Julie Beischel holds a doctorate in pharmacology and toxicology, but following the suicide of her mother and a convincing mediumship reading approximately around 2001, she decided to pursue research with mediums. Currently she is the only person in the US doing so full-time at the Windbridge Institute, which she co-founded with her husband. Since 2008 this has involved a team of mediums who were intensely screened over several months in an eight-step procedure. One of the main projects of the institute has been to examine the abilities of these mediums to report accurate and specific information about deceased individuals without prior knowledge or feedback, or using deceptive or fraudulent means (Beischel, 2015).

Beischel describes the research design as follows. A pool of over 1,000 individuals is identified who volunteered to serve as sitters by completing an online application, which includes a questionnaire about the deceased person (discarnate) they would like to hear from. This includes such items as the discarnate's physical and personality characteristics, interests or hobbies, and cause of death. One of the volunteer sitters is chosen at random from this pool and paired with a second sitter on the basis of his or her discarnate being very different from that of the first sitter. Two readings are scheduled with a randomly selected Windbridge certified research medium (WCRM), one for each sitter's chosen discarnate. Readings are given over the phone with the medium alone, who is only given the discarnate's first name and knows nothing about the sitter.

As soon as the medium has connected with the discarnate their reading begins to be recorded. They are asked several standard questions by an experimenter (over the phone):

What did the discarnate look like in his/her physical life?
Describe the personality of the discarnate.
What were the discarnate's hobbies or activities? How did s/he spend his/her time?
What was the discarnate's cause of death?
Does the discarnate have any comments, questions, requests, or messages for the sitter?
Is there anything else you can tell me about this person?

Usually a week later the same medium is given the name of the second sitter's discarnate and the same process occurs. Readings are transcribed to create lists of these items. Both of these are emailed to the two sitters, who each score each list without knowing which of the two was for his or her discarnate. Items are scored for accuracy, and a reading is given an overall global score from 0 to 6. Additionally sitters are asked which reading was intended for him or her.

The research protocol involves several types of blinding. Blinding refers to someone involved in a study being prevented from having certain information.

The WCRM is blinded to information about the sitter and the discarnate before, during, and after the reading, and is asked questions about the discarnate's appearance, personality, activities, and cause of death;
The sitters being read by a medium do not hear the readings as they occur. Instead, they score transcripts of two readings: one for their discarnate (target) and one for another sitter's discarnate (decoy), without knowing which is which;
Three experimenters are involved. The first who gets consent from and trains the sitters is blinded to which mediums read which sitters and which readings were intended for which sitters;
The second experimenter who interacts with the mediums during the phone readings and formats the readings into item lists for scoring is blinded to information about the sitters and the discarnates beyond the discarnates' first names;
The third experimenter who interacts with the sitters during scoring (i.e., e-mails and receives by e-mail the blinded readings) is blinded to all information about the discarnates, to which medium performed which readings, and to which readings were intended for which sitters.

At the time the first study was written up scoring was available for twenty-one readings. Sitters scored more of the items as correct in their own readings than the other reading, and this difference was statistically significant. They also gave their own readings higher overall scores than the second readings, again statistically significant. Out of the twenty-one readings, sixteen sitters correctly chose the one they thought was intended for them (statistically significant). Beischel summarized the results as supporting the initial hypothesis that certain mediums can report accurate and specific information about discarnates with no prior knowledge about the sitters or discarnates, without any feedback during the reading, and without fraud or deception.

She also points out that we can't conclude that the mediums are communicating directly with the deceased. Two competing hypotheses need to be considered. One is that there is some kind of psychic reservoir where all information since the beginning of time is stored somehow, somewhere, like the claimed Akashic record. The medium accesses this to acquire facts about the deceased. The second is the superpsi hypothesis just discussed. Beischel concludes that the survival hypothesis can't be considered to be better than these other two based on the results of this medium study.

To address the superpsi possibility, the Windbridge team investigated the mediums' experiences during their readings. Several things occur spontaneously in readings that suggest survival rather than psi. Sometimes the mediums are contradicted by the discarnates and surprised by the information they receive, which may be quite funny. This wouldn't be likely if psi were used to acquire the information. In one study WCRMs completed a questionnaire about their experience following a reading and another following a conversation with Beischel. In the reading they experienced higher levels of negative emotions, as well as alterations in sense of time, body image, perceptions, and general state of awareness than they experienced during the phone call. Conversely, they experienced a sense of lower levels of volitional control and memory.

Many of the WCRMs also perform psychic readings, and thus have experience acquiring information about the living using psi. In one study they were asked to describe in as much detail as possible doing both medium and psychic readings. While they reported similarities, there were also differences. In medium readings the WCRMs reported signs that contact had been made, such as rings, or whines, or light flashes, or feelings of vibration or heat. The mediumship experience involved independent, autonomous communicators who could surprise and sometimes frighten the mediums with their presence and sometimes voiced opinions with which the mediums didn't agree. They actually experienced the emotions of the discarnates, whereas they were only aware of the emotions of the living in psychic readings.

In an ongoing study WRCMs were given the first name of a living person and a discarnate without knowing which was which. They did readings for both and completed questionnaires about them. In 83% of the cases they accurately identified which recipient was living and which was deceased. These studies on the actual experiences of mediums, Beischel believes, more strongly support the survival hypothesis than those involving a psychic reservoir or superpsi.

An independent replication performed by researchers in Italy adapted the protocol first described by Beischel and included thirty-eight readings provided by nine mediums. The blinded sitters gave their own (target) readings significantly higher overall scores (on a scale of 0–6) than they gave decoy readings (3.36 ± 1.47 vs. 1.77 ± 1.3; p=.001). When asked to choose which of two readings was more applicable to them, the blinded sitters chose the target reading 66% of the time (25/38, p=.04).

Results were combined from three studies in two countries involving 112 readings by nearly 40 mediums collected under controlled conditions. The 75 sitters chose target readings over decoy readings 68% of the time, when only 50% could be expected to do so by chance (p=.0001). That is, the sitters were able to recognize their discarnates in the information reported by the mediums. Beischel points out that these findings provide evidence that certain mediums can report accurate and specific information about discarnates under conditions that exclude ordinary, sensory explanations. These data, she says, demonstrate the ability of mediums to be able to obtain accurate and specific information about discarnates without prior knowledge of the discarnates or sitters, in the absence of any sensory feedback, and without using deceptive or fraudulent means (Beischel, 2015).

CHAPTER 2

PARAPSYCHOLOGY

While researchers appeared to give up on the lofty goals and grand explorations of the early pioneers following their deaths, interest in psi research resumed in the 1920s, thanks largely to William McDougall, a physician and psychologist from England. McDougall, a cofounder of the British Psychological Society, taught psychology at Oxford, and in 1920 was named president of the British Society for Psychical Research. That same year he was offered the chair in psychology at Harvard that had been vacated since James's death.

McDougall was a staunch empiricist, allowing him to fit well with the growing shift in academic circles toward emphasizing objective experimental evidence, but he was uncomfortable with the growing trend in American universities that was proclaiming behaviorism, with its purely external focus and neglect of inner experience, as the future of psychology. At Harvard, home of fellow psychologist and leading behaviorist proponent B. F. Skinner, this trend was particularly popular. McDougall was delighted when he was asked to leave Harvard to create a psychology department at Duke University in North Carolina.

At Duke, McDougall was given the freedom to design his own psychology program, which he envisioned would include research into anomalous mental capacities, an endeavor that he labeled parapsychology. As he set about selecting faculty he became aware of a young scholar, Joseph B. Rhine (Mayer, 2007).

THE RHINES

Rhine and his wife, Louisa, had become interested in paranormal abilities after attending a lecture by Sir Arthur Conan Doyle who, in addition to being the author of the Sherlock Holmes stories, had a keen interest in Spiritualism. Doyle pointed out that several eminent scientists and academics were strongly interested in psychic phenomena, among them William McDougall. Rhine began reading in the field and became convinced that further research was needed.

He and Louisa contacted McDougall, who at the time was about to leave for Europe. He put them in touch with members of the SPR, who in turn invited them to attend a séance with Margery, a famous medium at the time. Rhine happened to be seated next to her in the semi-darkened room where the séance was held and soon became suspicious of some of her activities. Physical signals supposedly coming through her from the Spirit of her deceased brother he observed were actually produced by hidden devices she was cleverly manipulating. In an angry letter to the SPR Rhine publicly exposed the medium as a fraud. McDougall was impressed by Rhine's observational skills and scientific integrity, and initially offered he and his wife funding to do research for one semester. Soon this led to an appointment to become founding faculty in McDougall's new psychology department.

The Rhines proposed the establishment of a parapsychology laboratory dedicated to the study of anomalous mental capacities that would be based on the following essential principles:

First, they proposed studying ordinary people using thoroughly conventional scientific methods and procedures.

Second, their procedures would involve simple, easily controlled and restricted choices.

And third, this would yield data that would be readily quantifiable and easily subjected to objective measurement, as well as formal statistical analysis.

The overall goal was to discover whether by experiments completely in accord with all standards of the accepted scientific method they could show that anomalous mental capacities actually exist.

Initially they ran experiments asking whether a subject could identify, with an accuracy significantly beyond pure chance, a specific card from a series preselected from a standard deck by someone having no sensory contact with the subject. To improve their experimental design the Rhines asked a colleague, Karl Zener, to design a deck specifically for the simple guessing tasks their experiments required. Zener developed a deck of twenty-five cards, each depicting one of five simple geometric designs: a star, a square, wavy lines, a circle, and a plus sign. These became known as the Zener cards.

The Rhines conducted tests of two kinds of ability with these cards: telepathy, in which subjects were asked to name a card that another person was thinking of; and clairvoyance, in which subjects were asked to name a card selected but not observed by another person. On average a subject could be expected to guess five of the twenty-five cards correctly by chance alone. The question was, could more than five correct guesses be achieved with enough consistency to suggest that something beyond chance was operating.

One subject in particular, Hubert Pearce, a young divinity student, in a series of experiments with Rhine's assistant, Joseph Pratt, produced amazing results. An experiment began with the two synchronizing their watches. Pearce then went to the Duke library and Pratt to the physics building 100 yards away. At a rearranged time Pratt shuffled the deck of twenty-five Zener cards, picked the top card, and without looking at it, laid it face down. During the ensuing minute Pearce would write down what he thought the card was. They proceeded in this way through the twenty-five-card deck. Pratt then turned the cards over face up and wrote down what each one was in the order he had actually picked them. He then reshuffled the deck and repeated another run of the twenty-five cards. Immediately after a session of a certain number of runs each person sealed his results and gave them to Rhine to be compared.

In the first experiment involving 300 trials with the Zener cards Pearce averaged 9.9 hits per run of twenty-five cards, far exceeding the chance expectation of five hits. He then moved from the library to the medical school 250 yards away from Pratt, achieving similarly impressive results. The experimental protocol was then changed, with Pearce making a series of guesses before Pratt actually shuffled the deck and laid the cards face down one at a time. Again the results remained impressive. Neither distance, nor even time seemed to prevent Pearce's amazingly successful hit rate. The overall Pearce-Pratt experiments involved 1,850 trials, out of which Pearce achieved 558 hits. If nothing but pure chance were involved he would have recorded 370 hits. The odds of making 558 correct guesses out of 1,850 were an astounding 22 billion to 1.

In deciding how to characterize the abilities that appeared to be confirmed in his research, Rhine wanted a label that would distance them from Spiritualism or the occult. He settled on the term extra-sensory perception, which placed the work firmly within the study of perception, a well-established subfield in psychology. Rhine believed extra-sensory perception (ESP) only differed from ordinary perception in terms of being generated by another yet unknown sensory modality, one beyond the familiar five senses of sight, hearing, smell, taste, and touch.

Rhine published a monograph in 1934 describing the lab's findings with the simple title *Extra-Sensory Perception.* Even though it was an academic treatise, the book soon attracted a great deal of popular attention. The *New York Times*, *Scientific American*, and a number of other large newspapers and magazines gave it major coverage. As the first publication of sober systematic experiments on anomalous mental capacities Rhine's findings also generated no small amount of controversy in the scientific community. Some viewed it as "epoch-making," while others unleashed a series of assaults that ranged from respectful methodological critiques to vicious attacks on his character.

Laboratories similar to Rhine's were soon established at other universities, professional associations were formed with peer-reviewed journals and annual conferences, and a mushrooming literature developed, all concerned with anomalous mental capacities. Beyond an occasional flurry of public and scientific attention, most of this activity was to go on outside both the public eye and everyday scientific and academic life.

In the meantime the Rhines, as good researchers, carefully considered those criticisms of their work that seemed valid and took measures to improve their procedures. They completely isolated subjects from the experimenters on the very slight chance the latter, in some unwitting way, provided cues as to the cards. To eliminate any patterns in the card shuffling they employed a machine to accomplish this. They also instituted additional steps for checking and double checking their results. To meet a barrage of questions and criticism concerning their use of statistics they invited the American Institute of Mathematics to look at their procedures. The resulting full validation pretty much quieted this major source of criticism.

In 1937, Rhine published a book on ESP for the general public; *New Frontiers of the Mind* became a Book-of-the-Month Club selection and attracted wide attention. That same year Rhine and fellow ESP investigators were able to establish their own scientific publication, "The Journal of Parapsychology." In 1940 the Rhines published another book containing a highly detailed report of all the experiments undertaken at their lab since its inception, along with an enumeration of and response to every major criticism leveled against them. *Extra-Sensory Perception After Sixty Years*—ESP 60 as it came to be known—proved as highly popular as their earlier book and, much to the Rhines' astonishment, even became required reading for introductory psychology classes at Harvard.

For a time it seemed that anomalous mental abilities might finally gain the respectability to be considered worthy of study by mainstream science, but soon strong voices arose, denouncing ESP as pseudoscience. The book vanished from Harvard's assigned reading list and mainstream professional scientific organizations stopped discussing it. The Rhines' laboratory sank into scientific obscurity, although experimental results were regularly published in "The Journal of Parapsychology," which was read only by a small group of dedicated subscribers (Mayer, 2007).

Rhine encountered difficult challenges that his carefully controlled research designs couldn't overcome. As common sense would suggest, when people do the same monotonous task over and over they get bored and lose interest. This happened with his card experiments. A few months after the conclusion of the Pearce-Pratt experiments Pearce lost the ability to score highly on card guessing tests that he had demonstrated during the prior two years. To build up enough results to be statistically significant and eliminate chance as an explanation subjects had to participate in a very large number of trials. When they got bored and lost interest their scores dropped, a phenomenon Rhine labeled "the decline effect." Unfortunately this eliminated the possibility of a repeatable experiment that could automatically produce ESP every time for millions of times in a row. Human beings just don't function like physical processes.

To combat the decline effect and have subjects performing at their best he had to abandon the scientist's objective, neutral, emotionally uninvolved attitude toward an experiment and its outcome. What was required was to be a cheerleader encouraging the subjects, varying the procedures, and making the research setting comfortable and pleasant. However, getting too involved would mean that the investigator could open themselves up to charges of weak controls against cheating, experimenter bias, and unconscious collusion.

Rhine had hoped to show that ESP is a normal human ability, not something reserved for special unusual people or only present in abnormal situations, such as being in a trance. He was able to show that the average person off the street did exhibit some degree of ESP, but he discovered that some people were clearly better at it than others. One of Rhine's strongest discoveries was the importance of motivation. Highly motivated people scored better than those who didn't care about their results.

Most importantly, Rhine had strived to establish the kind of carefully controlled research procedures that would enable any other scientist using the same approach to produce the same results. Unfortunately this didn't turn out to be the case. Skeptical researchers, and sometimes even those open to the possibility of ESP, following Rhine's experimental protocol to the letter couldn't necessarily achieve his successful results. Why this was the case was never fully explained, other than the possibility that ESP originating from the experimenter, in spite of the best controls, did have an influence. And perhaps most troubling for everyone, in spite of all of his efforts, Rhine never succeeded in fully determining how, why, and when ESP would occur (Schmicker, 2000).

But what he did accomplish is truly impressive. In the some seventy years following Rhine's work at Duke new and more sophisticated methods of evaluating experimental studies have evolved which give even more credence to his findings. These will be discussed when we consider more recent research strategies for investigating psi.

During the many years the Rhines conducted their research people from all over the US, upon hearing about it, began sending them anecdotal stories of their own spontaneous psychic experiences. In 1948 Louisa Rhine began to systematically analyze these accounts. Based on an impressive database that by 1978, when she retired, had reached some 14,000 entries, she was able to draw important conclusions.

Nearly 60% of the reported ESP experiences occurred during dreams. The majority involved receipt of important life or death information. However, a significant number involved trivial, unimportant things, such as the color skirt a friend might wear the following day.

Louisa Rhine was interested in those ESP experiences that appeared to foresee some future event, and particularly in the question as to whether a person could take action to prevent a glimpsed undesirable future event from happening. She analyzed 191 carefully selected accounts of precognitive ESP where people had acted on that information. In almost 70% of the cases they were indeed able to do something to avoid the undesirable event.

One such incident involved a streetcar operator in Los Angeles who one night dreamed he was operating a tram through a busy intersection. A red truck, making an illegal turn, blocked his view, resulting in a crash in which two men died and a woman was injured. The injured woman, who had large blue eyes, repeatedly shouted at him that he could have avoided the accident. The next day the exact same scenario started to actually unfold. He was able to cut the engine and apply the brakes just in time to avoid an accident. Two men and a woman with blue eyes were in the truck. As they passed by the startled woman gave him an okay sign with her thumb and forefinger, thanking him for stopping. The streetcar operator was so upset he had to be taken off the job (Schmicker, 2000).

PSI IN DREAMS

As Louisa Rhine and others discovered through their surveys, about half of all spontaneous psi experiences occur in dreams. This stimulated interest among researchers as to whether this phenomenon could be studied under controlled laboratory conditions. In 1960 psychiatrist Montague Ullman, along with psychologist Karlis Osis, tested medium and president of the Parapsychology Foundation Eileen Garrett. Garrett spent a night in a sleep laboratory at the Parapsychology Foundation. The investigators selected a pool of three pictures from *Life* magazine, which were sealed in envelopes and given to Garrett's secretary to take to her home several miles away. The plan was for them to monitor Garrett and, when she had fallen asleep and appeared to be dreaming as indicated by a rapid eye movement state, to call the secretary, asking her to choose one of the envelopes at random, look at the enclosed picture, and try to send the image telepathically to Garrett. However, the investigators didn't think Garrett had entered a dreaming state and didn't call the secretary. In fact, the next morning Garrett reported that she did have a dream that reminded her of the chariot race from the movie *Ben-Hur* that she had seen shortly before. In checking the pictures enclosed in the envelopes Ullman discovered that one was indeed a color photo of the chariot race from *Ben-Hur*. Ullman was intrigued and decided to set up a series of dream experiments at his sleep laboratory at Maimonides Medical Center (Radin, 2009).

From 1966 through 1973, Ullman and psychologist Stanley Krippner conducted a total of 379 dream psi sessions. The typical experimental procedure was for a volunteer receiver, Jill, to spend a night in the Maimonides dream lab. When she was about to go to sleep she was taken into a soundproof and electromagnetically shielded room, where electrodes were attached to her head to monitor her brainwaves and eye movements. Following that she had no further contact with anyone else until the session was completed. A second volunteer, the sender, Jack, was given a sealed envelope containing a picture randomly selected from a pool of eight to twelve images. When he was alerted by a technician monitoring the receiver that she appeared to have entered the dream state he was to look at the picture and try to send it telepathically to Jill to influence her dream.

Prior to the start of an experimental session Jill had an opportunity to talk with Jack and meet the investigators. During the actual session she was completely isolated, with the sender located at distances from her of 32 feet, 98 feet, 14 miles, and in one case 45 miles. To make sure that no one could accidentally figure out what the target picture was during a session the only contact between the sender and the investigators was a buzzer tone or series of telephone rings alerting him to start sending.

When Jill was observed—via monitoring—to have stopped dreaming, a signal was sent to Jack to stop trying to send. Jill was then awakened and asked to describe her most recent dream on audio tape. She then could go back to sleep. Each time during that night she was observed to be in the dream state the process was repeated. This happened three to six times over the course of a typical night's sleep. In the morning Jill was roused again and asked for her overall impressions of the picture that Jack was trying to send. Her responses were recorded and transcribed for later analysis.

Following completion of a dream session one or more independent judges examined the transcript of the descriptions of each dream and compared it to the full pool of possible pictures the target was chosen from. They didn't know which one was the actual target the sender was using. They were asked to rank how well each picture matched the description of a dream. The picture with the highest correspondence was ranked one and the lowest (say eight) if there were eight possible pictures in the pool. If the picture was ranked in the upper half of the pool it was considered a hit, if in the lower half a miss. If nothing but chance was operating, with no psi, then the chance of a hit would be 50%.

These laboratory psi dream studies were time consuming, requiring seven years to complete 379 sessions. More recent investigators designed a sped-up process that could be completed in a volunteer's own home based on the fact that everyone dreams every night and most people can learn to recall their dreams the next morning. A computer was programmed to automatically select a target picture from a random pool and display it repeatedly, usually between 3 and 4 a.m., on a computer monitor. The computer was in a locked room, shielded from view, so nobody could figure out what the target was. Participants kept track of their dreams at home, then gathered at the lab the next morning, where they viewed four pictures, the target and three decoys. They each ranked the four pictures according to how well each matched their dreams. The ranks were combined to create one consensus selection for the best possible match. Participants then got to see if their choices were correct.

Both the dream lab and at-home experiments demonstrated, under controlled conditions that excluded such obvious explanations as sensory cues or recording mistakes, that information at a distance could be perceived in dreams. In 2003 psychologists Simon Sherwood and Chris Roe employed meta-analysis to review all of the dream psi studies from the original Maimonides series through the latest at-home dream experiments involving 47 experiments with a total of 1,270 trials. Overall the hit rate was 59.1%, which was a 9.1% increase over chance. The odds against chance of a rate this high is 22 billion to 1. Coincidence can be ruled out convincingly as a viable explanation (Radin, 2009).

META-ANALYSIS

Because some of the most impressive results in psi research strongly show up in meta-analysis, as in this case, it is important to look more closely at this procedure. Meta-analysis is a method of statistical analysis that involves the results of independent studies as the units of analysis, rather than the responses of individual subjects. In single experiments the participants' individual responses are typically the raw data points. In meta-analysis the results of separate experiments are the raw data points. In recent years meta-analysis has become an essential tool in what are known as the soft sciences, including sociology, psychology, and medicine.

Thousands of meta-analyses have been published in scientific journals. Three major questions are frequently raised about this statistical procedure. The first asks whether it is valid to combine studies using different investigators, designs, and subjects. This depends on the kind of effect in question. If one is interested in fruit, then it is perfectly acceptable to combine studies involving apples and oranges. In studies involving psi, researchers generally want to look at the possibility that some kind of paranormal ability beyond chance is operating. Exactly how that ability is conceptualized and understood—is it an apple or an orange?—is a question that can be explored after the existence of psi itself has been convincingly established.

Second, aren't there problems if the studies being combined are not equal in quality? A poorly designed experiment shouldn't carry as much weight as a good one. To combat this potential difficulty many ways have been developed to assess the experimental quality, and only sound studies are included in meta-analysis.

The third question involves what is known as the file drawer problem. Investigators tend to publish only successful studies. Perhaps there are stacks of unsuccessful studies of the same phenomenon languishing in the file drawers of those investigators. We need to remember that with a study shown to have results successful at the .05 level of confidence, where 20 such studies were conducted, one could be successful simply by chance alone. A researcher could conduct 19 unsuccessful studies, put the results in their file drawer, then publish the one chance successful study. Fortunately sophisticated methods for estimating the size and effect of the file drawer are available.

In terms of the psi dream studies examined with meta-analysis, the first two potential difficulties just discussed do not apply. Only general psi is in question, and the studies involved, as we have seen, were all very sound. It turns out the file drawer issue wasn't a problem either. To bring the results down to chance expectations an additional 700 studies averaging chance would have had to be conducted and not reported. Considering that around 20 different investigators have reported dream psi results, each would have had to conduct, yet not report, 35 failures for every experiment with positive results they did report. Since the average dream experiment involved 27 sessions, the 700 supposedly missing experiments would have involved 700 × 27, or 18,900 sessions conducted but not reported. Given one dream session per night, this would involve 18,900 nights, or over 50 years' worth of unreported data. That just isn't plausible (Radin, 2009).

PSI IN GANZFELD EXPERIMENTS

Researchers intrigued by the evidence for psi in dreams and other altered states of consciousness developed what is known as the Ganzfeld procedure for investigating these phenomena. Ganzfeld is a German word that means "whole field" and relates to a mild form of sensory stimulation originally developed to examine the nature of visual imagery. The experimental set up for studying psi using this procedure requires that a volunteer receiver relax in a comfortable reclining chair. Halved ping-pong balls are placed over the volunteer's eyes, as well as headphones that play pink noise—a whooshing sound like rushing water. A red light is then shined in the receiver's face while eyes are kept gently open under the balls. All that is then seen is a red glow. For most people, within a few minutes this produces a pleasant dreamy state of awareness. The receiver is allowed to relax in this state for 15 minutes, then is asked to speak aloud anything that comes to mind over the next 30 minutes. The "mentation," as it is called, is audio recorded. A second volunteer, the sender, views a photograph or a repeatedly played video clip and attempts to send this target telepathically to the receiver. The target is randomly selected by a computer from a pool of four images as different from one another as possible. Typically, in modern Ganzfeld studies, the sender can listen to the receiver's description of ongoing imagery over a one-way audio link and use it to adjust the sending strategy. The sender might attempt to send the target some 10 times over the 30-minute period with brief rest periods between each.

Following the sending period the receiver is removed from the Ganzfeld condition. The receiver and the experimenter, who is also blind to the target, discuss receiver impressions while looking at the four possible targets and is then asked to rank the four possibilities in terms of which most closely matches impressions. By chance alone the receiver could be expected to make a correct match 25% of the time.

The Ganzfeld investigations have generated more close scrutiny and debate among scientists than any other type of psi studies and, as a result, have been improved to the point where, according to Radin, they are "as close to the perfect psi experiment as anyone knows how to conduct" (Radin, 2009).

By 1982 the results of 42 Ganzfeld experiments had been published conducted by 10 different labs all over the world. Honorton conducted an overall assessment reviewing every one and, for the 28 showing actual hit rates, found those averaged 35%, which yielded combined odds against chance of 10 billion to one (Mayer, 2007).

Although he presented his findings before the Parapsychological Association the Ganzfeld studies remained relatively unknown. In 1984, the Army commissioned a report by the National Research Council (NRC) of the National Academy of Sciences to assess the effectiveness of a number of controversial approaches claiming to enhance human performance including biofeedback, neurolinguistic programming, accelerated learning, mental practice, and parapsychology. In 1988 the NRC issued its report that came to the sweeping and startling conclusion: "The Committee finds no scientific justification from research conducted over a period of 130 years for the existence of parapsychological phenomena."

Several of the most highly regarded researchers in the field immediately issued a formal and carefully reasoned reply in which they protested the NRC's negative assessment. One of those was statistician Jessica Utts who, in 1989, published a refutation of the report. Only years later did it become clear how thoroughly the NRC had stacked the deck against any evidence supporting the existence of psi. A telling example is the situation with Robert Rosenthal. The NRC had asked Rosenthal, a Harvard psychologist, to review the experimental evidence for a number of the performance-enhancing techniques. He was renowned as an excellent experimental psychologist, brilliant in evaluating research strategies, as well as spotting methodological flaws or sloppy thinking. In his report to the NRC Rosenthal concluded that of all the research in the five areas he and his associate examined, only the Ganzfeld ESP studies regularly met the basic requirements of sound experimental design. It would be "implausible," he stated, to suggest that the positive findings obtained in the studies they evaluated resulted from chance. The evidence for parapsychology was sound and deserved further investigation. Rosenthal publicly revealed several years after the release of the NRC report that the chair of the NRC committee directly asked him to delete the parapsychology section of his paper, which he refused to do, but it was not cited anywhere in the NRC report (Mayer, 2007).

In 1994, psychologists Daryl Bern and Charles Honorton published a meta-analysis of Ganzfeld studies showing strong evidence of psi in the *Psychological Bulletin*. Their analysis involved two collections of studies: earlier studies with positive results indicating odds of 48 billion to one against chance and later fully automated experiments specifically designed to eliminate all known criticisms of the earlier studies with odds against chance of 517 to 1. A later comparison of these recent studies indicated those using standard visual targets produced odds against chance of 5,000 to 1, whereas those using such variations as musical targets yielded only chance results. In 2001 psychologists Lance Storm and Suitbert Ertel conducted a meta-analysis of all known Ganzfeld psi studies up until that time which produced results with overall odds against chance of 131 million to 1 (Radin, 2009).

REMOTE VIEWING

Probably no area of psi research in recent years has attracted as much popular attention as what is known as remote viewing. These experimental investigations of clairvoyance actually have a long history dating to picture-drawing studies published by Myers and Gurney in 1882. The modern story begins in the early 1970s with Harold Puthoff, a theoretical and experimental physicist who had been conducting laser research at the Stanford Research Institute (SRI), a scientific think tank affiliated with Stanford University. In regard to a side interest, Puthoff circulated a grant proposal to explore questions involving implications of quantum theory for biology. This came to the attention of artist Ingo Swann, who suggested that Puthoff might be interested in some apparently successful parapsychological experiments he had been involved with as a subject. Intrigued, Puthoff invited Swann to his laboratory to attempt to demonstrate some of the effects he described.

As Puthoff described this, he took Swann to the physics lab and asked him to perturb the operation of a magnetometer in a vault below the floor of the building and protected by metal shielding, an aluminum container, copper shielding, and a superconducting shield. Swann doubled the rate at which the magnetic field in the magnetometer was decaying, then, upon request, stopped the field change altogether for a period of roughly forty-five seconds. He then went on to "remote view" the interior of the apparatus by drawing a reasonable facsimile of its rather complex construction. Puthoff stated that he was even more impressed by this feat than the former (Mayer, 2007).

Shortly thereafter representatives of the Central Intelligence Agency (CIA) contacted Puthoff to inquire as to whether he was interested in working with the intelligence community to carry out some low-profile classified preliminary experiments to see whether it was possible for subjects to identify and describe a distant "target" hidden from their view.

What resulted was the initiation of a 24-year, $20 million remote viewing research project sponsored first by the CIA, then the Defense Intelligence Agency, and which eventually, in 1991, was transferred from SRI to Science Applications International Corporation (SAIC), a major defense contractor. It is not surprising that governmental agencies would be interested. Even if the information that might be obtained would be only partially correct, it could be used as one piece of the overall puzzle that characterizes the typical intelligence operation. It could be obtained secretly at a distance, apparently couldn't be blocked by any known form of shielding, and would be available at a very minimal cost without the necessity of sending agents into the field in potentially dangerous areas (Radin, 1997).

Puthoff served as the founder and director of the program, to be joined soon afterward by physicist Russell Targ, and a few years later by another physicist, Edwin May. In 1985 May took over as director. The research protocol in the early investigations as described by Puthoff was as follows.

An individual called a beacon would be sent to a series of locations some distance from SRI randomly selected from a huge list—typically six to ten. The beacon would then spend thirty minutes at each site. At the same time the remote viewer back at SRI, sitting in a locked room, would attempt to draw the site and offer verbal impressions of where they imagined the beacon to be. This whole procedure was double-blind, insofar as neither the experimenters nor the viewers were given any information about any of the sites where the beacon was located. The list of trial targets was then given to outside blind judges who had nothing to do with the experiment and who were asked to go to each site in the series. While there, these judges were asked to match up the viewers' drawings and descriptions with the series of sites, pair for pair, based on how closely they resembled each other. The investigators then examined the resulting matches to see if they were more accurate than chance would predict. After a few months of experiments using this procedure enough data had been gathered to suggest that the positive matches achieved were highly unlikely to have resulted from chance alone. Puthoff published the results without revealing any link to the CIA.

At that time the CIA increased their interest in the project and indicated they wanted some new experiments in which they themselves chose the targets. A target would only be geographic coordinates—latitude and longitude—of a site they wanted the subjects to remote view. There would be no "beacon," and no one, including the experimenters, would know what the coordinates referred to except themselves. This would establish a rigorous long-distance test under external control. They sent Puthoff the first coordinates.

At that precise time a retired police officer, Pat Price, heard about this work and contacted Puthoff, indicating that he had used ESP as police commissioner to achieve some spectacular successes. Puthoff asked Pat Price if he thought he could remote view the indicated site from the coordinates alone. Here's Puthoff's description of what transpired.

Price agreed and immediately sent Puthoff a five-page report in which he first described a few log cabins and a couple of roads, and that was it. He then added that over a ridge was an interesting place, a highly sensitive military site surrounded by the heaviest security. He described this in great detail, supplied the code names that all centered on the game of pool, and provided other information about what was going on there and personnel involved. Puthoff sent the verbatim transcripts back to the CIA for confirmation. He also asked Ingo Swann to focus on the same coordinates and write a report, which he sent along with the one prepared by Price.

The CIA initially found that the viewings were way off, as the coordinates they had sent pinpointed the location of a staff member's vacation cabin in West Virginia. However, the CIA officers noted a striking correlation between the two independent descriptions from Price and Swann. Because this seemed unlikely they then sent an OIS officer to the site itself. What he discovered was that just over the ridge was a highly sensitive underground government installation that the cabin's owner knew nothing about. While some of the details in the Price and Swann descriptions were wrong, a lot were right, and some were precisely so. For example, the labels of each file folder in a locked file drawer inside the underground building were all designated by pool terms: cue ball, cue stick, and so on. Price had even gotten the actual code name of the site.

Price was intrigued by this experiment, and as a personal challenge he decided to try scanning the other side of the globe for a Communist bloc equivalent to the site he'd just scanned in the US. He located a site in the Urals that he remotely viewed. The CIA confirmed that this viewing was substantially correct based on several classified sources within the agency (pp. 110–111).

Shortly after this experiment the CIA provided Price with another set of geographic coordinates. He was locked in a small electrically shielded room with an experimenter who was blind to all aspects of the experiment. Price spoke his impressions into a tape recorder, saying that he was lying on his back on the roof of a brick building on a warm sunny day. A giant crane was moving back and forth over his head. He drifted up in the air and was able to look down. The crane appeared to be riding on a track, with one rail on each side of the building. He had never seen anything like it. After the viewing was completed the CIA revealed that the site was a top secret Soviet test site facility. They had drawings rendered from satellite photographs that featured a large crane. The CIA's and Price's drawings were extraordinarily similar (Mayer, 2007).

Pat Price died in 1975 and the experimenters were left hoping another experimental subject as talented as he and Ingo Swann would come along. Fortunately Joe McMoneagle arrived on the scene. He was initially discovered on the basis of a profile of individuals who might be good remote viewing subjects put together by the military. At the time McMoneagle was a senior projects officer for the US Army Intelligence and Security Command. In a series of interviews where he was questioned about his attitude concerning possible paranormal forms of knowing he indicated he was neither a believer nor a scoffer, but if such things existed they could pose a serious security threat. He was flown to California, and after passing preliminary remote-viewing experiments with flying colors began an eighteen-year career as a remote viewer in a secret Army project that came to be called Star Gate.

Puthoff described one of the most impressive of McMoneagle's remote viewing ventures as follows. In fall 1979 Puthoff's team was given a photo of a massive industrial-type building some distance from a large body of water somewhere in Russia. The US government didn't know what the building was, what it was used for, nor its strategic importance. McMoneagle was given only the geographic coordinates. He immediately said that they identified a very cold wasteland with an extremely large industrial-looking building that had enormous smokestacks not far from a sea covered with a thick cap of ice. Since his impression closely matched the photograph he was asked what might be going on inside the building.

In his remote viewing session McMoneagle described imagining himself drifting down into a building easily the size of two or three huge shopping centers, all under a single roof. He described what looked like cigars of different sizes, sitting in gigantic racks in giant bays. Everywhere were thick mazes of scaffolding and interlocking steel pipes. What appeared to be two huge cylinders were being welded side to side, forming what he had an overwhelming sense was going to be a really big submarine with twin hulls. After the session he did a very detailed drawing of the submarine, adding dimensions, as well as noting the slanted tubes, indicating eighteen to twenty in all. This material, along with the typed transcript of his session, was forwarded to the NSC. Soon thereafter McMoneagle was asked to return to the site and to try to provide an estimated time of completion. He revisited the site and, based on the speed of construction and the differences in the condition of the submarine from one session to the next, guessed that it would be ready for launch about four months later. This would put it in January, which seemed a singularly crazy time of year to launch a submarine from a building not connected to water, near a sea frozen over with ice yards thick. In mid-January of 1980, satellite photographs showed a new canal running alongside the facility and out to sea. A two-hulled submarine with twenty canted missile tubes was clearly evident in the photographs. This turned out to be the first in an entirely new class of submarine, the largest ever built, named the *Typhoon* (Mayer, 2007).

McMoneagle performed a number of other functions for the project in addition to that of remote viewer and, in 1984, was awarded the Legion of Merit by the US government for distinguished service, including his instrumental efforts "in developing a new revolutionary intelligence project."

In the certificate that accompanied the award McMoneagle is credited with "the execution of missions for the highest echelons of our military and government, including such national level agencies as the Joint Chiefs of Staff, DIA [Defense Intelligence Agency], NSA [National Security Agency], CIA, and Secret Service, producing critical intelligence unavailable from any other source" (Mayer, 2007).

During the years remote viewing work was being carried out at SRI articles describing the results were published in prominent scientific journals, including *Nature* and the *Proceedings of the IEEE*, as well as in a few popular books. This generated criticism that the researchers used to continually tighten their experimental design. Strict guidelines resulted for eliminating any possibility that factors other than clairvoyance might account for the results, including rules such as:

No one who knows the identity of the target should have any contact with the remote viewer until after his or her description of the target has been safely secured;

No one who knows about the target, or whether the session was successful, should have any contact with the judge until after the judging has been completed; and

No one who knows about the target should have access to the remote viewer's responses until after the judging has been completed (Radin, 1997).

The method of evaluating results utilized rank order judging, a procedure that had been used in the dream psi studies. First, a pool of five possible targets was created of the following type: a geographic site, photograph, video clip, or hidden object. One was randomly selected to be the actual target and remote viewed by the subject, who recorded impressions consisting of a verbal description and sketch. These are then given to a judge, along with photographs or videos of the five possible targets. With no awareness of which was the actual target the judge is asked to rank each of the five possibilities in terms of how well it matches the viewer's impressions.

In 1988 May analyzed all the psi experiments that had been conducted at SRI since 1973, which involved 154 experiments consisting of more than 26,000 separate trials. Just over a thousand of those trials were laboratory remote-viewing tests. The statistical results revealed odds against chance of a billion billion to one [*Conscious Universe*, p. 101]. This analysis appeared in an internal report that was not made public for some years.

Between 1989 and 1993 the government sponsored psi research carried out at Science Applications International Corporation (SAIC) that involved a rigorously controlled set of ten experiments, six of which involved remote viewing supervised by a distinguished oversight committee of experts from a variety of scientific disciplines. Because the earlier SRI studies had established the existence of remote viewing to the satisfaction of most of the government sponsors the SAIC experiments were not designed to prove its existence, but to try to gain some insight into how it operates.

In 1995, at the request by President Clinton for more open government, the CIA declassified a massive number of documents describing the remote-viewing research. A myriad of accounts describing the history of the Stargate Project soon appeared, some sober appraisals from those involved, and some more sensational, with little grounding in fact. For the first time Puthoff and May were able to go public about the involvement of the CIA, the DIA, and the Department of Defense in their work.

In that same year the CIA commissioned a review of the government-sponsored remote-viewing research, primarily those experiments conducted at SAIC, but also to include a review of the SRI studies to see if the SAIC experiments replicated the earlier experiments. In its official assessment of the twenty-three-year remote viewing program, what was reported appeared starkly contradictory to prior reports, to say the least. In fact, the investigation conducted by the American Institutes for Research (AIR) forcefully discredited the government-sponsored remote-viewing research done by SRI International and by SAIC. It concluded with a statement to the press that "there was no case in which ESP [remote viewing] had ever been used to guide intelligence operations." Clearly that is very different from a number of other documented observations, including the statements in the Legion of Merit award for Joe McMoneagle (Mayer, 2007).

The key players from Project Star Gate immediately issued criticisms of the report. In an article in the 1996 *Journal of Scientific Exploration*, which published a series of articles addressing the controversy, Star Gate director Ed May questioned the validity of CIA/AIR's conclusions. He noted such serious problems with their evaluation methodology that he had become convinced that "their conclusions were set before the investigation began and that methodological and administrative choices were made to assure that the results of the investigation would support the CIA's pre-determined perspective."

May went on to provide a blow-by-blow account of scientific failure on the part of the CIA/AIR evaluation, claiming that the evaluators had been instructed to examine radically incomplete data sets, directed to exclude a wide range of experiments and backup reports that might have challenged their eventual negative findings, that a significant proportion of the evaluators were known to have an anti-ESP bias, that they made deliberate decisions not to interview a number of crucial participants and ignored previous program reviews, and that they used the National Research Council's negative review of parapsychology as the basis for their review.

May was particularly surprised that statistician Jessica Utts, a major contributor to the AIR evaluation, did not mention her difficulties with the NRC report on the Ganzfeld research. When directly questioned about this Utts told May that she had been asked by the AIR staff not to mention the NRC report. She had thought it had been forgotten about and was very surprised at the prominent weight it was subsequently given in AIR's evaluation of remote viewing. She also informed May that she had been directed to not personally have any direct contact with a number of key remote viewing figures who May had told her about, including a former DIA project officer, a former senior DIA official, a military general who had program responsibility, and Joseph McMoneagle.

In her background report in the AIR evaluation Utts expressed an unequivocal conclusion that anomalous cognition was possible and had been demonstrated. The phenomenon, she believed, had been replicated in a number of forms across laboratories and cultures.

"No one who has examined all of the data across laboratories, taken as a collective whole, has been able to suggest methodological or statistical problems to explain the ever-increasing and consistent results to date" (Mayer, 2007).

Puthoff, in summarizing the SIR/SAIC work, spoke of it as an "extraordinary twenty-four-year collaboration between top-flight scientists, major government agencies, and a few people with apparently remarkable intuitive talents." He found that "at the upper echelons, in government and other venues as well, there's solid acceptance of remote viewing and real excitement about its potential. But," he noted, "although a solid body of evidence had been generated," the ability to use remote viewing as an intelligence tool "isn't ready for prime-time TV." While the results produced by remote viewing have been truly impressive, "they're inconsistent, unpredictable, and we know very little about who's good at it or why. This makes the findings vulnerable to criticism" (Mayer, 2007, p. 127).

As Mayer notes, the controversy about remote viewing remains ongoing, with a large number of books, websites, and associations involved. But maybe most intriguing for the future, as Puthoff informed her, are open boxes of SRI/SAIC data that remain barely tapped for what they have to teach us (Mayer, 2007).

PRECOGNITION

One of the most widely reported characteristics of ESP is that it operates across time as well as space. This raises fundamental questions. Nothing seems so basic to our sense of reality than that time flows in one direction from the past to the present and on into the future. Our personal lives and our civilization are built around the notion of this one-way flow of time. Yet, perhaps surprisingly, physicists are not at all sure what time really is. Einstein wrote in a letter of condolence to the wife of his best friend, "for us faithful physicists, the separation between past, present, and future has only the meaning of an illusion, though a persistent one" [Premonitions p. 179]. In 2001 around two-dozen top physicists, historians, and philosophers gathered at a symposium in Minnesota to debate the nature of time. There was such a marked lack of agreement that one professor of physics reported, "I don't see any evidence that they're talking about different parts of the same elephant" (Dossey, 2009).

People have no doubt reported experiencing glimpses of the future in all cultures throughout recorded history. Often referred to as foreknowledge, future knowledge, premonition, or as the parapsychological term precognition, this experience continues to assume major importance in today's world. A Gallup Poll in 2005 found that three in four people in America believe in the paranormal and that dreams of future events make up more than half of the ESP experiences people report.

The presence of precognition can very easily be studied in controlled conditions using Rhine's Zener cards. The subject simply names the order in which the cards will appear before they are shuffled and examined. Rhine conducted a large number of these forced-choice tests. Over the years the research design has been improved, with cards being shuffled by machine, and still more recently using random number generators (RNGs) to produce truly random number targets. In forced-choice studies the subject is asked to guess which one of a fixed number of possible targets will be randomly selected at some point after the guesses are made. Targets might be ESP card symbols, the face of a tossed die, or colored lamps. If the subject's guess matches the selected target a hit is recorded.

In 1989, Honorton and Ferrari published a meta-analysis of all forced-choice precognition experiments that had been conducted between 1935 and 1987, consisting of 309 studies by 62 different investigators. This huge database involved nearly 2 million individual trials by more than 50,000 subjects. The interval between the time guesses made and the future targets generated ranged from milliseconds to a year. The odds against chance for the combined 309 studies turned out to be ten million billion billion to one. For the results to have resulted from a file drawer problem would have required 14,268 unpublished unsuccessful studies, clearly highly unlikely. Of the 62 different investigators 23 had reported successful studies, eliminating the possibility that the overall results could have been due to a few wildly successful experiments. The only reasonable conclusion that can be drawn is that precognition is a genuine effect demonstrated by scientifically controlled studies successfully replicated across many different experimenters (Radin, 2009).

In recent years researchers have sought other ways of looking at precognition to get around the incredibly boring nature of forced-choice tests. One approach that proved fruitful relates to the observation that precognition appears to operate on an unconscious as well as a conscious level. Unconscious precognition, known as presentiment, is based on the assumption that we are constantly and unconsciously scanning our future and preparing to respond to it.

We know that our body has a predictable reaction to a novel stimulus, known as the "orienting response," in which it momentarily tenses up while evaluating whether to fight or flee. If presentiment occurs then one way to demonstrate it would be to test whether this body response occurs before the novel stimulus occurs.

Radin designed a research strategy to do this. A subject is seated in front of a blank computer screen. Electrodes are attached to the palm of one hand to record tiny fluctuations in skin conductance; in the other hand the subject holds a computer mouse. To begin a trial the subject presses the mouse button and waits for a picture to appear on the screen. The computer selects a picture at random from a large pool of images, waits a certain period, say five seconds, then displays it for three seconds, after which the screen goes blank again for ten seconds. A message then appears on the screen telling the subject to start the next trial whenever ready.

The subject's skin conductance is continuously monitored while 30 to 40 trials are repeated in one session. The images appearing on the computer screen are either calm pictures of such things as landscapes, nature scenes, or peaceful-appearing people, or emotional pictures involving the erotic, violence, or accident scenes.

Radin describes four such experiments that he conducted of this type involving 24 to 50 participants in each. "The combined odds against chance for these four experiments was

125,000 to 1 in favor of a genuine presentiment effect." According to Radin: "These studies suggest that when the average person is about to see an emotional picture, he or she will respond before that picture appears (under double-blind conditions) (Radin, 2009).

The concept of presentiment holds that not only will a physiological response occur before the emotional stimulus, but that the strength of that response will increase as the emotionality of the future stimulus increases, indicating that specific information about the emotional content of the future image is perceived in the present. Radin investigated this effect in his four experiments and found this to occur with odds against chance of 125 to 1.

Radin is very aware of the difficulties presentiment poses for scientists and philosophers because it challenges commonsense beliefs about causality and time. To provide a persuasive case for evidence supporting its existence every conceivable loophole would have to be carefully examined and tightly closed. A number of alternative explanations would have to be ruled out, which he noted might include sensory or statistical cues about the upcoming targets, data collection errors, measurement or analytical artifacts, selective reporting biases, participant or experimenter fraud, or a variety of conscious or unconscious anticipatory strategies. In the process of designing, running, and analyzing his experiments Radin stated, "all of these factors were considered and none could explain the results."

Serious consideration of precognition immediately raises the issue of free will. If we see the future, are we locked into acting out the preview? And if not, and we do act to change the future that we've glimpsed, then could it really be the future, since it didn't actually happen?

The Rhine Research Center in Durham, North Carolina, has gathered the largest collection of ESP cases in the world. Among these are 433 reports of precognition in which there was enough threat of danger to merit intervention. In two-thirds of the cases nothing was done. In the one-third of cases in which individuals did try to intervene to change the future they had foreseen success attempts outnumbered failures two to one.

Although reports trickle in to the Rhine Center at a steady rate, they flooded in following September 11, 2001. Anecdotal reports and news stories revealed that scores and probably hundreds of individuals all over the country had premonitory dreams and waking fantasies prior to the events of 9/11. These took the form of inexplicable dread or sudden illness that kept them away from their jobs that day, or intuitions that prompted them to simply turn around and go home before the planes crashed into the WTC or the Pentagon. Shortly after the tragedies on 9/11 stories began to surface from people who had changed their travel plans at the last moment because of a vague, gnawing feeling that something was not quite right.

Some years earlier William Cox, a North Carolina researcher and businessman, was able to investigate a possible precognitive effect involving train crashes. He compared the number of passengers present on trains involved in accidents between 1950 and 1955 with the passenger load on the same run of each of the preceding seven, fourteen, twenty-one, and twenty-eight days. In every case he discovered that fewer people rode the trains that crashed or were wrecked than rode similar trains that did not crash. The odds against a chance explanation for this were greater than one hundred to one.

The four planes that were involved in 9/11 were only 21% full. Knowing if premonitions caused the high-vacancy rates on the doomed planes would require Cox's approach. That is, vacancy rates throughout the year would have to be compared against the rates on that date. Researchers have been unable to do this because the airlines have been unwilling to provide vacancy information. In fact, all the data for the September 11 flights has been impounded by the FBI (Dossey, 2009).

PSYCHOKINESIS (PK)—MIND OVER MATTER

The fact that our thoughts influence our behavior is a fundamental principle in psychology. And in an indirect fashion, through our behavior our thoughts can influence others and the material world. This can also occur on an unconscious level. If we expect something to happen, we often act outside of our awareness in such a way as to bring that about—a self-fulfilling prophesy. But can we directly influence the nonliving material world with our thoughts alone? Certainly we have all heard stories about people causing something to happen through the power of their thoughts. In myth and religion supernatural figures do it all of the time.

Some of the most dramatic examples of material things being directly impacted by some kind of unknown influence, purportedly the Spirits of the dead, occurred in the séances of the physical mediums of the nineteenth century. Such things as tables tilting, rotating, or rising into the air on their own accord; rapping noises; and ethereal music were common.

The most famous of the physical mediums, D. D. Home, was observed by credible witnesses to levitate his whole body, a table with several persons sitting on it, a heavy piano, an accordion on which he played without touching its keys, and even to elongate his body up to six inches. Unlike most other mediums, he conducted his demonstrations in full daylight. As we discussed, well-known physicist William Crooks tested Home under laboratory conditions and was convinced that what he was able to do could not be explained on the basis of any known factors, including outright fraud.

In modern times, one of the best known producers of mind-over-matter effects was Israeli mentalist/psychic Uri Geller. In public demonstrations around the world Geller exhibited the ability, using mental energy only, to bend or plasticize steel, platinum, and other metals by softly stroking them; change the readout on a Geiger counter; move a compass needle; dematerialize objects; make things fly through the room and broken watches and clocks run again; influence a magnetometer; and imprint a picture on a roll of photographic film using only mental energy. Although he admitted that early in his career he mixed standard magic tricks in with his PK demonstrations, in later years he gave many impressive demonstrations in scientific laboratories where his activities were closely observed and controlled. Although well-known ESP skeptic and magician James Randi claimed that Geller deceived the scientists who investigated him by employing sleight of hand tricks, other magicians strongly supported the legitimacy of his PK effects, notably parapsychologist and magician William E. Cox, who had once organized a committee within the Society of American Magicians to investigate false claims of ESP. Cox pointed out that given the controlled conditions imposed on Geller, including frame-by-frame videotaping from multiple angles with close-up lenses, it would be easy to catch deception by even the best of magicians. [*Best Evidence* pp. 88–89] Before his work with remote viewing in the Stargate program, Ingo Swann had demonstrated psychokinesis ability under experimental controls at Gertrude Schmeidler's laboratory at the City College of New York (Schmicker, 2000).

One of the most intriguing demonstrations of psychokinesis was produced by people whose original interest involved Spiritualism, not PK. In the 1970s eight ordinary men and women in Toronto, Canada, all members of the Toronto Society of Psychical Research, decided to see if they could produce an apparition, or ghost, using only their minds. They met together several hours each week in a séance, attempting to "contact" an imaginary deceased person they had decided to call Phillip. Although they didn't succeed in producing an apparition, they did produce a number of PK effects, including levitating a table and making it rock, slide, spin, twist, and flip over; making lights flicker or turn off and on; keeping a round object from rolling off a table tilted at a 45-degree angle; and creating rapping sounds as Philip "answered" their questions about his life. The group scientifically measured the intensity of the rappings and acoustically recorded the sounds. From this endeavor they concluded that séance-like PK phenomena are produced not by disincarnate Spirits, but by the mental energy of the persons participating in a séance.

In his discussion of the Toronto PK experiments, Schmicker notes that they suggest a kind of recipe for producing group PK that could be testable by anyone following certain steps. These include recruiting at least four people, establishing good group rapport, promoting a curiosity and excitement about PK and a desire to test it, encouraging the group to expect PK effects to happen, and if/when they do trying to accept them as natural, normal phenomena.

On a personal note, in 1998, while attending a hypnotherapy conference in San Francisco, I was intrigued by one of the workshops on the agenda, a "spoon bending party" being conducted by Jack Houck. I had never heard of him, but had been interested in the claims and controversy surrounding Uri Geller and his spoon bending and other demonstrations back in the '70s. Houck, I was to learn, was at the time a systems engineer at a large aerospace corporation who, after conducting his own research in ESP and PK, developed the idea that the best way to produce a paranormal phenomenon like psychokinesis was to create conditions like those suggested by Schmicker, particularly an emotional atmosphere. To test this idea, in 1981 he found 21 friends and associates willing to participate in a party-like environment where he supplied silverware. Upon giving his instructions 19 out of the 21 succeeded in bending spoons. Houck went on to hold hundreds of these PK parties for everyone from army generals at the Pentagon to famous writers.

Michael Schmicker, in his *Best Evidence* book (2000), describes his experience attending such a "party," which was very similar to my own. He and his brother John were among several hundred excited, expectant people gathered in the ballroom in a large circle around Jack to hear his instructions. They had been told they could bring their own silverware if they wanted or could pick a fork or spoon from the big box of cutlery Jack carries to each event. (Since the event I attended was part of a three-day conference we didn't have the opportunity to bring our own. I did test some of the silverware in his box and couldn't bend any of it.) There is no "mumbo-jumbo," Schmicker pointed out, "no New Age incantations, no dimmed lights, no elaborate formalities." Jack gave a brief history of his PK research, showed samples of spoons and forks bent by people in earlier PK parties, went over his theory of how he thinks PK is produced, and led them through the three steps they were to follow to hopefully produce bent spoons. These were:

Make a mental connection with what you want to affect, focus your attention and concentration on the spoon.
Command what you want to happen by shouting "Bend! Bend! Bend!!"
Release, let go mentally, and let it happen.

Within 20–30 seconds of shouting their commands people were bending spoons. Schmicker and his brother quickly mastered "kindergarten" level spoon bending, which involved waiting until they felt the spoon go warm and soft, then twirling and bending the handle in tight circles.

Unlike Schmicker and his brother I initially didn't even get to this point. My spoon simply didn't bend. This was disappointing but not surprising. I simply do not seem to have a "psychic" bone in my body. I signaled Jack in the crowd of excited participants and he came over. He placed his hands lightly on my forearms but did not exert any direct physical force or pressure. What it felt like was some kind of energy traveling down to my finger. My spoon began to feel warm and I easily bent it with barely any effort. I have kept my bent spoon as a reminder of what I personally experienced.

I will add here one more very unusual experience that I had involving a PK-like effect. Again, I'll reiterate that I don't consider myself in any way "psychic," although I have a long-standing interest in the field. A bit of background is important. I had traveled from the Rosebud Sioux Reservation in South Dakota, where I was living at the time (late 1970s), to a conference of the Association of Transpersonal Psychology held at a hotel about twenty miles north of Boston. My flight and bus to the conference were late and I had to hurry to get registered, grab my room key, and rush to the event I particularly wanted to attend. It was a talk and experiential workshop conducted by anthropologist and practicing shaman Michael Harner. I had met Michael a year earlier and had invited him and his wife Sandy to stay with my wife and I on the Rosebud while he participated in a small conference we held there annually with local medicine men.

In the Transpersonal workshop Harner, after discussing his research and personal experiences with shamanism, led us in what he called a "Spirit canoe" exercise. Briefly this involved entering a mild alteration of consciousness produced by drumming and "venturing to the underworld" to help Michael obtain a guardian Spirit for a participant. (Her presenting difficulty resulted in this shamanistic model, from being "dispirited"—losing her guardian Spirit.) During this experience I became increasingly aware that I should have used the restroom before rushing to the workshop. By the time it ended I was in such discomfort that I practically ran to my hotel room not far away. In reaching into my front pants pocket I discovered that my room key, a standard heavy metal key, was bent at a right angle. I was in such desperation I tried to insert it in the lock and bend it enough to work, but I could not completely straighten it. Some hours later I was able to spend a couple minutes with Harner, and I asked him what he could make of this experience. His only comment was to ask if, on the Rosebud, I was involved with any medicine men having "contrary" powers. I was not.

I have never been able to find a good explanation for my bent-key experience. I do know the key was fine when I used it to leave my suitcase in my room. There was no way I could have sat on it with enough force to bend it. Even if I had been pushed by someone, which I don't recall, it couldn't have bent the key. This experience remains for me the most unusual thing that I have ever encountered.

In terms of the apparent ability to employ psychokinesis, one of the most fascinating and incredible accounts features Ted Owens, who called himself the "PK man." This account, while clearly strange, may well be true, as Jeffrey Mishlove, who followed and documented Owens' activities for years and presented them in his 2000 book *The PK Man*, enjoys a sound reputation. On a number of occasions Owens very publicly announced plans to cause major changes in the weather, which turned out to occur as reported in the media. Owens often vacillated between claiming that he was solely responsible for causing these things through his PK powers or that they were actually produced by other-dimensional beings he called the Space Intelligences. He would send them his plans telepathically and they, for their own purposes, would carry them out.

PK RESEARCH

This supposed ability to influence the material world directly through thought alone was one of the first things that Rhine and other early parapsychologists studied in the laboratory. The principle research procedure they followed to do this involved dice. A subject chose a particular die face and then attempted to mentally influence it to come up when one or more dice were tossed. If the subject's intention matched the resulting face then a hit was scored. With one die a hit would occur by chance alone one in six times.

Over the years a large number of such studies were conducted, but no definitive conclusions emerged. In 1989, Radin and psychologist Diane Ferrari searched all English language journals for reports investigating whether mental intention could cause a preselected die face to land face up after being tossed. For each study they calculated a 50% equivalent hit rate, as well as noting the presence or absence of a series of 13 quality criteria, such as whether automatic recording was employed, whether witnesses were present, and whether control tests were performed. They discovered 73 relevant publications containing reports of 52 investigators involving 148 different experiments with a total of 2,569 subjects and 2.6 million dice throws. There were also 31 control studies involving just over 150,000 dice throws in which subjects did not attempt to mentally influence the results. The overall hit rate for the control studies was 50.02%, just as expected. However, the overall hit rate for all the experimental studies was 51.2%. While this may appear to be quite insignificant, statistically it results in odds against chance of more than a billion to one. To eliminate the possibility of a "file drawer" problem Radin and Ferrari calculated that to bring the odds against chance of a hit rate down to less than 20 to 1, for each published study there would have had to be 121 additional, unretrieved, and unsuccessful studies involving 52 investigators (Radin, 1997).

In the 1960s, physicist Helmut Schmidt developed a much more sophisticated method of investigating small-scale psychokinesis utilizing random-number generators (RNGs). An RNG is an electronic circuit relying on a random source, such as electronic noise or radioactive decay, to create sequences of bits (the numbers 1 and 0). Because RNGs are computer-controlled the random sequence can be perfectly recorded. Modern RNGs are highly sophisticated, employing features such as electromagnetic shielding, environmental fail-safe alarms, and fully automatic data recording. Subjects attempt to mentally influence the RNG's output so that in a sequence of predefined length it produces, say, more 1's than 0's. Often they get feedback about their efforts in the form of a digital display, audio feedback, computer graphics, or the movement of a robot's arms.

Some of the most extensive RNG PK research has been conducted at the Princeton Engineering Anomalies Research Laboratory (PEAR Lab). In 1997 engineer Robert Jahn and his colleagues published a review of 12 years of experiments conducted there involving over 100 subjects. What they found was a PK effect approximately equal to 1 bit out of 10,000 being shifted away from chance due to mental influence. While this seems like a tiny effect, over the entire database it resulted in odds against chance of 35 trillion to 1 (Radin, 2009).

In 2000, a large-scale study was jointly conducted by the PEAR Lab and two German labs to attempt to replicate the PEAR results. Similar research design and equipment were used for a preplanned series of trials. Although this study failed to provide a significant outcome, the results were significantly similar to the original PEAR findings, with odds against chance of 20 to 1. Radin observed that "while the outcome of the mega-trial was not independently successful in demonstrating PK effects there was evidence that the same basic trend was repeated."

Radin conducted a meta-analysis of all known PK studies involving the RNG procedure published up to then involving 490 studies by 90 researchers. While the overall effect seemed small in magnitude, it was nevertheless associated with odds against chance of 50,000 to 1. In terms of a potential file drawer problem, each of the 90 researchers would have had to conduct an additional 29 nonsignificant studies and failed to report any of them. Radin found in this meta-analysis that higher-quality studies did not result in significantly lowered effects, thus reinforcing his conclusion that chance, selective reporting, and variations in study quality were not viable explanations for the positive results.

In conclusion, observations about the results of studies suggesting that mind can influence matter, Radin sounds both a cautionary and a challenging note.

While consideration of the results of PK studies could prompt people to start "conjuring up wondrous images of future-oriented psychic technologies," the PK-as-influence finding has not yet been solidly confirmed. "Much more basic research is required to turn the fragile phenomena that have been observed into useful technologies" (Radin, 2009).

Radin points out that while these studies seem to imply that mind literally influences matter, there are alternative interpretations. Perhaps mind and matter are like two sides of the same coin. He suggests that if we were to take a ribbon and write mind on the inside and matter on the outside and wiggle the ribbon we would find very strong correlations between mind and matter, yet in a fundamental sense "never the twain shall meet." Suppose that unknown to us a mischievous friend cuts the ribbon, creates a half-twist, and carefully tapes it back together. Later, as we ponder the "abyss" between mind and matter, we absentmindedly trace a finger along the matter side of the ribbon. To our astonishment we find that our finger ends up on the mind side. The ribbon had been transformed into a Mobius strip by our friend's half-twist. The lesson, Radin says, is that "sometimes simple twists in conventional concepts can unify things that appear to be quite different, like mind and matter."

Although some people believe that consciousness may be the unifying "substance" from which mind and matter arise, Radin believes that defining one mystery in terms of another isn't particularly illuminating.

"At this point, all we can say is that when you begin to pry apart the mind-matter interface it's as though that crack releases a dazzling and profoundly mystifying light" (Radin, 2009).

FIELD CONSCIOUSNESS

In speculating about the nature and limits of psi phenomena Radin posed an intriguing question. Are we dealing with a personal perceptual skill that can be used to our private advantage, like an improved form of visual acuity or more sensitive hearing, or is something bigger going on, something that transcends the individual altogether? If psi is real, as the experimental results strongly suggest, then "in the same way that networks of neurons combine to form our brains, maybe psi forms an interconnective web of brain/minds that results in a collective mind" (Radin, 2009).

How to study such a phenomenon poses an intriguing challenge. Perhaps, Radin speculated, if a group of people engaged in some highly focused activity and it did bring about a significantly increased order or coherence in their mental activity this might infuse the environment with an "ordering field" that could be detectable. Random number generators (RNGs) seemed the logical choice to do this, as they had been shown in studies of psychokinesis to detect mind-matter interactions. RNGs are designed to produce pure randomness or entropy, and any fluctuations in entropy can be detected using statistical procedures. They can be programmed to automatically run in the background, where they function as a kind of passive observer of mind-matter interactions.

In 1997 an opportunity to test this idea presented itself. On August 31, Princess Diana and her companion Dodi al-Fayed were killed in a car accident in Paris, an event that was featured in the world's news broadcasts for the next few days. Radin and others interested in field consciousness decided to use her upcoming funeral, to be broadcast live worldwide with hundreds of millions of expected viewers, as an opportunity to examine the possibility of global mental coherence. A dozen researchers with RNGs located throughout the United States and Europe each ran them before, during, and after the funeral. The combined outputs of the 12 RNGs yielded a significant deviation, with odds against chance of 100 to 1, in alignment with the predicted effect.

The researchers ran a similar study when Mother Theresa died only a few days after Princess Diana, but the results were not significant. The difference between the two outcomes, they speculated, might lie with the fact that Mother Theresa was 87 when she died and known to be in poor health. Although her funeral was also broadcast live the proceedings were conducted in several languages without translation, and the quality of the broadcast pictures was poor. These factors might have reduced the extent of highly focused attention associated with the Princess Diana funeral.

The success of the Princess Diana experiment and the failure of the one involving Mother Teresa convinced Radin and the other researchers that "global mind" experiments should be pursued. That same year the Global Consciousness Project (GCP) was initiated under the leadership of Princeton psychologist Roger Nelson. The idea was that within several minutes of major news events attracting worldwide attention a degree of mental coherence would result that could be measured by RNGs around the world.

Radin explains how this would work by asking us to imagine a vast, windswept ocean with scores of buoys dancing in the waves. Each buoy has a bell attached to it to alert passing ships about hidden dangers. The sounds from each buoy's bell are broadcast by radio to a central receiving station on land. This station receives the transmissions from all the buoys and consolidates them to form a single collective tone reflecting the "ocean's grand dance." Most of the time there would be no pattern to this sound. But imagine that every so often these buoys that are isolated from one another by thousands of miles "mysteriously synchronize and swell into a great harmonic chord." This would alert us that something large has affected the entire ocean. Whatever the cause might be, when the random bell tones spontaneously "coalesce into a great chord" we would be interested in two types of analyses. One would be how loud it is, that is, the amplitude of the tone, and the second how coherent it is, or the degree of its harmony.

The Global Consciousness Project, Radin tells us, can be considered analogous to monitoring the ocean's surface for the presence of a tsunami. In this case researchers are not looking for massive movements of water and trying to infer what is happening in the depths of a great ocean, but are monitoring "massive movements of entropy generated by a network of RNGs" and attempting to infer what is happening in "the depths of a grand mind."

Each random number generator (RNG) in the GCP network is attached to a computer that collects one sample of 200 bits per second. Every five minutes all data are automatically assembled and sent over the internet to a central web server in Princeton, New Jersey. RNGs in many places around the world were set up that would run continuously and automatically to see whether large scale coherence was generated during both events that are planned, like New Year's Eve celebrations, and also during unexpected events, like natural disasters, the tragic deaths of celebrities, and terrorist attacks (*Entangled Minds*, pp. 196–197).

One unique event that was studied was what was known as Y2K. On the stroke of midnight from 1999 to 2000 many people around the world feared a worldwide computer meltdown. Radin predicted that as each time zone approached midnight the increasingly coherent attention of millions of people would increase the order detected by the RNGs.

When he analyzed the data this turned out to be the case. The variance or "noise" among the RNGs dropped precipitously at the stroke of midnight. The probability of observing a drop of this magnitude in comparison to similarly generated random data is associated with odds against chance of 1,300 to 1.

No doubt the most dramatic event in recent history was the terrorist attack on the Twin Towers and Pentagon on September 11, 2001. As might be expected, numerous striking changes were recorded by the 36 involved RNGs.

Radin suggests that to understand the nature of these anomalies, to appreciate why the results the researchers found are not due to any number of mundane flaws or mistakes, it is important to understand the nature of the data collected. Each RNG in the network continually generates sequences of random bits and, if they sample periodically, they form a distribution resembling a bell-shaped curve. There are four simple ways, he points out, that a bell curve can deviate from a theoretically perfect bell shape. It can be shifted to the left as compared to chance expectation, shifted to the right, squashed flat, or squashed thin. The first two deviations in this case are not suitable because there is no clear way of predicting which direction the curve might shift. The focus in these studies was on the second two methods, how the width of the bell curve changes from one day to the next.

In examining the results of their analysis, the researchers noticed that on September 11, 2001, the curve deviated wildly as compared to all the other days they examined June 16–20. The curve peaked nearly two hours before a hijacked jet crashed into the World Trade Tower at 8:46 a.m. EDT, and dropped to its lowest point around 2 p.m., roughly eight hours later. The huge drop in the curve within an eight-hour period was the single largest drop for any day in 2001. The GCP "bell rang loudest" on that day because all of the RNGs behaved in the same way, even though they were scattered around the world, hundreds to thousands of miles apart.

Radin pointed out that positive results in field consciousness studies do not necessarily prove that coherent states of mind literally influence the environment. What they reveal is that intention and RNG outputs are correlated, and correlation doesn't necessarily imply causation. The movement of sunflowers over the course of the day is closely correlated to the apparent movement of the sun, but sunflowers do not cause the sun to move. In this example we know what causes what; the direction of causation is simply reversed. In circumstance involving mind-matter interactions determining what causes what is not so obvious.

Radin proposed that one way to examine the question as to whether mind-matter coherence effects are actually caused by mind would be to see whether mind interactions with nonliving systems such as RNGs would also simultaneously correspond to changes in a living system.

He teamed up with molecular biologists Ryan Taft and Garret Yount from the California Pacific Medical Center (CPMC) Research Institute to conduct experiments similar to those mind-living systems investigations previously described, but with the added element that any field consciousness effect would also be investigated. Their procedure involved exposing cultures of astrocytes, the most abundant cell type in the human brain, to healing intention to see whether this would increase their rate of growth compared to when they were not so exposed. For a nonliving target system they used three RNGs, each based upon a different type of random source.

This procedure lent itself to the examination of still another question. Would healing intention practiced repeatedly at the same location change the actual physical site itself into a healing location? Stories of spontaneous healings at sacred sites, such as Lourdes, suggested that perhaps with sufficient exposure those sites themselves might generate healing properties similar to those produced by a healer. Stories also abound of particular physical and psychological sensations repeatedly being experienced at traditionally haunted sites, again suggesting that certain physical sites become charged with some kind of energy. Of course, in both cases there is a strong possibility that such effects could be brought about by the expectations of those reporting them.

The researchers conducted a three-day experiment involving four experienced Johrei practitioners. Johrei is a Japanese Spiritual healing practice based on the concept of a universal Spiritual force or energy that can be cultivated and directed by intention. When focused on the body this energy raises its Spiritual vibrations, bringing about improved health and Spiritual purification.

The experimental procedure involved cultured human brain cells that were placed inside a thermally insulated box. Treatment sessions took place within an electromagnetically and acoustically shielded chamber. During a treatment session a Johrei practitioner directed their healing intention toward the box from about two feet away for twenty-five minutes, without touching the box. This process was repeated four times a day for each of three days, with healing sessions and control sessions being randomly alternated. Ten days later the cells in all flasks were "fixed" to stop further cell growth. Two lab analysts not otherwise involved in the experiment independently counted the number of cell colonies in each flask. Two RNGs were hidden behind a curtain inside the shielded room and a third RNG was six feet outside the shielded room in a hidden location. This one was a computer-monitored Geiger counter device that monitored background ionizing radiation, including ambient alpha, beta, gamma, and X-ray particles, in ten-second samples.

The results indicated that repeated exposure to Johrei treatment resulted in increased brain cell growth, whereas there was no such increase that occurred among untreated cells. The odds against chance of this effect was 1,100 to 1. Examination of the results of the three RNGs indicated that the three devices combined produced a peak response in the morning of the third day with odds against chance of 1.3 million to 1. Each of the three RNGs independently peaked at the same time. Both the treated cell cultures and three RNGs significantly deviated from chance at around the same time on the third day. The researchers carefully considered and ruled out alternative explanations for the results. This experiment, Radin points out, "suggested that certain forms of focused attention appear to causally influence both living and nonliving systems."

To investigate the possible influence of distance on this effect Radin obtained data from 36 other RNGs located from 24 to 10,500 miles from the lab that were not part of this experiment but had been set up to run continuously as part of another investigation. Comparing measures of deviation in the three RNGs in the lab with similar measures for the distant RNGs revealed strong evidence of a distance effect with odds against chance of 37,000 to 1 (*Entangled Minds*, p. 191). To further explore this distance effect the combined deviations from chance in the five RNGs within 100 miles of the lab were compared with six RNGs 6,000 or more miles away. The five closer RNGs peaked significantly above chance at the same time as the three in the lab, whereas the six distant RNGs hovered around chance. The combined effect for the three RNGs in the lab and the five nearby was associated with odds against chance of 5 million to 1. These results suggested that healing intention can act at a distance, but perhaps not at arbitrarily long distances.

One characteristic of psi [Radin noted] as revealed by both spontaneous reports and in lab tests is that psi is not tightly bound to "now," in either space or time. But there is also evidence, like the results of this experiment, that psi may not be completely independent of distance (Radin, 2009).

Other than Radin's unique effort investigating mental influence on both living systems and RNGs just described, the field consciousness studies so far discussed have involved highly dramatic, major global events. Radin wondered if ordinary daily fluctuations in the world's attention to news accounts might also influence the RNGs. As an objective measure of newsworthy events he used all of the news events listed in the "Year in Review" feature on the Information Please website for the year 2001, a total of 394 news events for 250 days. If the GCP was actually responding to the world's attention to global events Radin predicted that those 250 newsworthy days would have a larger average inter-correlation value than the remaining 115 non-newsworthy days. This turned out to be correct, with odds against chance of 100 to 1.

It would seem that field consciousness may well be a reality. Just what that may mean and how it fits with the world as we know it are intriguing questions.

In the concluding section of the book we'll discuss criticisms that have been leveled about psi phenomena.

SECTION II

SPIRITS

A huge range of spirits can be found in all cultures everywhere on earth, including in the US. They permeate our culture, but we typically do not view them as actually being real. We see them as vestiges of old superstitions, important primarily as entertainment.

The term "spirit" has many different meanings, but for our purposes a very general definition for spirit is a living, conscious, nonphysical entity. Very broadly they roughly fall into two groups: nonhuman spirits and human spirits. Nonhuman spirits are independent from us and never were human. Human spirits were once living people and are also referred to as souls or sometimes, when they appear to us, as ghosts.

CHAPTER 3

NONHUMAN SPIRITS

In her marvelous and comprehensive 2010 book *Encyclopedia of Spirits* Judika Illes tells us that nonhuman spirits have permeated every culture for thousands of years and continue to do so today. They have filled literature from its earliest days to today's best sellers. Fairy tales, an entire literary genre, is named for a branch of the spirit world. Mythology from around the world can be defined as stories about and involving spirits.

Illes emphasizes that spirits do more than pervade literature, games, myths, and movies; they also walk among us. For many people coming from all walks of life, unconventional and conventional alike, this is a statement of basic, obvious fact. There has never been a time when a large number of people did not consider the presence of spirits to be part of normal reality, including today. There has never, ever been a time when people and spirits did not communicate and interact with each other.

There are many different types of spirits. Some possess unlimited power, while others are comparatively limited. Many possess powerful links with specific locations, such as a mountain or city, or with general regions such as lakes, oceans, forests, deserts, swamps, or the moon. Some spirits also possess their very own realms where shamans journey (Illes, 2009).

WORKING WITH SPIRITS

Working with spirits is a shared and universal human experience. Every group of people everywhere on Earth has some history of spiritual interaction, whether or not it is publicly acknowledged, and whether or not it is currently celebrated, condemned, or suppressed. Right now, somewhere on Earth, on each and every continent, people are actively interacting with, petitioning, pleading with, thanking, or channeling spirits. They are seeking assistance in the form of healing, protection, prosperity, happiness, contact with spiritual power, or direct contact with the sacred.

Spirit veneration has survived and thrived despite thousands of years of brutal opposition because it produces joy, success, and positive results. In fiction people run from vicious spirits, but in real life people actively seek their presence and have historically suffered tremendous persecution to maintain relationships with spirits because the rewards are immeasurable. Thousands of years of propaganda to the contrary, encounters and experiences with spirits are generally positive. That's why people keep seeking them out.

In *Encyclopedia of Spirits* Illes offers a wealth of information about nonhuman spirits and how to secure their assistance. Methods of working with spirits have remained fairly consistent over millennia and all over the world. In a nutshell this is how it works.

Identify a spirit who can help you. For those who are generally unfamiliar with the huge number of spirits who might be available she describes hundreds—their likes and dislikes, and the particular kind of services they offer.

Familiarize yourself with this spirit to determine whether you are comfortable requesting its assistance.

Respectfully, but straightforwardly and clearly, articulate what you are looking for, going into as much detail as seems to be needed.

Remember that relationships between people and spirits are mutually beneficial. Spirits expect to receive something in return for favors rendered, if only sincere gestures of thanks, love, and veneration.

When petitioning a spirit, what you are looking for may show up in some quite ordinary thing someone does. Spirit contact may be more obvious, such as a spirit openly identifying itself by name to you in a dream or showing itself in a very recognizable form. Its personal attributes, its signs and symbols, may begin to make constant appearances in your life. Sometimes you'll know you've made contact because the spirit has clearly fulfilled a request.

It is not necessary to believe in spirits, but you need to believe in the possibility that just maybe there is something out there that can help you. If you are helped, it is crucial to acknowledge the reality of what helped you. Whatever you think spirits are, if you intend to work with them it is crucial to see them as something alive and independent from you. Many people have difficulty accepting spirits as distinct living entities, yet they live among us.

Spirits most often show themselves to people in dreams, but sometimes people see spirits while they are awake, even when other people present are unable to do so. Some people just see spirits, whether they want to or not. It is crucial to remember, Illes tells us, that regardless of how they appear, whether in exalted or humble form, spirits are really sacred beings of spirit and energy. While they may resemble a person, animal, or a bird, that guise is a cloak. Most spirits are aware that humans generally find it difficult to communicate with anything except another human. When they wish to communicate or make their presence known many do so in a form that we can understand and handle.

Countless means that have been devised over time to encourage communication with spirits include divination, visualizations, spells, and rituals. Illes tells us that summoning spirits can involve courtship, seduction, and bribes. You can create an atmosphere that appeals to a spirit and makes it feel at home. Many possess associations with specific colors, numbers, images, fragrances, and objects, and these are the tools used to beckon them.

The most common method of venerating and maintaining contact with spirits is feeding them human food or drink on a regular basis. Food, beverages, and gifts make spirits feel welcome and are influential tools of communication. Other common methods of attracting and venerating them involve construction of some sort of altar, lighting candles, and offering flowers (Illes, 2010).

SHAMANISM AND SPIRITS

At some point, many thousands of years ago, a class of individuals that today we might call psychic or spiritually gifted learned to communicate with nonhuman and human spirits and to secure their help in carrying out healing and spiritual activities for the benefit of their community. Anthropologists call them shamans, skeptics, or witch doctors, and the actual community members medicine men or women. Shamans were the first religious specialists, predating mystics, prophets, and priests by thousands of years, and they continue to perform their work today. Best known for entering alternative states of consciousness where they are able to draw on the help of spirits, shamans often journey out of their bodies to nonmaterial regions or dimensions where those spirits reside. One of the major practices they employ to do this involves ingesting psychedelic plants.

Until recently shamanism was utilized on all inhabited continents by indigenous peoples. The word "shaman" comes from the Tungusic-speaking peoples of Siberia and north China, but due to the worldwide similarity of the basic practices anthropologists began to apply the term generically. Because of wars, missionaries, persecution, the introduction of new diseases, and a radical erosion of their cultures' shamanic knowledge, the numbers of indigenous shamans were drastically reduced over the last five centuries. Fortunately, in the last few decades this situation has started to change (Keating, 2021).

MICHAEL HARNER

One of the best-known experts on shamanism, Michael Harner, is a practicing shaman. His account of how this interest began is fascinating. In 1960 and 1961, Harner was invited by the American Museum of Natural History to make a year-long expedition to the Peruvian Amazon to study the culture of the Conibo Indians. For a year he lived with them; although his anthropological research on their culture had been going well, his attempts to obtain information on their religion were not successful. Finally, they told him that if he really wanted to learn, he would have to take the shamans' sacred drink made from ayahuasca, the "soul vine."

He was given a concoction poured into a gourd bowl that he drank quickly, finding that it had a strange, slightly bitter taste. As he stared upward into the darkness, faint lines of light appeared that grew sharper and burst into brilliant colors. A sound like the rushing water of a waterfall grew stronger and stronger. The faint lines overhead gradually interlaced to form a canopy that resembled a geometric mosaic of stained glass. He could see dim figures engaged in shadowy movements. A gigantic, grinning crocodilian head seemed to be presiding over the activities and a torrential flood of water gushed from its cavernous jaws. The waters slowly rose, as did the canopy above them. The scene then changed into just blue sky above and sea below, and the creatures vanished.

Then he began to see two strange boats floating through the air toward him. They slowly combined to form a single vessel that had a huge dragon-headed prow like that of a Viking ship. As the boat floated back and forth above him he saw that it was a giant galley with several hundred oars moving back and forth, making a rhythmic swishing sound. At that point he heard the most beautiful singing he had ever heard in his life coming from the myriad voices on the galley. Large numbers of people became visible with the heads of blue jays and the bodies of humans like the bird-headed gods of ancient Egyptian tomb paintings.

Harner was certain that he was dying and that the bird-headed people had come to take his soul away on their boat. The extremities of his body became deadened and his entire body slowly began to feel like it was turning into concrete. As he struggled to accept his fate he began to receive more visions and information. This new material, he was told, was being presented because he was dying and, therefore, safe to receive the secrets reserved for the dying and the dead. The givers of these thoughts appeared to be giant reptilian creatures that he could only vaguely see in the gloomy lowermost depths of the back of his brain.

Harner was then shown a scene of the planet Earth eons before there was any life on it, with only an ocean, barren land, and a bright blue sky. Hundreds of large black creatures with stubby pterodactyl-like wings and huge whale-like bodies dropped from the sky. They explained to him in a kind of thought language that they were fleeing from an enemy out in space. They showed him how they had created life on earth to hide within all of its forms to disguise their presence. They are inside of everything, including humans, and are the true masters of humanity and the entire planet. Humans are only receptacles and servants of these creatures.

Harner began to struggle against returning to the ancient ones, who seemed increasingly alien and possibly evil. With a great last effort he managed to utter the word "medicine" to the Indians with him. They made the antidote, and upon drinking it the dragons gradually disappeared back into the lower depths and the soul boat vanished.

Eager to obtain an opinion about what happened from an expert, he consulted a blind shaman who had made many excursions into the spirit world with the aid of ayahuasca. He only related the highlights and told him the creatures were something like great bats who said that they were the true masters of the world. The shaman said with a grin, "Oh, they're always saying that. But they are only the Masters of Outer Darkness." He then waved his hand toward the sky. Harner relates that he felt a chill along his spine because he had not told the shaman that he saw them coming from outer space. The blind shaman was already familiar with what he had experienced because he had explored the same hidden world. At that moment Harner decided to learn everything he could about shamanism.

Three years later Harner returned to South America, this time to be with the Jívaro. He wanted to learn firsthand how to practice shamanism the Jívaro way. He was introduced to Akachu, a famous shaman, and explained that he had come to acquire spirit helpers, "tsentsak." For this privilege Akachu asked for his gun. Akachu prepared a concoction of juice from maikua (a Brugmansia species of datura) plant cuttings. That evening Harner drank about an eighth of a cup of the liquid, which had a disagreeable taste slightly similar to green tomatoes. He felt a numbing sensation. The next thing he was aware of he was being awakened by a flash of lightning and a thunderous explosion. He was pummeled by hurricane-like wind and stinging rain.

His companions had disappeared. Suddenly, a gigantic reptilian form floated directly toward him. Its body shone with brilliant green, purple, and red hues. As the serpentine creature drew closer, coiling and uncoiling, it separated into two dragons, both facing him. They had come to take him. Then they coalesced back into one. Harner picked up a small stick and desperately charged. It uttered an earsplitting scream and abruptly vanished.

Following this experience, with the shaman's guidance he began to acquire the tsentsak—the magical darts or spirit helpers that are essential to the practice of Jívaro shamanism. They are the main powers believed to cause and cure illness. Normally they are invisible, and even shamans can only perceive them in an altered state of consciousness. Bad shamans send these tsentsak into the bodies of victims to make them ill, or to kill them. Good shamans, or healers, use their own tsentsak to help them suck out spirits from the body of a sick person. New shamans collect all kinds of insects, plants, and other objects which become their spirit helpers.

Almost any object can become a tsentsak if it is small enough to be swallowed by the shaman. Different types cause and can be used to cure different kinds of illness. The greater the variety of these spirit helpers that a shaman has in his body the greater his ability is to doctor. Tsentsaks have an ordinary and nonordinary aspect. Their ordinary aspect is an ordinary material object that is seen without drinking ayahuasca. Their nonordinary true aspect is revealed to the shaman by taking the drink. When that occurs the magical darts appear in their hidden forms as spirit helpers, such as jaguars, serpents, giant butterflies, birds, and monkeys that actively assist the shaman in their work.

The first task of a shaman called to treat a patient is diagnosis. They drink ayahuasca and green tobacco water that changes their consciousness and allows them to see into the patient's body. If the illness is due to sorcery the shaman will see the intruding nonordinary entity clearly enough to determine whether they possess the appropriate spirit helper to suck it out. This can only be done in darkness, because only then can they perceive nonordinary reality.

When the sun sets they alert the tsentsak by whistling the tune of the power song they have been given. When they are ready to suck they keep a tsentsak in their mouth identical to the one they have seen in the patient's body. It incorporates both its material and nonmaterial aspect and functions to catch the nonordinary aspect of the tsentsak when the shaman sucks it out, so that it can't enter their body and do them harm. The essence of the offending tsentsak is caught by, and incorporated into, the material substance of the one that the shaman has in their mouth. They then vomit this out and display it to the patient and their family.

Harner points out that the shamanic practice of the Jívaro and the Conibo stand apart from many other tribal peoples who have long practiced shamanism without employing psychedelics. In the years since his work with them he has briefly studied with these other groups and learned how shamanism could be successfully practiced without the use of ayahuasca or other drugs. This knowledge has been especially useful for him in introducing Westerners to the practice of shamanism (Harner, 1990). In his more recent book *Cave and Cosmos* (2013) Harner expands on his discussion of shamanism:

> While the work of shamans encompasses virtually the full gamut of known spiritual practices, shamanism is universally characterized by an intentional change in consciousness ... to engage in purposeful two-way interaction with spirits ... What they [shamanistic traditions] all ... share is disciplined interaction with spirits in nonordinary reality to help and heal others.
>
> These interactions occur through "out-of-body" journeys to otherworldly realms where these spirits reside, and it is this activity that distinguishes shamanism from other forms of spiritual practice.

Harner emphasizes that for shamans, spirits are absolutely real. Shamans differ from those who believe in spirits because they know from firsthand experience that spirits exist. They see the spirits, touch them, hear them, and converse with them.... Shamans no more believe spirits exist than you believe your family, friends, and acquaintances exist. You know your family, friends, and acquaintances exist because you talk and otherwise interact with them daily. Similarly, shamans know spirits exist because they interact with them daily or, more often, nightly, for it is usually easier to see spirits in darkness (Harner, 2013).

According to shamanic understanding, the cosmos contains three worlds: the upper, middle, and lower. We live in the middle world, which has both nonspiritual and spiritual aspects, what Harner calls ordinary and nonordinary reality (OR and NOR), whereas the upper and lower worlds are purely spiritual and exist only in nonordinary reality. Shamans travel to them to seek assistance for healing and divination from compassionate spirits there. While there are a huge variety of helping spirits, among the most common and compassionate are those of human and nonhuman beings who once lived in ordinary reality and left the middle world after their death to enter NOR in the upper and lower worlds. They are in the process of ongoing development, gaining increasing compassion and power as they move toward closer union with the loving hidden universe.

Harner points out that these compassionate beings want to alleviate suffering and pain in our world because, while now merged within realms of divine love without pain, they understand and empathize with our pain and suffering because they formerly lived in our ordinary reality. They are known in various forms in virtually all human cultures. A number of tribal societies have ancestral spirits, as well as spirits of animals and plants. Christianity and Hinduism know ancestral spirits as the spirits of saints.

Harner offers a major distinction between shamans and ordinary people and priests, who commonly appeal to these spirits by means of prayer. Although such supplication can often facilitate spiritual help from the other reality and is used in shamanic practice, prayer is not usually recognized as being as effective as their two-way interaction with one or more helping spirits because compassionate spirits in the upper and lower worlds are limited in power to affect circumstances in the middle world. They need allies in ordinary reality to help create openings and passageways to alleviate pain and suffering. Shamans can do this through their journeys, establishing strong healing connections to the middle world.

The upper world is not only home to a great variety of compassionate spirits, but modern people who have journeyed there have reported experiences heretofore generally assumed to be reserved for the founders of the great religions. These experiences included hearing heavenly choirs and celestial music, entering realms of splendor, meeting deities and the deceased, celestial dismemberment, cosmic union, and the discovery of indecipherable scrolls and books.

The lower world is also home to a variety of compassionate spirits and powers.

Contrary to cultural expectations [modern people who journeyed there] did not find the Lower World to resemble the Christian hell, but rather the opposite. Many later said that upon dying they would prefer to go down rather than up, based upon the knowledge they had gained for themselves through core shamanic journeying (Harner, 2013).

Harner points out that their reports cast doubt on the argument that these peoples' experiences in the upper and lower worlds were simply products of cultural projection.

Of major importance to shamans in their work are animal spirit helpers or power animals. Harner likens them to an electric transformer that receives the immense power of the universe and modulates it into a form that can be safely transmitted to humans. However, this power or energy differs from what we think of as physical power insofar as it also contains knowledge of the nonordinary reality. While they are clearly not the only power connection shamans have to the universe, as there are a great variety of helping spirits with some degree of power, they are somewhat unique. When connected with a power animal one becomes power-filled.

The middle world where we live also has a complex variety of spirits, including nature spirits and such helpers as power animals who occupy all realms. Many middle world spirits have limited compassion. Some, in fact, may have none, and can even be the source of illness and other difficulties. Among these problematical entities are spirits of deceased persons that have significant determination and power to remain in the middle world to look after their surviving family members. They usually linger in locations that had long been familiar to them and provide power and protection only to their own descendants. However, they may undertake hostile action against outsiders who seem to threaten those individuals and their interests. The middle world is also home to amoral spirits who lack any compassion for anyone but whose powers can be used by sorcerers to affect the lives of others without their permission. They include the spirits of elements and certain small objects and creatures.

In our middle world there are also the spirits of deceased persons who are involuntarily here. These spirits typically do not know that they are dead. They are aware that they are lonely and unhappy and may seek to enter a living person's body or mind, or simply hover close to that person. They can become confused with living people's dreams, and those people may erroneously assume that they are having their own past-life experiences. These lost or wandering spirits normally do not have much power, but still can be a widespread source of illness. Shamans are able to heal all of these various afflictions (Harner, 2013).

From a shamanistic perspective, spiritual factors can contribute to illness in two main ways. Patients may lose a spirit important to their well-being, or they may acquire a spirit detrimental to their well-being. Shamans determine the precise nature of their difficulty (conduct a diagnosis) by entering the shamanic state of consciousness and performing a diagnostic divination by consulting their helping spirits, or by shamanically "seeing" the spiritual causation of an illness, or both.

Several different healing strategies can be used depending on a patient's difficulty. Soul retrieval is typically employed in cases of mental and emotional trauma, which restores the portion of the patient's soul that had left at the time of an emotional or physical trauma. It is also useful to treat cases of dependency on alcohol and other drugs.

When the protective power of a personal guardian spirit is lost and the patient also has suffered significant soul loss that individual becomes especially vulnerable to illness in the form of involuntary possession of his or her body and mind by a spirit, typically that of a confused deceased human being. This is another common factor in cases of mental and emotional illnesses. In these situations the shaman employs depossession strategies.

For cases involving depression and chronic illness unresponsive to normal medical treatment guardian spirit retrieval is the preferred strategy to restore the patient's spiritual power. When there is chronic localized pain or illness that hasn't responded adequately to medical treatment and a shaman has diagnosed the intrusion of a spirit as the cause shamans can use noninvasive procedures to extract the harmful spirit. One is to suck the spirit out of the patient's body (Harner, 2013).

During my time on the Rosebud Reservation I invited Harner to attend a small healing workshop presented by my college and to attend two ceremonies with me. During one the medicine man said of Harner, "I see we have a sucking doctor among us. We don't see many of those anymore." I have no idea how he could have known this as Harner hadn't mentioned it.

Most people who have some awareness of shamanism are likely to believe shamans are a rapidly dwindling group of rather exotic primitive people living in cultures far removed from our own. It may be surprising to learn that Harner has not only spent more than sixty years studying this practice among a wide range of currently active shamans around the world, but that he has trained thousands of Western people to enter the shamans' reality for their own spiritual development.

He offers reports of these people detailing their voyages to the upper and lower worlds. In most respects they closely resemble accounts obtained from native shamans around the world. It might seem reasonable to assume that through this training students would learn what to expect in their journeys to these worlds and then have these expectations fulfilled. Harner makes clear that he has carefully avoided this possibility by giving them little information ahead of time other than the methods to employ. They then learn directly through their own experiences, and what they encounter often surprises them by running counter to what cultural norms would have suggested (Harner, 2013).

CHAPTER 4

THE LAKOTA SIOUX AND SPIRITS

VISION QUESTS

Lakota holy man Black Elk described the vision quest, or *hanblecheyapi*, as one of the basic ancient sacred rituals. Everyone can seek a vision, and in the old days men and women both frequently did so. There are many reasons for seeking a vision, which helps us to realize our oneness with all things, to know that all things are our relatives; then in behalf of all things we pray to Wakan-Tanka that He may give to us knowledge of Him who is the source of all things, yet greater than all things (Brown, 1989).

Most importantly, visions are sought to secure the assistance of spiritual beings to bring healing and help to members of the community. When this is acquired in a vision the medicine man (shaman) is said to have power.

The person seeking a vision goes with a filled sacred pipe to a holy man, saying he (almost always male) wishes to do this and asks for his help. They smoke the pipe, then decide on a day for the seeker. On the chosen day the seeker goes with his pipe to the tipi of the holy man, who advises him to build an *inipi* lodge (sweat lodge) for him to purify himself.

Following this he, along with his two helpers, are now ready to go up to the mountain, where he will cry for a vision. When they arrive at the foot of the mountain the helpers go on ahead with the equipment that will be needed to prepare the sacred place. They go directly to the center of the spot they have chosen and first make a hole in which they place some tobacco. Then they set up a long pole in the hole with the offerings tied at the top. Another pole is placed about ten strides to the west with offerings tied to it. Poles are set up in the same manner in the north, east, and south. The other helper makes a bed of sage at the center so that when the seeker is tired he can lie having his head against the center pole and his feet stretching towards the east.

They return to him and he walks alone and naked up to the top of the mountain, holding his pipe in front of him and carrying his buffalo robe that can be used at night. Entering the sacred place, he goes directly to the center pole and faces west. Holding up his pipe with both hands he cries, "O Wakan-Tanka, have pity on me, that my people may live!" Then he goes to each of the poles, offering the same prayer, always returning to the center each time. After completing each one of these rounds he raises his pipe to the heavens and asks the wingeds and all things to help him. He then points the pipe stem to the Earth and asks for aid from all that grows upon our Mother.

Following this he remains silent, directing his whole attention to the Great Spirit, and alert to recognize any messenger that may be sent to him. Often helping beings come in the form of an animal, even one that seems small and insignificant. Although none may speak to him at first, they are important and should be observed. All day long he walks along the sacred paths among the poles while asking Wakan-Tanka for help. In the evening he may sleep on the bed of sage with his head against the center pole. Very often during sleep the most powerful visions come, which are not merely dreams, but much more real and powerful. They do not come from ourselves, but from Wakan-Tanka. The seeker should get up in the middle of the night and again go to the four quarters, returning to the center each time, all the while praying for help. He should always get up with the morning star and pray silently in his heart. The seeker continues all of these behaviors for the three or four days of his quest. He is not permitted to eat or drink during this entire time.

At the end of this period the helpers come to take him back to the camp, where he immediately enters the sweat lodge. The holy man, his spiritual guide, enters next, with others coming in. The seeker is asked to tell everything that happened and not leave anything out. As he does so his guide comments on what each element may mean. When he has finished the *inipi* takes place. This completes the vision quest.

A person may not receive a vision or message from the Great Spirit the first time that he undertakes a vision quest. However, he should remember that Wakan-Tanka is always anxious to help those who seek Him with a pure heart. A lot depends on him and upon the extent to which he has purified and prepared himself. If no vision is received he may decide to engage in a second quest (author's personal interaction with Lakota medicine men).

LAKOTA SIOUX SPIRITUALITY AND HEALING

In this discussion I will depart from a strict academic stance to introduce some of my personal experiences and observations. In 1976, I secured a position as a college teacher in the human services field at Sinte Gleska College (now university) on the Rosebud Sioux Reservation in South Dakota. My wife and I remained there for four years. The main goal of the college was to help young reservation inhabitants acquire the education to offer services in the teaching, health, and human services fields, while at the same time to help them gain a deeper understanding, appreciation, and respect for their Lakota heritage so they could bring much-needed healing to their families and communities. That heritage involves a world view much different from those that whites were raised in and accepted as simply the obvious way things are.

The college at the time was in its fourth year and owed its existence largely to two people: Gerald Mohatt, the founding president and a former Jesuit who had come to the Rosebud in 1967; and Stanley Red Bird, representing the Rosebud people. While Jerry and Stanley, among many others, were laying the groundwork for the college, they were also attempting to strengthen the work of the local Lakota healers or medicine men. The result was the formation of the Rosebud Medicine Men and Associates, which came to include most of the practicing medicine men on the reservation and their helpers. Stanley became the chairman of the association, as well as the chairman of the college board of directors.

The Human Services office at Sinte Gleska served as a kind of informal meeting place for people who wanted to talk with Stanley, so almost on a daily basis one or more of the medicine men's group would be there. I had the good fortune to be responsible for organizing and facilitating one of the courses the college began to offer titled Lakota Medicine. Members of the group came to class to give talks and led students on field trips to find medicinal plants and other natural things used for rituals and sacred purposes. My association with Stanley and members of the group gave me an opportunity to be invited to healing ceremonies whenever I wanted.

To appreciate the work of Lakota medicine men it is crucial to understand that although functioning fully in contemporary reservation life, they simultaneously participated in an ancient heritage with a world view quite different from that of us modern folks.

HEALING CEREMONIES ON THE ROSEBUD

Most of the ceremonies, or *lowanpis*, I attended were held by medicine man Robert Stead at his house out on the prairie. The person seeking help and requesting a ceremony would have first gone to him, presented a sacred pipe, and asked for help. To prepare for the ceremony the help seeker or friends would have made tobacco ties and made or purchased food items. I would have made some tobacco ties to bring with me also. Tobacco ties are small pieces of material a few inches square tied at the corners to contain a small amount of tobacco and tied on a string some 4–6 inches apart.

On the evening of a ceremony, typically with my friend and fellow human services instructor Frank Pommersheim, I would arrive early so we could participate in the sweat that the medicine man and helpers did to purify themselves. When this was concluded it would be dark and we would go into the house. Everyone else, typically 15–25 people, would be there in the main room of the simple Stead home. The altar would be set up consisting of what looked like fine sand placed on the floor in the form of a circle maybe sixteen inches in diameter. Strings of tobacco ties would be placed around it. Four cans with sticks with attached colored materials would be placed surrounding the altar to represent the four directions. The medicine man's sacred materials, including his pipe, would be placed in a certain way. If a medicine was required, typically it would be in a container next to the altar. Blankets would then be put over the windows to keep out any possible light and the door would be locked.

The medicine man and helpers would then begin praying and singing songs of welcome to invite the spirits in. Robert's spirits were *wanagi*, spirits of former medicine men. What then occurred was the help seeker would explain his/her situation and request aid. The medicine man would consult with his spirits and follow their direction. The "doctoring" was done by the spirits. They might give the medicine man instructions to pass to the person. Other people in attendance would then in turn have an opportunity to ask the spirits through the medicine man for general guidance if they wished. When this was completed more songs and prayers of thanksgiving would be offered, the spirits would leave, the lights would be turned on, and the ceremony would be over.

Robert would typically go around to those present and talk to them about any advice the spirits had for them. (Maybe this was only for those of us not speaking Lakota, as everything in the ceremony was conducted in that language.) After this we would all eat. Because the ceremonies did not start until dark, which in summer months in South Dakota came quite late, it might be after midnight by the time we left to drive home.

I remember my first ceremony. I was quite nervous. Once the lights were turned out the room was in pitch darkness. As I mentioned, everything took place in the Lakota language. Shortly after the initial praying and singing ended there was a very loud rap on the wall right above my head. A bit later the medicine man's rattle could be heard shaking in various places in the room. It came very close to me, right in front of my face. I remember being aware that

I could have reached out and touched it, but I was much too scared. While this was going on there were no other sounds in the room.

I have often wondered about what was going on, and in my most critical moments have speculated that maybe there wasn't anything involving supposed spirits at all. Maybe the medicine man or his helpers were doing these things in the darkness to convince the help seeker, whose own inner resources would be stimulated to produce the healing, a kind of placebo effect. However, for someone to have been rapidly moving about shaking the rattle without making any other sound, and to have done so while not bumping into the attendees sitting on the floor all around the room, would have required some very special abilities or procedures that just did not seem plausible.

As mentioned, healing ceremonies are preceded by the sweat lodge purification for the medicine man and his helpers, the *inikaga* or *inipi*. A sweat lodge ritual can also be used by itself for healing or other purposes. Robert Stead's sweat lodge was some distance from his house. The framework for the lodge is constructed from willow saplings formed in a circle about ten feet in diameter and lashed together to form a cone about four feet high. It is covered with blankets and tarps, with a small entrance that can be opened and closed with a flap. In the center a small hole is dug some two feet in diameter.

Some time before a sweat lodge purification is to be held a fire is built several feet away to heat rocks that have been carefully selected so as not to crack or explode. When the ritual is to begin the medicine man or leader enters first with his pipe and burns sweet grass to create smoke that is whirled around to make everything pure and sacred. The participants then crawl in counterclockwise, sitting with their backs against the outside. If there are six or seven people it is very crowded and you have to have your knees drawn up to keep them away from the pit. If it was necessary to wait for the rocks to become hot enough in Robert's sweat lodge some light teasing or even somewhat earthy jokes were exchanged (sometimes translated for Frank and I). This greatly surprised me, as I was used to anything involved with religion and church being very strict. When ready a helper outside brings in the heated rocks with a pitchfork and places them in the center pit.

The entrance flap is then closed, making the lodge completely dark—unless the rocks are hot enough to emit a glow. The medicine man dips water from a bucket and pours it over the rocks.

Lame Deer describes what happens in his book *Lamedeer Seeker of Visions*. "The water is ice-cold and the stones red-hot, so here is a unifying, the earth and the sky, the water of life and the sacred breath of the spirit, grandfather, and grandmother coming together. There is a great surge of power. You inhale that breath, drink in the water, the white, steam. It represents clouds, the living soul, life" (Lame Deer, 1972).

The lodge becomes extremely hot. Before entering we were told that if it became unbearable we should just pray harder. If we still couldn't take it we could get down with our face near the edge of the lodge and some cool air might be seeping in.

As Lame Deer describes it, the sweat lodge shakes and trembles as the men sing "Tunka–shila, hi-yay, hi-yay." [Sometimes water might splash out of the bucket.]

"The heat, the earth-power, hits you. You inhale it, get filled with it. That power penetrates into you, heals you. That steam stops at the skin, but that earth-power penetrates your body and mind. It cures many sicknesses—arthritis, rheumatism. It heals the wounds of your mind" (Lame Deer, 1972).

As the ceremony concludes the Sacred Pipe is passed around and each participant prays with it. Everyone says "Mitakuye oyasin" (all my relatives), the door flap is opened, and the participants leave.

JOE EAGLE ELK—LAKOTA MEDICINE MAN

To present a real flavor of Lakota healing I will draw extensively on Jerry Mohatt's book co-written with medicine man Joe Eagle Elk, *The Price of a Gift*. Eagle Elk was a highly respected member of the Rosebud medicine men group, but he did not often come to the college. The one ceremony of his I attended was memorable for something unusual that occurred. Prior to the start of the ceremony, a Lakota man who served as a janitor at the college asked me if I would give him a ride to the ceremony. I immediately was aware that he had been drinking, but thought if he wanted to go I would oblige him. At the ceremony, after the lights were turned off and the singing started inviting the spirits in, a loud commotion occurred. What it sounded like was an enraged bird with huge wings beating on the floor. The lights were turned on and urgent discussions took place in Lakota. I had no idea what was going on. Then the inebriated man who had arrived with me was taken out. What was said was that the spirits were highly offended by his behavior. It was only years later, when reading Eagle Elk's book, that I learned about his experience with the eagle and his eagle power.

Eagle Elk's first encounter with the spiritual powers that came to play such a significant role in his life occurred in the form of a persistent dream when he was around eight years old. He could not recall what was in it except for his grandma, a bow and arrow, and two gourds. He told his father and his grandparents about it and they told him it was bad and he should forget it.

When he was in his early thirties Eagle Elk started having unusual experiences with thunder. One night he dreamed that a thunderstorm was coming before it came, and sure enough, it came. Another night the same thing occurred, and then lightning came into the basement and continued to strike in different places steadily for about half an hour. He and his wife were terrified [p. 90].

Sometime later he was with his father, and they spotted an eagle that his father encouraged him to shoot. Eagle Elk did so and it fell on to the snow. As he walked over to pick it up, in his words: "He was ready for me and stood up and made his call. I jumped backwards really surprised!" He got his rifle to finish it off, but the eagle "looked like someone who was raising his hand like a stop signal. He opened his mouth and was screaming," but Elk shot him.

A week later he dreamed he met a man and they began arguing about something. He took his gun and aimed at the man's forehead. Then the man raised his arm "like a stop signal, just like the eagle. He told me, 'Don't do that; don't do that.'"

The next night while sleeping somebody came into his bedroom and spoke to him, saying that he had a dream a long time ago that he had done nothing about. If he didn't do something with the dream then he would do what he saw in last night's dream. He would then be removed from his family.

One day while he was employed as a farm hand milking cows, he happened to glance over toward the door and saw two small men. When he looked toward them they ducked away, only to reappear in a different place. He thought maybe he was "just seeing things."

However, the cow he was milking was spooked and began to shake. He then knew it was not just his imagination.

Eagle Elk attended a ceremony and described to the medicine man what had been happening. He was told that the two men were standing right outside of the ceremony, waiting for him, and that he had better take care of whatever was happening with him.

What he needed to do, Eagle Elk realized, was to undertake a vision quest. He went to a medicine man and asked to be "put on the hill." The medicine man agreed to help. He was told that he must pray and stay there for the whole time. Some things would happen that would make him want to run away, but he must not or it would be worse. Eagle Elk prepared as he was told and spent four days and nights on the hill, but he was very scared and the spirits didn't come to him. He had to do it again.

As mentioned earlier, for the next two months "the thunder would not stay away from me." He prepared for another vision quest with two gourds and a bow and arrow like in his dream. Since his grandmother had died, he went to her grave and took some of the earth from the grave to be with him. Up on the hill he prepared everything like in his dream. A man came, stood near him, told him he was there to support him, and said another man was coming to speak with him, but nothing bad would happen. From somewhere somebody came right up behind him and took hold of him. This man started to talk directly to him saying he would be shown how to use his dream to help people. But if he attempted to push it out of the way his life was not going to last.

The man started to sing and told Eagle Elk that when he would use that song both of the men with him would come. Later others would also come, but he had to wait until they got used to each other. They told him their names were little thunder being and the single thunder being, they were the thunder powers he had seen on the farm, and they were to be his friends. They told me that the eagle he had shot would come to him later as a friend to help in his work. They told him four things to do to doctor people, how to set up his altar, the song for the ceremony, who to call, and to not to push for more until they were all ready for each other.

In subsequent years Eagle Elk undertook more vision quests that resulted in more powers. One involving yuwipi spirits is unusual in that it requires that the seeker be bound. He described his experience being all tied up like a mummy. When he was alone the spirits came fast and they took him away and showed him many places, including where his ancestors were now. They told him to tell the people about his journey and that there was a place he had seen where there was no more of the suffering he knew they were experiencing.

Two years after originally contacting the yuwipi spirits Eagle Elk was told by his spirit friends that he must do another vision quest. This time the one who came was the eagle he had shot the time with his father. He told Eagle Elk that things were going to become very difficult and that he would help him. He kept his word helping him with difficult cases.

In another vision quest two spirit women came to him, gave a song to call them into his ceremony, and told him that he should call them to help with very serious problems. These two women in ceremonies, Eagle Elk said, were really different than the other ones.

Two years later, in still another vision quest Eagle Elk received his final form of spirit help. The spirits of former medicine men visited him but couldn't get close. They told him that they would work with him, at first from a distance, and gave him songs. When he would "put down their altar and sing their songs" they would come and help him doctor.

Over the years Eagle Elk offered healing ceremonies for a wide variety of people and situations. One of the first he recalled involved a woman brought to him who had a very bad case of arthritis and could not move. She was "thin and her hands were already crooked." Although she had been to the hospital a number of times over the years she just kept getting worse. When Eagle Elk saw her he didn't know what could be done for her and wondered if his spirits could help her. During the first of four ceremonies the spirits told him they could help her and what medicine to use and how she should take it. He "went and found the medicine," prepared it, and gave it to her. Each day after the ceremonies she got better and was able to sit up and move about.

Another time Eagle Elk was asked to go and see a man in a hospital in Salt Lake City whose leg had been badly crushed in a car accident. He held a ceremony in the hospital. His spirits came and examined this man. They said they "would go in and redo the leg with the help of this one medicine." They did it and he was able to walk. The doctors x-rayed his leg and found it was "all put back together."

Eagle Elk encountered all kinds of difficulties for which his assistance was sought. The following is not only unusual, but also involves a past lives connection which he does not amplify.

One time the parents of an adolescent brother and sister were brought to him because they were infatuated with each other and wanted to get married. His spirits "looked them over." They told him that there once were two young men who were really good friends, but they died. About the same time the parents of the adolescents were having them the two young men's spirits were put in a boy and girl, so they were really close, like the originals, but "got mixed up" at adolescence because they wanted to get married. His spirits "had to stop this." They helped the boy and girl "to know themselves and to understand what had happened to them."

Eagle Elk describes one particular ceremony involving his own nephew when the healing power was particularly strong. His young nephew was accidentally shot in the stomach. They rushed him to the hospital and he was almost dead. The doctors were able to keep him alive but couldn't give him the help he needed, so he was sent by plane to a hospital in Denver. Eagle Elk was sick with worry and held a ceremony that night. Many people came to his little home (including Mohatt). He asked to be tied up for a *yuwipi* ceremony. His singers sang a song and his spirit friends came into the ceremony. They looked at all of the people who were there for only one reason, to help this young boy survive. Eagle Elk commented: "Sometimes my spirits will play around or stay away or not cooperate. Everything is not quite right. Not too often does the power really come into a ceremony. But that night, it was right; we were of one mind."

He told the spirits what had happened and that the boy was not expected to live. "I told them that they had to save him. I told them I had done everything they had told me to do. I had suffered and followed their directions. I threatened them. Either they saved this boy or I would quit my life as a medicine man. There was no other choice, no other way. They owed me."

The spirits listened to him and the prayers of the people. They agreed to go to Denver and help the doctors with the surgery. In spite of what everyone expected the boy survived. From that experience Eagle Elk said he learned "how great power comes when we are one."

"In my many years of practice I have not seen the power really come that often. But when it has come, we were all of one desire, one thought locked on the person to be doctored.

I also learned about how my spirit friends could respect me. I shamed them out; they had to do as I told them."

There are, Eagle Elk noted, expectations and rules involving ceremonies and the medicine man's work. They are hard but necessary rules. The medicine man should never ask for money. People give him a gift after the ceremony. Sometimes they give money, sometimes food or animals, or a quilt, or sometimes a handshake or a cup of water. They give whatever they can afford, and he should always be happy with whatever they give him. Another rule is that he should thank the spirits for what they received by holding a ceremony after the doctoring. The rules, he said, "are not just for us, but also for the people, so they can live and become strong. We depend entirely on the people who come to us, so the cycle of healing is completed."

Throughout my personal experiences with the Lakotas I never attempted to verify that any of the claimed successes in the healing ceremonies actually occurred. I viewed my work as primarily a teacher. I was not there to study Native American culture, nor Lakota healing practices, except insofar as gaining a greater understanding might facilitate my ability to function as a better teacher. I do know that the people I worked with believed that Lakota healing practices were helpful in alleviating suffering and promoting the overall health of those involved as the accounts from the Mohatt and Eagle Elk's book indicate. Jerry Mohatt, who spoke the Lakota language fluently and was closely involved with the medicine men for years, clearly believed in their effectiveness. I would guess, although I never asked, that he did have occasion to talk with a number of people who had been helped as Eagle Elk claimed.

CHAPTER 5

CHANNELING

Channeling has been defined as the communication of information to or through a physically embodied human being from a source that is said to exist on some other level or dimension of reality than the physical as we know it, and that is not from the normal mind (or self) of the channel (Klimo, *Channeling* 1998).

Channeling is a universal phenomenon that can be found in most or all religions throughout history. It can be thought of as differing from revelation, which is a religious concept involving communication that flows from the Divine to humans. Channeling involves communications or information from supernatural sources or entities that do not fall into the realm of God or the Divine. A huge number of such nonphysical entities have been mentioned.

A distinction is sometimes made between mediumship, which is restricted to communication with deceased humans, and channeling, which includes all other communication with any intelligence not occupying an embodied mind or associated with physical reality, such as the channel's higher self, ascended masters, nonhumans from angelic and other realms, extraterrestrials, group entities, gods, God, the collective unconscious, and the universal mind.

Channeling may be intentional, with the individual deliberately initiating and controlling the phenomena, or it may occur spontaneously in an intrusive manner. During channeling the individual may enter a complete trance state, during which he or she has no awareness of what is taking place and a source entity takes control of the channel's voice or body (automatic writing). Some individuals enter only a light trance, or remain fully conscious while channeling.

The range and variety of channeled information is vast. In addition to the personal information delivered through mediums to their sitters, Klimo identifies the following categories of channeled material: Ageless Wisdom, descriptions of the realities experienced by the sources, information about the future and past, "proof" of the identity of discarnate sources, subject matter for creative expression, and scientific and medical/healing information.

It is the Ageless Wisdom that primarily links channeling with other forms of visionary experience. Ageless Wisdom refers to a common view of the greater reality running through world religions and the various esoteric, metaphysical, and mystery schools. Klimo summarizes the broad features of this reality as follows:

> There is a consensus within the channeled material of all ages that the universe is a multidimensional, living Being, which some call God. Within it as aspects of itself are sentient beings of consciousness existing on many or all of its other dimensions besides the physical as we currently experience it. We have continually received messages about, and from, the etheric, astral, mental, causal, and other dimensions of this expanded

nature. Wherever a being, personality, or entity may be within this cosmological hierarchy, that entity is always in a process of learning for the purpose of evolving toward greater unity with the one being that is the source and destiny of all separate beings. Reigning over wisdom, light, and pure force or energetic power is love, the supreme reality of all creation. We humans on Earth are in a kind of classroom in which we are slowly learning to be loving beings that reflect the nature of our creator. Essentially, we are of the same quality or nature as our creator and thus undying with many opportunities and contexts for this learning and evolution to take place. There is a recurrent theme of reincarnation, or multiple projections ourselves as the experience-gathering vehicle of consciousness (Klimo, *Channeling* 1998).

Two bodies of channeled work of this type in the last half of the twentieth century stand out as classics: the Seth material and the Course in Miracles.

THE SETH MATERIAL

The Seth material was channeled by poet and science fiction writer Jane Roberts over the course of twenty years. She described her first encounter with channeling in 1963, as she sat quietly at the table in her apartment in Elmira, New York.

Quite suddenly "a fantastic avalanche of radical, new ideas" burst into her head with tremendous force, as if her head were some sort of "receiving station turned up to unbearable volume." What she was receiving was not only ideas, but intensified and pulsating sensations. It seemed to her as if "the physical world were really tissue-paper thin, hiding infinite dimensions of reality," and she was "suddenly flung through the tissue paper with a huge ripping sound." As she sat at the table her hands were furiously scribbling down the words and ideas that flashed through her head. Yet, at the same time, she seemed to be somewhere else, "traveling through things." She went "plummeting through a leaf, to find a whole universe open up, and then out again, drawn into new perspectives." She felt as if knowledge was being "implanted" in the very cells of her body so that she couldn't forget it. This was "feeling and knowing," rather than intellectual knowledge. When she came to, she found herself scrawling what was obviously meant as the title of that "odd batch of notes: *The Physical Universe as Idea Construction*" (Hanegraaff, 1998 p. 29).

Inspired by this experience, Roberts and her husband started experimenting with a Ouija board to see what might happen. After a few tries they began to receive messages from someone claiming to be "Frank Withers." Soon a larger entity began coming through of whom Withers was but a fragment. This entity, calling himself Seth, was to become the best known channeled entity in the twentieth century. He described himself as an individual consciousness, "an energy personality essence no longer focused in physical reality."

Roberts soon abandoned the Ouija board and began to receive Seth's communications in full trance and dictate them to her husband, who took them down in shorthand. Mostly the communications consisted of monologues on a wide variety of topics. In 1969 Roberts published a summary, with substantial excerpts from the Seth personality, in a book titled *The Seth Material.*

Beginning in 1970 Seth began to dictate his own books, with Roberts claiming no authorship beyond her own role as channel. The five resulting books, according to Roberts, were verbatim accounts of Seth's remarks with only minor editorial corrections.

Roberts, throughout the twenty years she channeled Seth, continued to question what was actually going on. Was Seth merely part of her own psyche, or did he represent some kind of separate being? What she said she was sure of was that Seth was her channel to reveal knowledge, and that this knowledge was not discovered by the reasoning faculties.

As to who or what Seth is or was, his term "energy essence personality" seems as close to the answer as anyone can get. "I do not believe he is a part of my subconscious, as that term is used by psychologists, or a secondary personality.... I do think that we have a supraconscious that is as far above the normal self as the subconscious is *below* it... . It may be that Seth is the psychological personification of that supraconscious extension of my normal self" (Klimo, Channeling 1998 pp. 30–31).

In her introduction to one of "Seth's" books, *Adventures in Consciousness*, Roberts further explored this issue, describing our present personalities as "aspects of a far greater consciousness of which our individual awareness is but a part, though an inviolate one." Other aspects of our personalities are dominant in other realities. If, like Seth, they become activated, they would have to communicate through the psychic fabric of ourselves as the focus personality. Although their own reality might exist in quite different terms than ours, they would have to appear in line with our sense of personhood. Roberts noted that she always sensed that Seth was a "personification of something else—and that 'something else' wasn't a person in our terms" (Roberts, 2005. p. 31).

The Seth material discusses a wide range of topics, including the origins of the universe, the theory of evolution, the nature of physical reality, the nature of God, the Christ story, and the purpose of life.

THE COURSE IN MIRACLES

Only two years after Roberts began to channel Seth, equally portentous experiences started to happen in the life of psychologist Helen Schucman who was, at the time, employed at the Psychiatry Department of New York's Columbia University College of Physicians and Surgeons. As she described her experience, at first she began to vaguely sense what soon became a clear inner voice. As a psychologist, atheist, and disbeliever in the paranormal, Schucman could not make sense of what was happening. The voice wouldn't leave her alone. It kept saying "This is a course in miracles. Please take notes."

When she decided to comply in her first session taking dictation the voice spoke what was to become the first introductory page of a volume that came to be called Text. The central theme of the work was announced: "Nothing real can be threatened. Nothing unreal exists. Herein lies the peace of God."

Schucman immediately became alarmed by the alien nature of what was happening and broke off the process after taking down only fifteen lines. She tried to describe what the voice was like.

"It's hard to describe. It can't be a hallucination, really, because the Voice does not come from outside. It's all internal. There's no actual sound, and the words come mentally, but very clearly. It's a kind of inner dictation, you might say. It's not automatic writing ... because I'm perfectly aware of what I'm doing" (Klimo, Channeling, 1998).

For eight years Schucman continued to take down everything the voice said. What resulted was a self-study text of spiritual psychotherapy in a three-volume set containing some 1,200 pages which was published in 1975. Volume I is the text; volume II is a workbook for students, with an exercise for each day of the year planned around a central idea; and volume III is a manual for teachers.

Schucman continually questioned her role as the recipient or channel of the material. At one point she asked, "'Why me?' I'm not religious; I don't understand these things; I don't even believe them. I'm about the poorest choice you could make..." The clear answer she received was: "On the contrary: You are an excellent choice. In fact, the best." "But why?" she asked. The answer was: "Because you'll do it."

The central question was, and remained, what was source of the material she was scribing? Schucman said this:

> Where did the writing come from? Certainly the subject matter itself was the last thing I would have expected to write about, since I knew nothing about the subject... At several points in the writing the Voice itself speaks in no uncertain terms about the Author (i.e., as Christ) ... which literally stunned me at the time... I do not understand the events that led up to the writing. I do not understand the process, and I certainly do not understand the authorship. It would be pointless for me to attempt an explanation (Schucman, 2007).

A number of passages in the material itself clearly say that the author is Christ. "You cannot forget the Father because I am with you, and I cannot forget Him. To forget me is to forget yourself and Him Who created you. ... The name of Jesus Christ as such is but a symbol. But it stands for love that is not of this world. It is a symbol that is safely used as a replacement for the many names of all the gods to which you pray... This course has come from him."

While the Course clearly makes this claim and uses terminology and theological elements found in traditional Christianity, it is not aligned to the doctrines of this religion. In fact, it appears to be more closely aligned to fundamental premises of Eastern religion and has been characterized as a Christianized version of non-dualistic Vedanta. The physical world of our separate perceptions is viewed as basically illusory and can only offer us violence, sorrow, and pain. This world is to be differentiated from the "real world," where there are no dreams of hatred or revenge. Students of the Course seek an ultimate goal of existence in a radically different mode of being than that found in this physical world. This can be attained through a unified vision with the Holy Spirit, or that part of the mind that sees all actions as rooted in love. (Wikipedia, *A Course in Miracles*).

The introduction to the Workbook for Students states that it is divided into two main sections: the first "dealing with the undoing of the way you see now" and the second with the "acquisition of true perception."

"The purpose of the workbook is to train your mind in a systematic way to a different perception of everyone and everything in the world."

Following are a few of the 365 daily lessons:

1. "Nothing I see means anything."

2. "I have given everything I see all the meaning that it has for me."

32. "I have invented the world I see."

43. "God is my source. I cannot see apart from Him."

67. "Love created me like Itself."

121. "Forgiveness is the key to happiness."

195. "Love is the way I walk in gratitude."

222. "God is my life. I live and move in Him" (Schucman, 2007).

CHAPTER 6

EVIL AND ATTACHING SPIRITS

DEMONS

Traditionally religions have been very concerned with a dark dimension or force, the opposite of God, heaven, and divine beings. Here we find hell, the devil or Satan, and those entities, forces, and dynamics associated with them: demons, demonic possession, and the like. Transpersonal psychology, that branch of psychology that addresses the spiritual dimension of the psyche, largely ignores these kinds of phenomena. Even psychical research that has been investigating psychic phenomena for well over a century has tended to avoid this area. For a number of years published reports from those who had near-death experiences pretty much only discussed the positive elements. Yet if we are to accept that the kinds of spiritual experience we have been considering are actual aspects of reality and not just projections from our own psyches, then it seems only logical that we ought to give those nonordinary experiences on the flip side of positive spirituality equal respect.

While science and psychology long ago pretty much concluded that these "dark phenomena" reside only in our imagination, or in the warped minds of the mentally unbalanced, they continue to attract a large number of believers. A 2023 Gallup poll found that 59% of Americans believe in hell and 58% in the devil. According to a 2019 YouGov poll, more than one in five (22%) say that demons "definitely exist." From as long ago as Babylon and the Egyptian pharaohs, ancient cultures speak of demonic entities and forms of exorcism.

To understand the place of angels and demons in Christianity and other religions it is important to recognize the way those religions view the nature of cosmic reality. For the most part they have conceived of a cosmos structured in one of three basic ways:

In monistic religions, such as Hinduism, the totality of all reality is regarded as wholly sacred, or as participating in one single divine principle.

In dualistic religions, such as Gnosticism, there are two basic realms: the world of matter, which is regarded as evil, and the realm of the spirit, which is regarded as good.

The third view of the cosmos, found in Monotheistic religions including Christianity, Judaism, and Islam, posits a tripartite cosmos with celestial, terrestrial, and subterrestrial realms.

In the Christian cosmos of biblical times the celestial, or highest realm, is the home of the divine spiritual beings and powers. At its highest level is the ultimate sacred, God, Yahweh, Allah. The middle or terrestrial realm is the home of us humans. Like all other inhabitants in this realm we are limited by time, space, and cause and effect. The subterrestrial, or lowest realm, is an area of chaos and the home of the spiritual powers of darkness.

Associated with the celestial realm are benevolent beings or angels that have as their primary function to serve God and do His will. They act as revealers of divine truth, to assist us to achieve a proper rapport with God and to attain salvation or special favors. Angels serve as guardians over individuals and entire nations.

The subterrestrial realm in the tripartite Christian cosmos is, of course, hell. Hell is typically thought of as the home of Satan, the devil, and his followers. However, it is unclear whether this is their current or final home. Revelation 12:9 states:

> And the great dragon was cast out, that old serpent, called the Devil, and Satan, which deceiveth the whole world: he was cast out into the earth, and his angels were cast out with him.

Yet in 1 Peter 2:4 we find:

> For if God spared not the angels that sinned, but cast them down to hell, and delivered them into chains of darkness, to be reserved unto judgment.

Over the years understandings of Satan have changed. In the Jewish Old Testament the term *satan* means adversary or opponent. Whenever he appears it is always as God's angelic servant who operates with God's permission against human beings, but certainly not against God himself. Apparently, with God's permission, he murders Egyptian children (Exod. 12:23), prompts King Saul to dishonorable behavior (I Sam. 16:14–16; 18:10–11; 19:9–10), sends a plague to Israel (2 Sam. 24:13–16 and I Chron. 21:1–30), and torments Job. He is portrayed in the Gospels as the tempter of Jesus and in the Book of Revelation in the form of a dragon (Turner, 1993).

Increasingly Satan came to be understood as a fallen angel. He once was Lucifer, among the highest of all angels, and the brightest in the sky, who would not bow to God. He led other angels in a rebellion to set himself up as the ruler of heaven. God prevailed and cast Satan and his followers out of Heaven down to Earth, where they could attempt to mislead humans against following God's will. In the Christian belief system these followers are known as demons.

Like angels that they once were, demons are noncorporal (without a body) spiritual beings. Although they possess intellect and free will, they serve Satan and function to carry out his will. While they themselves are sometimes referred to as devils, they are clearly subordinate to the supreme devil, Satan. Ultimately there is but one God in Christianity, Judaism, and Islam, and He is all powerful. Satan and his demons can tempt and afflict human beings only because God permits them to do so.

Demons have been identified with a wide variety of activities in their attempt to subvert the will of God. Besides tempting humans to sin, perhaps the best-known function of demons in Biblical as well as pagan religions was to cause disease, famine, war, accidental deaths, and various mental disorders. Demons were thought to directly influence human beings to experience physical and psychological difficulties in two ways. They can fill the mind of the victim with evil thoughts, called obsession, or they can physically take over the victim's body, called possession. Typically the term *possession* is used to describe both. The Christian gospels describe numerous accounts of demonic possession. In fact, one of Jesus' major activities involved healing those possessed through exorcism, that is, casting out the demons possessing them.

The gospel accounts offer a number of observations about these possessing demons. They were believed to be responsible for a wide range of afflictions. Luke 9:39 describes a case of epilepsy caused by a demon. Luke 11:14 mentions a person who was unable to speak because of an indwelling demon, and Luke 13:10–13 offers an account of a woman who had been unable to straighten her back for years because of an evil spirit. Some gospel passages describe the possession of one person by a number of demons. Luke 8:30 gives an account of a man who was possessed by so many demons that the term "legion" was used, which refers to a military unit of 6,000 soldiers.

Demons appear to have special abilities. Several accounts describe the possessing demon as using the vocal apparatus of the victim to speak directly to the exorcist. Mark 5:4 mentions an indwelling spirit causing its victim to have such superhuman strength that fetters and chains could not hold him. Matthew 12:45 gives an account of a demon leaving a person, only to return with seven others who were more wicked.

Over the centuries a large body of popular tales, as well as scholarly writing, accumulated describing hell, Satan, and his demons. Some early Christians believed that the devil lived in the air, from where he kept a watch on his victims. Saint Augustine believed that demons were made of air. The bishop of Marseille preached in the fifth century that demons had specialized duties. Some tempted humans, some performed cruel or lascivious acts, and others played pranks. Saint Thomas Aquinas pointed out in his writings that one of the main duties of demons is to torture the sinners in hell's fires.

Dante in *The Divine Comedy*, written between 1308 and his death in 1321, provided a detailed, precise view of hell, with nine circles funneling into the Earth. At the center of the ninth or lowest circle is a giant, terrifying beast, Satan himself, who chews on the very worst of the sinners.

Father Girolamo Menghi, in the middle of the sixteenth century, pulled together hundreds of post-Biblical writings on the devil, demons, and exorcism and added some of his own to produce a body of ideas that the Catholic church largely adopted. He concluded that there are many types of demons existing in a hierarchy of rank and responsibility. Some live almost beyond the sky and some closer to Earth. Some live on Earth, where they entice their victims with worldly and base temptations. Some lurk in seas and lakes to sink ships. Some live underground, where they collaborate with magicians and sorcerers. All demons are crafty and work with the devil's ability to see the future. Demons have sex with witches, teach them sorcery, and make pacts with them to control people. Father Menghi also published a handbook for exorcists that described each step for them to take. The Vatican endorsed his work and drew significantly from it in its own manual for exorcists issued shortly thereafter. The instructions provided are very similar to its current guidelines (Wilkinson, 2007).

HEALING THROUGH EXORCISM

Healing plays a central role in gospel accounts of Jesus, where He is portrayed as both a healer of physical illness and of spiritual distress through exorcisms, driving out unclean spirits. These accounts tend to fall in a standard form involving four items: first the description of the condition; second the response by Jesus, usually a verbal command or a touch; third the response or the reaction and what happens, the healing; and fourth the reaction of those who witnessed it.

A typical story of Jesus performing a healing is found in the Gospel of Mark, 1:39–45:

> So he went all through Galilee, preaching in their synagogues and driving out the demons. There came to him a leper appealing to him on his knees, saying to Him, "If you only choose, you can cure me. And He pitied him and stretched out His hand and touched him, and said to him, I do choose! Be cured!" And the leprosy immediately left him, and he was cured. And Jesus immediately drove him away with a stern warning, saying to him, "See that you say nothing about this to anybody, but begone! Show yourself to the priest, and in proof of your cure make the offerings for your purification which Moses prescribed." But he went off and began to talk so much about it, and to spread the story so widely, that Jesus could no longer go into a town openly, but stayed out in unfrequented places, and people came to Him from every direction (*The Complete Bible; An American Translation*).

Jesus gave the ability to cast out demons to His disciples:

> Then He summoned His twelve disciples and gave them authority to expel unclean spirits and to cure sickness and disease of every kind (Matthew 10:1).

Acts mentions several examples of them doing so. Judaism and Islam, along with a number of other religions, contain elements of exorcism, cleansing rituals, or "deliverance," as Protestants call it. The Roman Catholic Church has thoroughly codified and institutionalized these practices. The early church fathers, including St. Justin Martyr, Tertullian, and St. Cyril of Jerusalem, mentioned exorcisms in their writings.

In subsequent years, with the blessing of the Catholic Church, priests and other designated officials were given the ability to cast out demons by using Jesus' name. However, the Bible makes clear that only Christians can perform exorcisms. Acts 19:13 offers an account of seven non-Christians who attempted to exorcise demons in the name of Jesus and Paul. Not only did this fail, but all were attacked and beaten by the possessed man (Robinson, 2014).

Between the fourteenth and seventeenth centuries belief in the power of Satan reached a feverish level. By the eighteenth century the church had become increasingly influenced by Enlightenment, thinking that gave precedence to reason and the laws of nature over emotion and superstition. It sought to curb the religious frenzy of the previous centuries. As a consequence the rite of exorcism began to fall out of favor. During much of the nineteenth and twentieth century for church hierarchy exorcism became "an embarrassing, unsavory ancient ritual that was best forgotten" (Wilkinson, 2007). The Second Vatican Council, in 1962–1965, emphasized the positive, hope, and compassion while minimizing discussion of evil and demons, and what many church leaders saw as clearly medieval, controversial, and backward rites, such as exorcism.

Interest in exorcism was soon to make a comeback, both within the general public and at the top of church hierarchy, the Pope himself. Pope Paul VI, who took office during the last half of Vatican II, was alarmed at theological negation of the existence of the devil and his work. His successor, Pope John Paul II, frequently referred to Satan as a real and present dangerous force in the world:

> The battle against the devil ... is still being fought today, because the devil is still alive and active in the world. The evil that surrounds us today, the disorders that plague our society, man's inconsistency and brokenness, are not only the results of original sin, but also the result of Satan's pervasive and dark action (Wilkinson, 2007).

He viewed exorcism quite favorably and is said to have personally performed three.

Increasing popular interest in exorcism was stimulated by the steady growth of the Catholic Charismatic Renewal movement, a Pentecostal faction that promotes belief in healing and prophecy. In the US, the 1973 academy award movie *The Exorcist* stirred great interest in a subject that few people knew much about.

Prior to 1996 there has only been one trained exorcist in the entire United States. In that year the Catholic Church appointed ten priests to the position. The Vatican has now asked that every diocese in the United States have a trained exorcist (*Exorcism: Ancient Art or Hocus Pocus?*). Between 1986 and 2006 the number of exorcists in Italy increased dramatically from 20 to around 350.

There are also priests who are not official exorcists but claim to have permission from their local bishop to perform exorcisms at their discretion. Catholic priests are not the only religious people performing exorcisms today. In the United States alone an estimated 500 non-Catholic Christian groups perform exorcisms (deliverances).

In 1999 the Vatican issued the first significant revision of the rite of exorcism since the original document was written in 1614. This revised version kept most prayers and exhortations as they were, but included a new warning against confusing psychiatric illness with possession and urged priests to exercise maximum prudence and circumspection when deciding that exorcism should be used. It also formalized the requirement that bishops need to appoint an exorcist, or at least authorize specific exorcisms individually.

A short time later the church issued separate guidelines seeking to put a stop to unauthorized exorcisms and mass faith healing. With these two documents the church appeared to be acknowledging that exorcisms were again popular and in demand, yet wanting to keep their use carefully controlled so that they could not readily be seen as archaic rituals and would not become an embarrassment.

Pope Benedict XVI frequently spoke of evil as an omnipresent and tangible threat eroding faith and morality. In seeking to recapture Christian souls for the Catholic Church in an increasingly secular, godless world, he saw a role for exorcists. During the first months of his papacy he praised a group that was meeting for their annual convention, telling them, "I encourage you to pursue your important ministry in the service of the Church" (Wilkinson, 2007).

In Catholic Italy, where exorcism is particularly popular, priests see the manifestation of demonic influence as falling into several categories, some of which are considered more minor. These can be helped with prayer and may not require an actual exorcism.

Infestation of places, homes, businesses, animals, or objects. An exorcist can bless the place or object to rid it of evil Spirits.

Vexation. This is not possession, but a kind of haunting of the victim. He or she is dogged by evil in the form of what appears to be a long spate of bad luck in work, love, or health.

Obsession. The victim has uncontrollable evil thoughts that torment him or her, impeding the ability to enjoy life.

Possession. This is the most serious, and most rare form. An exorcism is the only recourse and can take years to cure the victim. Satan takes possession of the person and causes him or her to speak.

Willful subjugation to the devil. This is really in a category by itself because the person has sought out the devil through satanic worship, black masses, which are rituals that mock and blaspheme Christian beliefs, or other overt activities. Such people almost never undergo exorcisms (Wilkinson, 2007).

Today the Catholic Church is officially adamant about the need to establish that someone seeking an exorcism is not mentally or physically ill. However, this is not always carried out.

What should happen is that when a case of possession is reported to the church an investigation is begun to determine if there is any way to explain the subject's behavior besides possession. Often the priest investigator will consult a psychiatrist to determine whether the person's symptoms can be fully explained as mental illness. According to American Exorcism, Michael Cuneo's 2001 study, there were at that time about a dozen psychiatrists in the US whom the church used to do this. A medical examination is also conducted to rule out the possibility of a physical disorder or illness. Sometimes a church recognized expert in paranormal phenomena will be also consulted.

If all of these factors can be ruled out the investigator looks for the classic signs of possession that have remained pretty much the same through the centuries. These include:

Manifestation of superhuman strength;
The speaking in tongues or in a language the victim doesn't know or hasn't been exposed to, particularly archaic languages such as Aramaic;
The revelation of distant or hidden knowledge he or she doesn't know about, particularly the exorcist's personal life;
Blasphemic rage and aversion to holy symbols; and
Unexplainable physical phenomena, such as movement of objects with no apparent cause (Cumeo, 2002).

The investigator reports his findings regarding all of these criteria to the church. The bishop at this point decides whether possession is involved. True demonic possession is rare. The church officially reports about 1 out of every 5,000 cases investigated actually qualify, although some exorcists put the percentage somewhat higher.

As described by a prominent Italian exorcist, the process of exorcism begins with prayer. The exorcist places a purple stole over the patient, makes the sign of the cross, and may anoint him or her with oil and holy water. Prayers are said by the priest and patient in unison. A patient who is truly possessed will experience an uncontrollable aversion to the sacraments and to all things holy and sacred. This may begin with physical convulsions, followed by fury-filled bellicose reactions, a deep booming voice cursing the priest, as well as a small, effeminate voice pleading for help. The exorcist commands the demon to state its name (which it often has difficulty doing) and attempts to interrogate it. He asks a series of questions that are useful for the liberation, such as when it entered the person, under what circumstances, and when will it leave by order of Jesus Christ. The exorcism culminates with the priest ordering Satan to be gone (Cumeo, 2002).

Patients are rarely cured in a single session. Some may return to the exorcist a number of times and these sessions may stretch out over years.

DELIVERANCE

The practice of ridding people from the influence of evil spirits among those who are not Catholic priests is typically known as "deliverance," rather than exorcism. According to Francis MacNutt, author of several books on spiritual healing, and himself a former priest, deliverance is intended to free people from oppression of these spirits, which is common. Typically one area of the victim's life is invaded. Possession, which is quite rare, implies that "Satan has taken over and possesses the very core of a human personality." It is these cases that require exorcism (MacNutt, 2009).

MacNutt notes that in recent years worldwide interest in healing and deliverance has been growing rapidly. We are, he says, "seeing the beginning of a renewed, life-giving Christianity such as we have not known since days of the apostles." Although exorcism had pretty much died out in mainline Catholic churches in recent centuries, Pentecostals in the beginning of the twentieth century reawakened such spiritual gifts as the baptism of the Spirit, praying in tongues, prophecy, healing, and casting out evil spirits through deliverance.

Deliverance, including its more extreme version exorcism, MacNutt says, is rooted in the most fundamental of Christian beliefs and practices.

A major reason Jesus took on human flesh was to free us from demonic influence. For Him it was no side issue, no minor ministry.... He saw exorcism as one of His major missions.

There is a real need for deliverance because "multitudes of hurting people are looking for the help that can come only through prayer for deliverance." MacNutt certainly recognizes that many people are suffering from psychological problems and can be helped with counseling (his wife is a psychologist), but not those whose problems have demonic sources. In his book he offers guidelines for distinguishing between the two.

Although the authority to perform deliverance and exorcism have been restricted to a few priests since the early centuries of the church, the Pentecostals imposed no limits. In fact, mass deliverances began to be practiced, but often not without problems. MacNutt believes that there should be some limits on who can perform them, but this should not be completely restricted to priests and ministers.

An actual deliverance service involves the following:

The session begins with prayer. First we call on Jesus Christ to give us wisdom and guide us in our prayer. We call on His authority to cast out the spirits. We ask the Holy Spirit to anoint us with power and the love of God to heal as well as free the person. We ask God to fill the room with His power and love to overflowing. Nothing evil can survive in such an atmosphere. We call on the holy angels (especially the archangel Michael) to minister to us, surround us with their protection and do battle for us, while the "communion of saints" who are in heaven, the "great cloud of witnesses" of Hebrews 12:1, intercede for us. Lastly we forbid, in the name of Jesus Christ, any communication in the realm of evil spirits, as it might affect the spirits that are troubling the counselee; and we forbid these spirits to draw power from any spirits outside the person. Having finished praying for protection, we are now ready to proceed with the deliverance itself (MacNutt, 2009, Kindle Locations 2719–2721).

1. "In the name of Jesus Christ..."
2. "...I command you...".
3. "...you spirit of (name of spirit if determined)
4. "...to depart ...."
5. "...without doing harm to (person infested) or anyone else in this house, or in their family, and without making any noise or disturbance..."
6. "...and I command you to go straight to Jesus Christ to dispose of you as He will. Furthermore, I command you never again to return" (Kindle locations 2822–2824).

Sometimes the spirits go instantly, and sometimes it takes hours or even days, requiring several sessions, but when this is accomplished people report very strong feelings of relief.

The deliverance field appears wide open, with a large number of individuals and groups involved. One of the best known and controversial individuals involved in deliverance work is Bob Larson, long time Christian radio and television personality. He claims that he has performed more deliverances than any person on the planet. With his staff Larson travels around the world performing deliverance sessions for thousands of people a year. Larson believes more people are possessed today than ever have been in history. Demons cause virtually all our problems, as individuals and as a society.

Reporter Steve Lumbley attended one of Larson's Spiritual Freedom Conferences and described what happens in a deliverance session. Larson "calls up" the demons in a person and converses with them rather than simply telling them to depart in Jesus' name. He "forces" them to tell him how they came in to the person, by what "right" they stay, what generational curse they have brought with them, and the like. He also communicates with what he calls a person's "alters," or alternate personalities that he believes are not demons, but personalities developed by the person to "protect" themselves, for example from further emotional harm. Some of these alters, he believes, are good and some are bad. Working with the alters helps him determine which demons are present.

In the deliverance Lumbley observed, Larson placed the Bible, which he refers to as the "sword of the Spirit," physically on a demonized girl. While two male deliverance team members physically held her down she struggled, writhed around, and screamed, as if in pain, whenever Larson touched her with the Bible. He then "stabbed" the demon with the "sword" (Bible), which appeared to force the demon to tell him what he wanted to know. With questioning the demon finally admitted that it had gained entrance to the girl's family line seven generations back when her ancestors sacrificed pigs and called on demon spirits for power. Larson also communicated with all the girl's alters. He then sent the demons to "the pit" and to "torment" (Lumbley, 2006).

Larson has attracted a lot of criticism for the flashy showmanship quality of his conferences, and particularly for the high fees he charges for attendance and for the many books, tapes, and programs he advertises on his website.

THE OCCULT VIEW

Spirit possession, the involuntary takeover of a living human being by a discarnate spirit, has been described for thousands of years. In 90% of societies worldwide there are records of possession-like phenomena. Historically the treatment for this problem consisted of extracting, or casting out, the intruding spirits through the use of rituals and incantations. Shamans, healers, and priests were responsible for carrying this out. The understanding from the prevailing religious perspective was that the possessing entity was a demon.

Another less well known but equally ancient tradition takes a quite different view, and it is very important in the discussion to follow that this be recognized.

The occult, esoteric, or metaphysical beliefs about the afterlife are not widely known outside of certain spiritual groups. They developed within the ancient Indian Vedic tradition. According to this view human beings were thought to have a number of bodies, or vibrating energy fields, in addition to their physical body. These bodies form a hierarchy in terms of the rate of their vibration, with the physical being the lowest or most "dense." The higher bodies are nonphysical, and thus invisible to ordinary sight.

The body next higher and closest to the physical in terms of its vibration level is the etheric, or bioplasmic. The etheric body is a duplicate of the physical and interpenetrates it. It molds matter into the many organs making up the physical body and channels certain cosmic energies required to keep the body healthy and operational. The etheric body is involved in the chakras and in the meridian system forming the basis of acupuncture.

The next higher body is the astral. It interpenetrates the physical and etheric and extends several inches beyond them, forming an oval of colored lights visible to certain psychic sensitives. The astral body controls the emotional aspects of our personality. Normally it stays within the confines of the physical and etheric bodies, but can leave temporarily during sleep and in certain other circumstances. The astral body survives the death of the physical and etheric bodies.

Next higher beyond the astral is the mental body. It contains all of our memory banks and is connected to and works through the physical brain. Still higher beyond the mental are a number of spiritual bodies of increasingly high vibrations that reside partially outside the individual but are nevertheless part of our being.

Just as there are interpenetrating nonphysical bodies, so too are there an incalculable number of nonphysical realms or planes of reality that occupy the same space as the physical world. They too exist as a hierarchy based on their vibratory rates.

Closest to the physical world are the astral planes. There are said to be three general levels. The lowest astral planes are dark, dismal, dangerous, and often frightening worlds which are the dwelling place of greedy, self-centered, unloving, resentful discarnate people. Some traditions believe that less desirable beings of non-human lines of evolution also exist here. This plane is cluttered with thought-forms of humanity's hatred, greed, lust, and jealousy accumulated over the centuries. These thought-forms can be as real as any of the shadowy bodies of the poor lost souls existing there. This lowest astral plane is traditionally referred to as hell.

The intermediate astral planes are primarily a region where the deceased person rests and is helped to recuperate from the travails of physical life. Continued mental and spiritual growth is encouraged so that progress can be made to higher planes of reality.

The higher astral planes are wonderful realms of existence characterized by the most positive of experiences. The individual enjoys loving interactions with like-minded and spiritually developed people and encounters with angelic beings. There are unlimited opportunities for mental and spiritual growth. This realm corresponds to the Christian notion of heaven.

Beyond the astral planes are higher mental planes offering unlimited scope for the further development of the individual mind and soul. There is access to all of the accumulated wisdom of the ages on the Earth plane and throughout the cosmos. Still higher are a number of spiritual (causal and celestial) levels where the individual gods of various religions may be experienced. And finally, all form dissolves into the final absolute indescribable universal Godhead.

According to occult teachings, at death our physical and etheric bodies die, but the "real" us remains alive in our astral, mental, and spiritual bodies. In this nonphysical form we rise or float out of our physical body, often accompanied by spirits of departed loved ones who have come for us. Although we may remain in contact with the physical world and the familiar people in it for a time, we are generally unable to communicate or interact with them. What is said to happen next and in what sequential order varies among different occult systems.

A very common motif is that at some point, as our physical body shuts down we become aware of and may be drawn toward a very bright light, which is clearly spiritual in nature and that communicates great love. However, we do not remain with or in the light because we are not sufficiently developed spiritually. Usually within minutes to a few days after the death of the body we find ourselves functioning on the particular astral level to which the quality of our life on Earth has entitled us. If we have made more than average progress in this and/or past lives and our soul has evolved to the point that it is living naturally in harmony with the principles of the highest astral plane we will find ourselves there. This is likely to be only a very small percentage of the population. If we are an average adult or a child we will find ourselves on the intermediate astral planes.

According to general occult belief, if we have been cruel, greedy, and unloving, or addicted to drugs and sensual pleasures, the story following physical death is different. In our astral body form we may be met by malevolent entities and taken to, or just arrive automatically at the lowest astral planes. Even here there is hope. If we discover ourselves in this dark and unpleasant realm upon death, and if some part of our soul still strongly desires spiritual growth and calls out for assistance, sooner or later a compassionate being from a higher realm will come and lead us out of darkness.

Occult beliefs provide still another possibility following our death. We may remain tied to the physical plane and, even though we no longer have physical bodies, remain here in our astral form. We could be in such a state of confusion when we die that we simply do not realize we are dead. This is said to be more likely when death is sudden. We could be so convinced that nothing happens after death that we simply refuse to see the family members or spirit guides who come for us. If we are afraid of hell we may resist efforts of those who have come for us. We could be so ashamed of our former deeds that we do not want to meet spirit forms of our deceased family members or spirit guides. If we are addicted to drugs or sex a strong tie is created, binding us to the physical plane. Obsessive attachment to a living person can also have the same effect. Should we continue our existence on the physical plane we would be said to be earthbound spirits. Earthbound spirits seem to remain exactly as they were moments before death, including the same attitudes, desires, needs, interests, and addictions. They are likely to want to continue this same existence, and the only way they know how to do this is through a physical body. Thus they attach themselves to, invade, or possess a living person. But such possessions are always negative, both for themselves and for the host.

There are a number of reasons why a particular person might become possessed by an earthbound spirit and varying degrees of influence that possession might exert. Occult philosophy holds that each person has an aura relating to the etheric body that performs the same protective function in the emotional/mental/spiritual dimension as the immune system performs for the physical body. What the aura guards against is invasion of possessing spirits. When our aura is vibrating at high frequencies our energy field cannot be entered by spirits vibrating at lower levels. But should our aura be weakened, and its vibration be sufficiently lowered, invading spirits can enter.

A number of conditions can weaken the aura. Severe illness and drug and alcohol abuse are particularly troublesome. But excessive negative emotions like anger and depression, fatigue, exhaustion, and any illness also can temporarily lower the aura's frequency. Thus, under these circumstances a person is vulnerable. And once one spirit has succeeded in penetrating the aura it is weakened and more easily entered by others.

Some people may deliberately invite possession through participating in such activities as playing with Ouija boards and practicing automatic writing. Others may unwittingly open themselves to earthbound spirits when in times of loneliness and loss; without taking protective measures they seek the help of what they believe will be higher spiritual entities.

Possession by spirits can range from a very minor influence to nearly total replacement of the original personality. The more the afflicted person gives up control of their personality the greater the influence of the possession. When a person is possessed as a young child and grows up with the spirit's personality merged with their own it becomes very difficult to clearly discern the boundaries of the individual self. The possessed person is often afraid to have the possessing spirits leave. Possession early in life also makes a person more vulnerable to subsequent possession by subsequent spirits.

Spirit possession can lead to a number of problems, including all kinds of physical symptoms such as headaches, pain, lack of energy, insomnia, obesity, allergies, and many others; mental problems such as inability to concentrate and difficulties with memory; emotional problems including anxiety, phobias, and depression; drug and alcohol addiction; and relational and sexual difficulties. Serious mental illness such as schizophrenia most clearly can result from possession. The possessing spirits that have invaded their personalities speak to them, influence their thoughts, and direct their behavior.

All contact with nonphysical entities is of course not restricted to troubled, earthbound spirits. It is possible for souls from the astral or higher realms to visit the living. Usually this involves individuals or angelic beings who have a positive message for a living person. Spiritually advanced souls do not possess a living person but might work through them, as in the case of a medium or spiritual healer. At the moment of death the soul of a loved one, an angelic being, or a denizen of the low astral plane comes to take the newly deceased away (Fiore,1995), (Meek, 1998).

RELEASEMENT THERAPY

The traditional religious belief accepted the reality of demons and held that ridding a person from demonic possession could be done through exorcism. However, in the early decades of the twentieth century other understandings and practices developed based on the occult view.

In 1924 psychiatrist Carl Wickland published his *Thirty Years Among the Dead* that described his work, which he called "depossession." He invited the intruding spirits who afflicted his patients to channel through his wife, a gifted medium. When this occurred he gently guided each one to the awareness of its own death. Invisible helpers from the spirit world then assisted the confused earthbound soul to find its rightful place in the Light. In Wickland's approach it was not necessary for the patient to actually be present in the treatment room (Baldwin, 2003).

More recently William Baldwin and others built on Wickland's approach in what he calls releasement therapy, which he described in his 1995 book *Spirit Releasement Therapy* and more recently in his 2003 book *Healing Lost Souls*. In pursuing this practice for several decades he has identified three major main types of intrusive entity:

Earthbound souls, which is the most common, include deceased humans, as well as terminated pregnancies, and mind fragments of living people;

Dark force entities that claim that they have never been alive in human bodies and comprise the classic demons as described in religious literature;

Extraterrestrial entities involving aliens and otherworldly beings.

Baldwin notes that in most cases he works directly with the client, the person having the problem of spirit attachment, but he can conduct a remote spirit release with an individual serving as the medium, or connecting link, to the target person. This remote spirit releasement is very successful in removing attached entities from people at a distance.

The primary focus of releasement therapy is on newly deceased souls who try but cannot return to their own body and attach to living people, causing all kinds of difficulties. These lost souls can also be found in haunted houses and in cemeteries, at battlefields, and sites where natural disasters have occurred, such as earthquakes, floods, and volcanoes. Releasement procedures work in those cases as well (Baldwin, 2003).

The 1994 DSM-IV, the *Diagnostic and Statistical Manual of the American Psychiatric Association*, in an appendix identifies "dissociative trance disorder." Its essential feature is "an involuntary state of trance that is not accepted by the person's culture as a normal part of a collective cultural or religious practice and that causes clinically significant distress or functional impairment." Baldwin notes that the definition of this disorder is a clear description of entity possession.

Entity attachment is very common, and in almost any trauma can cause a vulnerability to it. Fortunately, most people manage to live reasonably successful lives despite its interference. Attaching entities can become enmeshed in the aura, that is, the energy field around the body. Emotional or physical trauma experienced by a person can render those energy centers vulnerable. When this occurs they are opened like doors to allow the entering and attachment. This situation may occur in past lives, as well as in the present. Entities can attach to any chakra and also to the surface of the body, to any interior space, or to any organ. In the case of organ donation an entity attached to an organ, such as the heart, can follow the transplanted organ into a new body. Baldwin notes that grateful organ recipients may get "more than they anticipated."

Children can be inflicted by entity attachment. Many people who die in hospitals and are confused about their death and reincarnation search for newborns and attach to them. Souls of infants and children can attach to other children or adults.

A number of things a person experiences can attract a discarnate entity if that same thing is a problem for the entity. These include strong feelings such as anger, rage, sadness, or guilt, as well as repressed negative feelings and unconscious needs. Physical trauma from auto accidents, beatings, or a blow to the head can cause a person to be vulnerable, even physical intrusions in the body such as surgery or blood transfusion. Baldwin points out that an attached earthbound entity may be present without producing noticeable symptoms. It can be benevolent in nature, self-serving, malevolent, or completely neutral. Sometimes attachment may be random, even accidental. It might occur simply because of physical proximity to a dying person.

Connection may be the purposeful choice of either the entity or the living human due to an emotional bond between them that might be in this life, or in a previous lifetime together. In about half the cases of spirit attachment Baldwin discovered some unfinished business between them. Spirit attachment only perpetuates a prior conflict with little possibility for resolution.

There are also positive beings Balwin refers to as Light Beings, including spirit guides and guardian angels. They do not attach or use the energy of living humans. Their purpose is to provide assistance, and they do not make decisions for the person or attempt to control in any way.

The third type of attachment Baldwin has worked with involves extraterrestrial or otherworldly beings. In therapy it is not unusual for a client to discover an entity that is nonhuman and not demonic. These beings appear to be highly intelligent and claim to be from "far away," and are only visiting here on some kind of mission. They are not the spirit of a deceased extraterrestrial, but an alien in their non-physical form.

Spirit releasement therapy (SRT), as practiced by Baldwin and others, is a clinical treatment to help those who are troubled by the various attached entities. With lost earthbound souls—the most common attaching entities—the objective is to help them find their way into the Light where they belong. In the case of extraterrestrial beings they are guided back to their own home. Dark force entities are transformed and taken back to their appropriate place in the Light.

Baldwin, in his practice of releasement therapy, follows several steps. In the first step with earthbound spirits he attempts to discover any and all attached discarnate entities. This involves directing the client to give words to sensations and feelings. "If that tension in your stomach had a shape, a size, what would that be?" "If that sadness and tightness in your heart could speak, what would it say?" "If that pain in your head wanted to speak what would it say right out loud?" Engaging in this way facilitates an altered state of consciousness. An attached entity seems to reside at the level of the subconscious mind. It can hear and respond to the therapist through the client's voice. By personifying the sensation or image and urging it to speak such questions often uncover an attached entity (Baldwin, 2003).

The second step is to identify what type of entity is present, because each type of attachment requires a different releasement method. The therapist wants to learn whether the entity is part of the client or something/someone else by asking it directly, "Are you part of [client's name] or someone or something else?" Past life entities, subpersonalities, or altered personalities in a person with multiple personalities will state immediately that it is definitely a part of the person. Dark force entities will be hostile in declaring they are something else. Extraterrestrial beings will often be condescending in making a firm statement that they are something else.

The third step in SRT is dialogue with the entity to determine why and how it came to the client. The circumstances are explored that led to the attachment, the vulnerability or susceptibility that first allowed it to attach, its motivation for joining, and its effects on the host.

In pursuing this the therapist asks such questions as: "What attracted you to them?" "Was it mutual in any way?" "Did they give you permission to join?" "What was the opening that allowed you to get in?" "How were they vulnerable to you?" The therapist uses this information to seal the leak and prevent future spirit attachments.

The therapist explores the nature and extent of the interference caused by the attachment by asking the entity such questions as: "How have you affected him/her physically?" "How have you affected him/her mentally?" "How have you affected him/her emotionally?" "How have you affected him/her spiritually?" The responses to these questions, indicating an outside influence, often eases the client's mind. However, Baldwin points out that in his twenty years of practice no client has sloughed off personal responsibility and placed blame on an attached entity.

The fourth step in SRT is the actual release of the attached entity into the Light. Baldwin instructs the entity to focus upward and describe whatever it perceives. Often this is a brightness, a brilliant light. Usually the entity is greeted by the spirits of family or friends who have already gone on to the Light. These guiding spirits extend their "hands" to help the entity cross into the Light. When this happens the entity can be released from the client without them being afraid of getting lost again or returning to the client. When the earthbound spirit is welcomed home there is often a tearful reunion.

Baldwin has found that there are often additional entities, a layering of attachments, to be discovered and released in further sessions. Some clients seem to carry hundreds of these attached entities.

The fifth step in SRT, as practiced by Baldwin, is a specific guided imagery called the Sealing Light Meditation. This is important and necessary to metaphorically fill the space left by the departing entities. He guides the client to imagine a brilliant spark of Light deep in their center, to imagine the light glowing and expanding to fill their body, then expanding outward about an arm's length all around. This forms a shimmering protective bubble of Light surrounding them. He instructs the client to silently repeat this visualization several times each day. It is like a "spiritual bandage over a spiritual wound."

The sixth step of SRT involves ongoing therapy to resolve the conflict and to heal the emotional vulnerability that first allowed the spirit attachment. Even though the condition caused by the attachment seems to be resolved after release, sometimes a personality dysfunction remains that is more easily treated through traditional psychotherapy once the attached entity no longer burdens the host.

Baldwin points out that groups of earthbound spirits can be released from disaster sites such as plane crashes, volcanoes, landslides, earthquakes, battlefields, sunken ships, and the terrorist attack on the World Trade Center in New York on September 11. Groups of dark-force networks can be released from locations such as the Nazi death camps, battlefields, geographical locations, and countries dominated by malevolent dictators.

Picking up from Wickland's work, Baldwin also uses spirit releasement done at a distance for another person. In other words, the person needing such assistance is not physically present in his office. The individual in front of him acts as an intermediary, a surrogate, on behalf of the target person, the one who needs the releasement work (Baldwin, 2003).

CHARLES AND NANCY TRAMONT

Releasement therapists have various ways to do this. Charles Tramont, now deceased, worked with his wife Nancy, who acted as what they called a surrogate spirit guide. In a 2023 interview with psychologist Jeffrey Mishlove, on his series "Thinking Allowed," she discussed this procedure.

He would interview the patient seeking releasement therapy by phone and arrange a remote session. At that point Nancy would be brought in and enter into hypnosis. She could then make contact with the patient and the attaching entity. After this occurred Charles would conduct the releasement protocol, through Nancy, following Baldwin's procedure. She told Mishlove that she would not remember the actual content of a session. After her husband had died she looked at his clinical notes to discover what had actually occurred with a given patient.

Over the course of their work together Nancy participated in some 400 sessions, some of which involved her serving as a surrogate in past lives therapy. In the releasement work three main types of attaching entities were encountered. Most commonly these were earthbound spirits and the procedure was straightforward. A second type she referred to as being connected with "dark energy." In that case Charles would invoke celestial entities to surround them with light and call in "rescue spirits" to encapsulate the dark force in the patient. Nancy would feel this happening. Charles then asked an archangel to come in and sever that force from the patient and take it to its destination.

Another type of attachment Nancy described was "mind fragments." These occurred when an individual had suffered from a traumatic event in their lives and part of their mind had split off to join someone else. In that case both the original person suffered because of the loss of part of their mind energy, as did the one to whom the mind fragment attached. Charles and Nancy also encountered and released extraterrestrial entities that Baldwin had described.

Nancy told Mishlove that in her conscious mind she could not have done this work, but being able to do it in trance was an awesome and humbling experience. It did not seem to matter whether a patient actually believed in attaching entities, just that they were willing to try releasement.

Following his death Nancy contacted a dozen former patients to inquire whether the releasement had been helpful. All but one were very enthusiastic. In fact, some had gone on to do their own releasement work.

CHAPTER 7

WITCHES AND WITCHCRAFT

In all societies through the ages there were people, mostly women, who used herbs, potions, spells, and other magical practices to bring about cures of illnesses and desired events in the lives of people who consulted them. Because bad things occurred in people's lives that could not be readily explained—sickness, misfortune, etc.—the cause of such things was often attributed to the nontraditional activities of these women. They were labeled witches and said to be practicing witchcraft. This was particularly likely if they were old and outcasts from society. Although some traditions recognized a positive or benign form of witchcraft practiced by "white" witches, in most cases the activities of witches were associated with evil and the causation of harm.

While cultural traditions have differed in how they define and relate to witchcraft, the one element that has consistently been associated with the activities of witches is magic. Magic involves the use of supernatural or paranormal powers to influence natural events. Traditions that accept magical practice in general have typically seen a clear separation between witches and those employing magic for legitimate reasons. Belief in witches as harm doers is very old and universal. Existing records from ancient Egypt and Babylonia indicate that it played a conspicuous part in those cultures. Most of the indigenous populations of the world believed that certain individuals could cause harm through magical means.

The word "witch" is a translation of the Hebrew word for sorceress. The Hebrew Bible contains a number of references to witchcraft and it is strongly condemned. Exodus 22:18 states: "Thou shalt not suffer a witch to live." The New Testament also spoke strongly against the practice of sorcery. During the early centuries of the Christian era it was prohibited by both Roman criminal and church ecclesiastical legislation. Roman law permitted torture, and a decree enacted in the third century called for witches who caused a person to die through enchantment to be burned alive. In reality, during these years only a few individuals were actually prosecuted for witchcraft. In the centuries to follow church officials attempted to stamp out popular belief in witchcraft ("Witchcraft," *Catholic Encyclopedia*).

Throughout the Middle Ages there was no clear separation between beliefs and practices constituting religion, magic, and science. It was common for learned people to have interests in all three. The Renaissance, along with its rediscovered knowledge of Greek philosophy and science, also stimulated interest in centuries old magical systems, including astrology, alchemy, and hermeticism. The Protestant Reformation, in its emphasis on returning to the purity of an original Christianity, began a long and arduous process of cleansing religion from the centuries-long influences of superstition and magic. The Catholic response to the spread of Protestantism was a major reorganization that led to a streamlining of its rituals and practices. Elements that had been permissible became no longer acceptable and led to greater persecution of such activities as witchcraft.

There was a universal acceptance that certain events lay outside the natural order of things. Clearly God has the power to cause supernatural things to occur in the form of miracles. In Catholic tradition, saints acting through God's power were commonly associated with miracles. Bad things also happened outside of what seemed to be the natural order and were attributed to witches. But witches alone could not be the real source of supernatural happenings. Since they clearly were not saints, then the only source of power behind their activities must be the devil. If a witch has supernatural powers, whether used for good or harm, they must come by way of the devil. Because she, like everyone else, has moral freedom, then she must have entered into some kind of explicit or implicit pact with him. This pact was considered the most important aspect in becoming a witch.

Guazzo's 1608 book *The Compendium Maleficarum* describes this in detail. An important element in the process of becoming a witch, he said, involved the devil, or one of his representatives, imprinting a mark on her body. The mark was usually depicted on the skin as a bat or toad and appeared to lack sensitivity. Typically it was found under the armpits, in the genital area, or under the eyelids. Also it occasionally appeared as a third breast or nipple.

The pact, according to Guazzo, bound the individual to Satan for a predetermined period of time, or perhaps an entire lifetime. The terms of the pact were specific, listing what the witch would be given in return for his help, typically power, wisdom, sex, wealth, and/or revenge. The pact was usually written in her own blood and placed at a crossroads.

The Compendium also described other acts required for the aspiring witch, including:

Abjuring one's faith,

Casting away rosaries and scapulars,

Paying homage to the devil or his representatives with obscene gestures,

Promising to gain followers for the devil,

Undergoing a sacrilegious baptism,

Giving a token to the devil, and

Entering the devil's magic circle (Ruiz, 2005).

A major activity that witches were said to be involved in was meeting in gatherings known as Sabbats. The greatest of these took place on Walpurgis Nacht, April 30. There were supposed reports of thousands of witches gathering on that day in some places in Germany. The devil himself, or one of his representatives, dressed in a goat skin presided over these meetings. The Sabbats featured great banquets with exquisite food and aphrodisiacs, along with lewd dances and sexual orgies. It was even said that child murder and cannibalism sometimes occurred. These same charges had been leveled throughout the ages against any oppressed minorities, even the first Christians themselves.

These lurid and dramatic accounts of witches and their activities increasingly came to dominate much of the popular interest and gave rise to attempts to stamp out the heresy of witchcraft through severe punishment. Between 1400 and 1700 as many as 80,000–100,000 people, mostly elderly women, were executed in Western Europe after being charged and found guilty of practicing witchcraft. These executions were not mindless hysterical acts of violence. Proceedings against suspected witches involved an official, systematic program of arrest, interrogation, trial procedure, and application of the principles of law based on the best current knowledge of human nature, crime, punishment, and evidence. The basis for these activities was the *Malleus Maleficarum*, written in 1486 by two Dominicans who provided a coherent theory of witchcraft, a set of tests to determine witchcraft, and a list of appropriate punishments. The book contained in its preface the apparent blessing of the Pope and was supported by the kings and princes of Europe. It became immensely popular, undergoing over twenty publications in the ensuing 200 years.

As spelled out in the *Malleus Maleficarum*, several types of evidence were to be used in the trials of accused witches. By entering into a pact with the devil, the witch had a diminished capacity for remorse. If statements were read to an accused woman about the love Mary had for her dying son Jesus, whose blood was spilled for her salvation by his ultimate sacrifice, and she did not weep, then you might well suspect she was a witch. This was known as the tear test. (We now know that one of the characteristics of aging is dry eye, or difficulty forming tears.)

Another test was the flotation test. An accused person was put in the center of a pool of water deeper than her height. People around the pool held her up by sticks under her body. On a signal they were pulled away. The question was, would she float? If she floated the presumption was she was a witch; if she sank, she was not. The rationale apparently was that when the soul has lost its saving grace a certain quality of levity is taken on.

As mentioned, when the devil enters a person's body he leaves a mark. The existence of this mark constituted another strong piece of evidence. Because it was often hidden the body of the accused had to be completely shaven. Special people known as witch prickers were employed who claimed to know exactly how to apply calipers to certain locations on the body to find the desensitized spots by which the devil had entered. If a person failed the tear and flotation test, and if the devil's mark was found on her body and, particularly if she had already confessed to being a witch, as many did, then her fate was sealed. She would be executed by burning.

Whether the witch trial took place in a Catholic or Protestant setting did not appear to make much difference. In comparison with a religious court, one's chances in a secular court were probably even worse. The practice of witch trials and executions went on during the scientific revolution that included Copernicus, Kepler, Descartes, Galileo, and Newton. It continued in the face of counter evidence and in spite of eloquent defenses raised on behalf of some accused. In fact, it gained momentum over the years and took on a life of its own that was to last until the end of the seventeenth century (Ruiz, 2005).

About the ending gasp of the witch craze occurred in Salem, Massachusetts, in the last decade of the seventeenth century. Between February 1692 and May 1693 more than 150 people were arrested and imprisoned for practicing witchcraft. Two courts convicted twenty-nine people of witchcraft, a capital felony. Nineteen were hanged, fourteen women and five men. One man was crushed to death under heavy stones in an attempt to force him to enter a plea when he refused. At least five more of the accused people died in prison.

Public outcry against these actions soon arose, and in ensuing years victims were exonerated, and those surviving or their families were financially compensated. With that the long ordeal was pretty much over. The last witch was executed in Europe in 1792 ("Salem witch trials," Wikipedia).

Before leaving the topic of witchcraft and the witch craze as a historical phenomenon, one very important point needs to be emphasized. The only sources of information we have come from outsiders who held strongly hostile and often fanatical opinions regarding what they assumed to be the practice of witchcraft. We do not have any surviving writings of witches themselves that explain what they believed and did. Many of the claims against them had been voiced against other minority groups before. The first Christians were believed by non-Christians (pagans) to be atheists. Because they offended the pagan gods by refusing to worship them, those communities that harbored Christians were believed to attract divine retribution in the form of crop failures, sickness, and the like. Christians were commonly believed to engage in such morally reprehensible activities as incest, infanticide, and cannibalism.

WICCA

A modern version of benign witchcraft known as Wicca is popular among some circles. The history of Wicca, known as The Craft, has been hotly debated. The most widely accepted opinion among academics is that it is a modern nature-based religion popularized, if not largely created, by Gerald Gardner in the 1940s and '50s. Gardiner set out to revive a kind of medieval witchcraft religion described by anthropologist Margaret Murray in her 1921 book *The Witch-cult in Western Europe*. In that book Murray laid out a central thesis, widely discredited by subsequent scholars, that the witches persecuted during the witch craze were members of a secret pagan fertility religion. Gardner claimed in his influential writings *Witchcraft Today* (1954) and *The Meaning of Witchcraft* (1959) to have been initiated into such a witchcraft religion in England that had existed in secret for hundreds of years. He described beliefs and practices he said were revealed to him, although he acknowledged that the rites were fragmentary and that he substantially rewrote them. Scholars believe Gardiner actually drew on metaphysical ritual magic and popular works about folklore and mythology along with Murray's ideas as the source for his writings.

Practitioners typically do not give that much weight to what the scholars say. They see their beliefs and practices, if not as a continuation of an actual religious tradition, at least grounded in ancient tradition. Certainly paganism, within which The Craft or Wicca is one form, is very old indeed. Since time immemorial there have been people who lived close to the Earth attuned to nature's cycles who worshiped a variety of gods and goddesses, practiced folk healing with natural remedies, and used magic to influence natural and human affairs.

Modern Wicca includes a number of traditions, each with its own distinctive beliefs, rituals, and practices. Many are secretive and require that members be initiated. Typically members function within covens which are groups of thirteen. However, there are a large number of Wiccans (witches) known as solitaries who choose to practice alone, outside of any particular tradition.

Because Wicca (The Craft) has no centralized church, organizational structure, or universal orthodoxy, its beliefs and practices vary substantially, although most practitioners subscribe to certain key principles. The Council of American Witches, in 1974, articulated the following basic principles:

We practice rites to attune ourselves with the natural rhythm of life forces.
We seek to live in harmony with Nature, in ecological balance offering fulfillment to life and consciousness within an evolutionary concept.

We acknowledge a depth of power far greater than is apparent to the average person. Because it is far greater than ordinary it is sometimes called "supernatural," but we see it as lying within that which is naturally potential to all.

We conceive of the Creative Power in the Universe as manifesting through polarity—as masculine and feminine—and that this same creative Power lives in all people, and functions through the interaction of the masculine and feminine.

We recognize both outer worlds and inner, or psychological worlds, and we see in the interaction of these two dimensions the basis for paranormal phenomena and magickal exercises.

We do not recognize any authoritarian hierarchy.

We see religion, magick, and wisdom-in-living as being united in the way one views the world and lives within it, a world view and philosophy of life which we identify as Witchcraft or the Wiccan Way.

A Witch seeks to control the forces within him/herself that make life possible in order to live wisely and well, without harm to others, and in harmony with Nature.

We acknowledge that it is the affirmation and fulfillment of life, in a continuation of evolution and development of consciousness, that gives meaning to the Universe we know, and to our personal role within it.

Our only animosity toward Christianity, or toward any other religion or philosophy of life, is to the extent that its institutions have claimed to be "the one true right and only way" and have sought to deny freedom to others and to suppress other ways of religious practices and belief.

As American Witches, we are not threatened by debates on the history of The Craft, the origins of various terms, or the legitimacy of various aspects of different traditions. We are concerned with our present and our future.

We do not accept the concept of "absolute evil," nor do we worship any entity known as "Satan" or "the Devil" as defined by Christian tradition.

We work within Nature for that which is contributory to our health and well-being (RavenWolf, 2012, pp. 6–7).

The activity most commonly associated with witches is their use of magic (sometimes spelled magick). RavenWolf defines magic as:

> The art and science of focusing your will and emotions to effect change both in the world around you and the world within you. Magick is neither good nor evil, positive nor negative. It is the use of the power that determines the path it will take.

One of the main acts of magic is spell casting. For the practitioner this is serious business. Simple spell casting is not so "simple." It truly is an art in itself. It is the practice of working magick— changing thought into some type of emotional or physical form—by your own will using specific words in conjunction with a magickal tool or entity. A successful spell is one that accomplishes the desired end without harming anyone in the process. Sometimes this is not as easy as it sounds. RavenWolf offers these suggestions for casting spells:

> Spells are tricky . . . and you have to plan them carefully. Don't expect to just stand in front of a candle, whisper some mumbo-jumbo, and have everything turn out just peachy. If you do, and it does, you were damned lucky!
>
> It is not that spells must be elaborate, but is imperative that they are specific. ... Spells should be written, and the wording considered with great care. Your requests and statements should somehow connect with a specific set of deities, or the Universe in general. A spell does not need to rhyme, but a good beat is helpful when trying to remember it if you plan to use it often. When chanting or dancing a rhyming spell adds to the magickal working.

Witches, RavenWolf tells us, often develop a particular way to begin and end their spells that they find through trial and error works. It might be a particular rhyme or phrase with a beat that helps them to raise their "vibratory note."

SECTION III

OTHER PARANORMAL PHENOMENA

Paranormal or supernatural phenomena are considered to be impossible to explain by known natural forces or by science. Perhaps the richest source of accounts of them can be found in spiritual and religious sources.

CHAPTER 8

SPIRIT-RELATED PHENOMENA

Spirit can be thought of as a universal aspect of reality that underlies religion, but is not exclusive to any one religion and can manifest outside of religious systems. The direct experience of spirit involves a kind of energy field or power. Typically this is transmitted through or by spiritual beings that vary in terms of their relationship with their source. Spirit is known primarily through experience. The behavior of truly religious people arises out of their beliefs about, and perhaps direct encounters with Spirit.

In the very long evolutionary history of life on Earth modern humans emerged some 200,000 years ago. Ever since becoming aware of themselves and the world around them anthropologists tell us they experienced a spiritual or sacred dimension of their lives and the cosmos. We know this on the basis of archaeological evidence involving ancient cave art and burial sites. Until roughly 10,000 years ago these people were hunter/gatherers, existing in small bands of twenty or fewer individuals. In a great many respects they remained very much tied to and, in a sense, embedded in the natural world.

The experience of spirit for thousands of years among these early people is likely to have been strongly influenced by two interrelated systems of belief and practice: magic and shamanism. "Real magic," as opposed to stage magic, refers to various acts that are undertaken to harness special powers to accomplish supernatural effects in the world. Although we can only speculate about how this earliest thinking came about and the form it took, it seems likely that emerging human consciousness must have been dominated by the demands involved in physical survival. After all, humans were far from the largest or strongest of the creatures with whom they shared living space.

While it has been standard anthropological practice to label early humankind as hunters and gatherers, the argument has been made that the greater likelihood is that they were not so much the hunters as the hunted. Of course wild animals were only one of the threats to survival. Loud crashes of thunder, fires set off by lightning, fierce winds, downpours of rain and parching droughts, bitter cold in some areas, floods, huge waves in larger bodies of water, and volcanic eruptions must have been very frightening. And should they be able to evade wild beasts and the extreme forces of nature, there was an ever-present threat of injury, sickness, starvation, and death. These very early humans must also have marveled at those forces and events that sustained and nourished them: the return of the sun every morning, changing of the seasons with the appearance of new plants in the spring, and the miraculous birth of animals and their own kind.

Behind these events they no doubt sensed a kind of unseen power, perhaps experienced as an impersonal force, perhaps as a spirit or spirits. Attracting some of this power or actually aligning oneself with it to increase one's effectiveness in the world no doubt assume prime importance.

SPIRITS AND MAGIC

Anthropologists believe the earliest attempts to attract the power of spirit in any systematic way involved magical beliefs and practices. Basically magic has three functions: protective, productive, and destructive. Productive magic is used to solicit desired outcomes from human endeavors or natural phenomena, such as success in a hunt, a bountiful harvest, or good weather. Protective magic strives to defend a person or community from adverse natural events, or the evil of others. Destructive magic, often referred to as sorcery, is intended to cause harm. The most basic practice to effect these results is the performance of a magical spell.

Magic rests on two underlying principles: the law of similarity and the law of contact or contagion. The law of similarity can be stated as "like produces like." Whatever happens to an image of someone will happen to them. Sticking pins in the stomach of a voodoo doll, constructed to resemble a particular person, will harm that actual person. The law of contagion states that things or persons once in contact can continue to influence each other when separated. If someone obtains hair or fingernails of a person they can perform magic with them to affect that person. Anthropologists speculate that, in its earliest forms, magic may not have involved spiritual or religious elements, but over time some forms of magic increasingly did so. In this sense magical practices sought to invite or compel spiritual agencies to accomplish the desired objective ("Magic," 2016 Encyclopedia Britannica Online Article).

CHRISTIANITY, JESUS, AND SPIRIT

Spirit played a central role in the origin and development of Christianity with its central figure, Jesus Christ. While from its outset there were major questions and controversy about who Jesus was, the majority of today's scholars agree that He was first and foremost a charismatic, a person who knows the world of spirit firsthand. His life was marked by an intense experiential relationship with spirit. Christians believe that, as God's son, Jesus continues to live among us as a life giving spirit.

The gospels tell us that He began his ministry with a vision from the other world of spirit that descended upon Him. He had gone to John the Baptist, a charismatic wilderness preacher of repentance, and during His baptism He had a vision. "He saw the heavens opened and the spirit descending upon Him like a dove" Mark 1:10.

Shortly after this experience spirit drove or led Jesus out into the wilderness for forty days where, in a desolate desert area near the Dead Sea, He underwent a period of extended solitude and fasting, during which He was tested by Satan and nourished by beneficent spirits. Borg describes these events as:

> ...typical of what other traditions call a "vision quest" [and notes that] ... the sequence of initiation into the world of spirit (the baptism) followed by a testing or ordeal in the wilderness is strikingly similar to what is reported of charismatic figures cross-culturally (Borg, p. 42).

From these events onward Jesus's life was marked by an intense experiential relationship with spirit. His connection to the world of spirit, Borg notes, can be seen:

> ...in central dimensions of His public life: in the impression he made on others, His claims to authority, and in the style of His speech.

Jesus, in the gospels, is portrayed as a person of prayer. In the Gospel of Luke, He prays at every significant moment in His ministry. In the gospel of Matthew, chapter 6, He teaches His followers to "pray in this way":

> Our Father, who are in heaven, sanctified be your name. Your kingdom come. Your will be done, on earth as it is in heaven. Give us this day our daily bread, and forgive us our debts, as we forgive our debtors. And do not bring us into a time of trial, but rescue us.

THE HOLY SPIRIT

According to Christian scripture, before Jesus died he promised the disciples that God would send the Holy Spirit to remain with them and carry out His task of salvation. They subsequently experienced this directly at their Pentecostal gathering in Jerusalem as an intense visionary encounter. The Holy Spirit is said to have descended into their group accompanied by a sound "like a mighty wind" that filled the room with "tongues as of fire" appearing above them. For the disciples this was overwhelming and indisputable proof that Jesus the Christ continued to be present among them in spite of His death on the cross. Acts of the Apostles reports that immediately after this occurrence the disciples were inspired to begin preaching ecstatically to the multitudes. This Pentecostal experience marked the beginning of a new age, with the pouring forth of the spirit upon all people within the Christian community.

Early on a problem arose in the first Christian churches when individuals claiming to be possessed by the Holy Spirit began producing charismatic phenomena such as speaking in tongues, spontaneous spiritual ecstasies, miraculous healings, prophesies, and assertions of new divine knowledge. These phenomena easily became disruptive when they occurred in church services. Wandering preachers proclaiming supposedly spirit inspired but unorthodox messages were clearly a problem to a church attempting to define and teach one correct set of beliefs. Increasingly, as more structured and formal church organization developed, these activities were discouraged. The Holy Spirit came increasingly to be seen as solely invested in the authority and activities of the institutional church and, over time, became accepted as the basis for the church itself, expressing itself in all aspects of the life of the church, its sacraments, prayer, and doctrine, its developing tradition, its official hierarchy, and its spiritual authority (Tarnas, 1991).

MANIFESTATIONS OF SPIRIT IN US RELIGIOUS HISTORY

Outbreaks of intense spiritual activity have occurred several times in American history. Following the Revolutionary War, in the early years of the nineteenth century a great wave of religious revivals swept through the new nation, known as the second awakening. (The first awakening occurred between the 1730s and the 1770s.) The movement was particularly strong in the newly developing frontier west of the Appalachians. This area was being rapidly settled by a diverse population of hardy individuals who eked out a living under harsh and isolated conditions. Serving them presented a serious challenge for the established churches.

A few clergy did venture out on the frontier. One, James McGrady, initiated what was to become a significant feature of nineteenth-century religious activity, the camp meeting. Rather than relying on tiny communities to construct or designate buildings to serve as a church, in 1800, at Gasper River, Kentucky, he designated a central place where people would come in and camp to hear sermons preached. This proved to be highly successful. A year later McGrady and another minister, Barton Stone, led a revival camp meeting at Cane Ridge, Kentucky, that attracted between 10,000 and 20,000 people, far more than inhabited any of the towns west of the mountains. From crude log pulpits ministers one by one preached highly emotional sermons that urged people to renounce their sins and convert to Christianity. Often, taken up in the emotionally charged atmosphere, they exhibited extreme reactions that were referred to as exercises. Barton Stone described the Cane Ridge revival as follows:

> The falling exercise was very common among all classes, the saints and sinners of every age and every grade. The subject would generally with a piercing scream fall like a log to the floor, earth, or mud and appear as if dead. The jerks cannot so easily be described. Sometimes the subject of the jerks would be affected in one member of the body, and sometimes the whole system. When the head alone would be affected it would be jerked backward or forward, or from side to side so quickly that the features of the face would not be distinguished. When the whole system was affected, I've seen the person stand in one place and jerk backwards and forward in quick succession, their head nearly touching the floor behind and before. A person affected by the jerks, especially in his head, would often make a grunt or bark from the suddenness of the jerk (Allitt, 2001).

People, Stone observed, rushed around in fits of manic laughter, howled, and sang together in strange ways, while crowds of women fainted on to the muddy and trampled floor. This strange scene finally ended after seven days when the food ran out.

Word of this traveled back east, meeting with mixed reactions. Clergy in the Congregational and Presbyterian churches were alarmed by what they perceived as hysterical breaches of established Christian decorum. Baptists and Methodists were more enthusiastic and went on to play to the frontier appetite for highly emotional religion.

The most famous of the second great awakening revivalist preachers was Charles Grandison Finney. He had a commanding presence and captivated his audience. Unlike his predecessors, Finney believed that revivals did not happen solely through God's action within the individual, but that they needed to be set up and run in a certain way to create the right kind of atmosphere and conditions. The intent was not meant to be cynical manipulation, but to get people worked up into an intense excitement where they were receptive to receiving spirit, God. To help other ministers do this kind of orchestration Finney wrote a how-to manual. He developed what he called an "anxious bench" in front of the pulpit where people experiencing doubt could sit and be prayed over by everyone else.

Finney understood that the revivals provided opportunities for lonely and isolated frontier families to gather and socialize, and that a good revival should be entertaining. Like other revivalist preachers before him he was soundly criticized, particularly by Congregationalist and Presbyterian clergy who said he was using theatrical techniques to stir up intense feelings. You do not need to be taken out of your right mind to receive God, they asserted, but just the opposite: you need to be fully rational to take God into your heart (Allitt, 2001).

SHAKERS

The Shakers originated in England in 1772, when Mother Ann Lee was told in a vision that she should come to the United States, where her mission would be fulfilled. In 1774, with a tiny group of nine people, she settled in New York. The group grew, and soon nineteen communal settlements were established. The Shakers participated in intensely spiritual rituals involving singing, shouting, speaking in tongues (*glossalalia*), and ecstatic dancing. The dancing would begin in a formal way, with ritualized steps, and go on hour after hour, with people whirling around with increasing excitement until they fainted in exhaustion. Often there would be trembling and shaking that Mother Ann taught was caused by sin being purged from the body through the power of the Holy Spirit. It is the latter that gave rise to the group's name, originally used by detractors in a pejorative sense.

In 1837, a period of intense religious experiences involving spirit manifestations began among the believers. Children told of visits to cities in the spirit realm where they received messages for the community from Mother Ann Lee, who had died in 1784. The next year, through messages received in glossolalia, sacred places were identified and set aside with names like Holy Mount. A few years later the spirits abruptly left. By the end of the nineteenth century the population of Shakers had begun to decline markedly, with little effort to gain new members ("Shakers," Wikipedia).

PENTECOSTALS

Pentecostalism is a charismatic religious movement developed in the early twentieth century that places special emphasis on a direct personal experience of *God* through *baptism with the Holy Spirit*, harking back to the Holy Spirit's descent upon the first Christians in Jerusalem on the day of Pentecost. This is believed to be accompanied by the gift of speaking in tongues along with other supernatural gifts, such as an ability to prophesy and to heal. Pentecostals emphasize conversion, moral rigor, faith healing, and a literal interpretation of the Bible. There are estimated to be more than 10 million Pentecostals in the United States today, including 5.5 million members of the Church of God in Christ and 2.5 million members of the Assemblies of God (Melton, 2011, Encyclopedia Britannica).

GLOSSOLALIA, OR SPEAKING IN TONGUES

Glossolalia is perhaps the most fascinating and controversial experience directly involving the power of spirit among the first Christians. It has been described as "an absolute, direct, and pure religious experience, ecstatic utterance" made possible through empowerment of the Holy Spirit. From the very first account of its appearance in Christianity glossolalia was met with a mixed response. Acts of the Apostles describes the Holy Spirit falling upon the disciples, who began to speak in tongues. Some people in the crowd thought they were drunk and mocked them, while others, convinced that the experience demonstrated the resurrection of Jesus, who had given them a prophetic power of speech, were persuaded by it to be converted and to join the new movement.

Luke, in Acts, offers a positive, straightforward evaluation of tongues. For him speaking in tongues is prophecy, pure and simple. Paul, although himself a practitioner, is more ambivalent. While recognizing glossolalia as a gift of the Holy Spirit, he sees a clear difference between the two. Glossolalia is prayer, not prophecy, which is a form of rational speech that strengthens the community. He allows tongues speaking in community worship only when it can be interpreted; that is, changed into prophecy.

By the fourth century the practice of glossolalia had largely disappeared among more orthodox groups. For them it resembled some pagan practices and sometimes fostered a kind of elitism. Those who did it viewed themselves as more spirit filled, "real" Christians. Most importantly, it could be disruptive and tended to subvert established authority (male), especially when practiced by women.

Today, most Christian denominations acknowledge that glossolalia did occur early on as described in the Bible as part of a miraculous outbreak of the Holy Spirit by which God enabled the movement to spread. However, they see themselves as having clearly matured since then and view speaking in tongues, with its potential for self-delusion and even deception, as something of an embarrassment. Charismatics or Pentecostals regard speaking in tongues as the most direct sign of the power of the Holy Spirit. It is the defining experience which, when first engaged in, is the sign that one has been baptized in the Holy Spirit and is fully initiated into the life of the living, spirit filled faith.

Pentecostal and charismatic groups tend to believe that those speaking in tongues are actually expressing some real but unknown language:

> [They] are full of folkloric accounts of how somebody spoke in tongues, and nobody knew what was going on, and then a stranger in the room stood up and said, "That's Urdu. I learned Urdu when I was a child," and then they proceed to say what the speaker wanted to say in Urdu (Johnson, 2002).

No one has ever been able to verify these accounts. Modern anthropologists and linguists define glossolalia as a form of ecstatic utterance that is non-rational. It is not a real language. It is not rational, and it involves some level of psychological dissociation. Johnson calls it a form of babbling. That is, what is given utterance in this state of ecstasy is a combination of sounds in syllable-like form that tend to be repetitious and rhythmic. For those practicing glossolalia it does not really matter what scholars want to call it. Speaking in tongues for them is a form of praise and prayer to God resulting from inspiration of the Holy Spirit which, when interpreted or translated, gives comfort (Johnson, 2009).

CHAPTER 10

NATIVE AMERICAN SPIRITUALITY

When we think about the many different expressions of religion in America, it is most important to recognize and appreciate that the first European settlers did not arrive at a new land where there was no religion. Quite the contrary, Native Americans had already been here some 11,500 years, and they were steeped in a sense of the sacred. Everything they thought, felt, and did involved an awareness and typically a direct experience of the presence of spirit. Although different groups had different particular local stories and practices, they all shared the sense of directly participating in a relationship with all that is, and that all is infused with spirit. This is an ancient way of seeing and experiencing that predates the monotheistic religions by tens of thousands of years.

RELATIONSHIP WITH OUR MOTHER EARTH

We saw in our opening discussion of current threats to the Earth the devastation we have inflicted, which, viewed from a long-range time perspective, has been very recent in the making. The Native American understanding of Earth as our mother, with whom we enjoy a harmonious relationship of respect, offers a much-needed corrective. Ed Mcgaa in his 1990 book *Mother Earth Spirituality: Native American Paths to Healing Ourselves* points out that the environmental threats we have examined are so serious as to require Native Americans to share with non-Indians their understandings and practices, the "old wisdom that has performed so well," so it can "work its environmental medicine on the world where it is desperately needed."

With our planet in great danger it is of utmost importance that we learn how to communicate with her, that we listen as she speaks through age-old Indian nature-based ceremonies. In spite of the great odds posed by environmental threats we can live, Mcgaa tells us, and our planet can also live. Mother Earth has natural self-healing powers, but without the help of knowledgeable humans she cannot set herself right. A reversal of world values, a spiritual concept of the Earth as God-created and sacred, is in order before we two-leggeds can be environmentally effective on a global basis.

The Sioux believe that all things are of the Great Spirit. Trees, mountains, rivers, grass, four-legged animals, winged creatures, and us two-leggeds all came from the Great Spirit called *Wakan Tanka*, the Supreme Being. Today traditional Sioux still practice their Way. Holy men and holy women continue to conduct sacred ceremonies. But these ceremonies do not belong to Indians alone. They can be done by all people who have the right attitude, who are honest and sincere about their beliefs in Wakan Tanka (Great Spirit), and who follow the rules. If we are sincere in wanting to stop the destruction of the Earth we should listen and learn.

Ceremonies keep Indians closely related to the Earth and to Wakan Tanka above and everywhere. Participation in ceremony brings about a deep realization from beyond of the spirituality that surrounds all. Mcgaa describes seven Mother Earth ceremonies that he says have evolved to be:

> a bridge across to the sacred in the natural world and to foster a regard for our planet as a living relative who must be sustained (Mcgaa, 2011, p. 42).

THE SACRED PIPE

The sacred pipe, commonly called a peace pipe by non-Indians, is central to Sioux ceremonial practice. The Sioux received the original Sacred Pipe many, many years ago from the White Buffalo Calf Woman. Two men, it is said, were hunting and saw something approaching in the distance. The figure drew closer and they saw it was a beautiful maiden dressed in white buckskin, who was carrying a bundle wrapped in buffalo hide. She walked slowly toward them, but one of the men had evil thoughts about her and started to approach. The other tried to restrain him but the evil man pushed him away. This evil man was enveloped in a cloud. When it lifted his body had become a skeleton that was being devoured by worms.

The good hunter was terrified, but the woman spoke to him, telling him not to be afraid. She instructed him to return to his people and get them ready for her coming. He did as she instructed and the beautiful maiden appeared among them. She held out her bundle, saying it was a sacred gift that they must always treat in a holy way.

> In this bundle (she said) is a sacred pipe
> Which no impure man or woman should ever see. With this sacred pipe
> You will send your voices to Wakan Tanka.
> The Great Spirit, Creator of All.
> Your Father and Grandfather. With this sacred pipe You will walk upon the Earth
> Which is your Grandmother and Mother. All your steps should be holy.
> The bowl of the pipe is red stone
> Which represents the earth. ...
> Who will smoke the pipe and send voices to Wakan Tanka. When you use this pipe to pray,
> You will pray for and with everything.
> The sacred pipe binds you to all your relatives;
> Your Grandfather and Father, Your Grandmother and
> Mother.
> The red stone represents the Mother Earth On which you will live.
> The Earth is red
> And the two-legged creatures who live upon it are also red" (Mcgaa, 2011, pp. 3–6).

The Buffalo Calf Woman instructed the people that they should send runners to other bands of the Sioux nation, to have them bring in the many leaders, the medicine people, and the holy people. When the people assembled she instructed them in the sacred ceremonies. When she was finished she walked away from them and sat down. When she rose she had become a white buffalo calf, which walked away, bowed to the four directions, and then disappeared in the distance. She left the sacred bundle with the people. Ever since a traditional Sioux family, the "Keepers of the Sacred Bundle," continues to guard the bundle and its contents (pp. 3–6).

Since 1966 the Pipe keeper has been Arvol Looking Horse, who was born on the Cheyenne River Reservation in South Dakota in 1954. When he was twelve he became the nineteenth generation Keeper of the Sacred Pipe, the youngest person ever given this responsibility.

At this point I will interject a personal experience. When I was living on the Rosebud Sioux reservation and teaching at Sinte Gleska University in the late 1970s I became involved with the Rosebud Medicine Men and Associates. At the time they had a grant to develop resources for strengthening traditional Lakota families and communities and I helped keep track of their funds. They received word that the Looking Horse family was struggling financially and in danger of losing their land where the Pipe was kept. The Rosebud group decided to give them money from the grant. About five members and I drove to the Looking Horse home to do this. We each were permitted to go one at a time into the tiny red building that housed the actual Pipe wrapped in a buffalo skin bundle. Arvol stood silently close by. I recall being very humbled and honored to be given the special privilege to put my hands on the bundle and pray. After we had all done this we participated in a *lowanpi* ceremony of thanksgiving.

Mcgaa suggests that those who want to develop their spirituality by learning Native American knowledge and wisdom inherent in ceremonies should get a sacred pipe. The pipe is not restricted to only one race or one culture, but it must be treated with respect and "deeply regarded as a spiritual instrument by the pipe holder." The pipe serves as a portable altar and using it involves a simple ritual. First, it is loaded with tobacco. No form of mind-altering substance whatsoever, Mcgaa emphasizes, is condoned by "true Native American religion traditionalists."

To load the pipe it is held firmly by the bowl in the palm of the hand. The individual faces east, holding the pipe in one hand with its stem pointed eastward and with the other hand takes a pinch of tobacco, sprinkles some on the ground, then places the remainder into the bowl. By sprinkling a portion on the ground the pipe holder recognizes that we must always give back to Mother Earth a part of what we have taken. This also demonstrates to the spirit world that a bit of the tobacco is for the powers from the east. As this is done a prayer is said to these powers. The pipe holder then turns to the south, the west, and the north, repeating this process. The pipe offering is concluded by holding the pipe with its stem pointed straight upward, out into the center of the universe, to Wakan Tanka, the Great Spirit (Mcgaa, 2011).

CHAPTER 10

MYSTICAL-TYPE PHENOMENA

MYSTICAL EXPERIENCE

Mystical experience involves the brief, intense experience of spirit containing insights into deeper aspects of reality. Each of the three major Western religions (Christianity, Judaism, and Islam) have sects devoted to the cultivation of this experience through the practice of mysticism. Yet mystical experiences also occur outside of formal religious settings. A 2009 poll conducted under the direction of Princeton Survey Research Associates International among a nationwide sample of 4,013 adults advised that nearly half of the public said they had had a religious or mystical experience, defined as a "moment of sudden religious insight or awakening." This is more than twice as high as a 1962 Gallup survey. Roughly one-fifth who described themselves as atheists, agnostics, or said that religion is not important in their lives reported they have had this kind of experience.

Following is a description of his mystical experiences by a professional who was not devoutly religious at the time. Over 100 years ago Canadian psychiatrist R. M. Bucke, at age 36, had a single brief mystical experience of what he came to call "cosmic consciousness" that led to a life-long investigation of similar experiences of others:

> I had spent the evening in a great city, with two friends, reading and discussing poetry and philosophy. We parted at midnight. I had a long drive in a hansom to my lodging. My mind, deeply under the influence of the ideas, images, and emotions called up by the reading and talk, was calm and peaceful. I was in a state of quiet, almost passive enjoyment, not actually thinking, but letting ideas, images, and emotions flow of themselves, as it were, through my mind. All at once, without warning of any kind, I found myself wrapped in a flame-colored cloud. For an instant I thought of fire, an immense conflagration somewhere close by in that great city; the next, I knew that the fire was within myself. Directly afterward there came upon me a sense of exultation, of immense joyousness accompanied or immediately followed by an intellectual illumination impossible to describe. Among other things, I did not merely come to believe, but I saw that the universe is not composed of dead matter, but is, on the contrary, a living Presence; I became conscious in myself of eternal life. It was not a conviction that I would have eternal life, but a consciousness that I possessed eternal life then; I saw that all men are immortal; that the cosmic order is such that without any peradventure all things work together for the good of each and all; that the foundation principle of the world, of all the worlds, is what we call love, and that happiness of each and all is in the long run absolutely certain. The vision lasted a few

> seconds and was gone; but the memory of it and the sense of the reality of what it taught has remained during the quarter of a century which has since elapsed. I knew that what the vision showed was true. I had attained to a point of view from which I saw that it must be true. That view, that conviction, I may say that consciousness, has never, even during periods of the deepest depression, been lost (Kelly, Edward & Emily, 2006, p. 499).

In his classic book *Varieties of Religious Experience* William James identified four elements that characterize strong mystical experiences. The first is ineffability. Those reporting such an experience typically say that it defies description; they cannot find words to adequately describe it. To fully appreciate what occurred one must experience it directly. In this respect mystical experiences seem more similar to states of feeling than states of thought.

The second of James' characteristic elements is their noetic quality. Those experiencing them report gaining insights into depths of truth beyond that obtained through the discursive intellect. They are certain they have gained fundamental insight into the nature of reality, but they cannot adequately communicate these insights so that the rest of us can fully understand them.

Two additional characteristics, not as definitive but commonly present, particularly in spontaneously occurring experiences, are transiency and passivity. Typically mystical experiences are very intense, but can be sustained only for brief periods from a few seconds to a few hours. Even when brought on voluntarily through such practices as meditation they tend to "break in upon and engulf" the experiencer as if they originated in some area outside of normal consciousness.

VISIONS

One of the major ways that spirit becomes manifested in people's lives is through their experience of visions. Visions played a dominant role in the development and growth of Christianity, and they continue to have a major impact in the lives of people who experience them today. It is important to note that the scientific and psychiatric community hold a markedly different view of visions, regarding them as hallucinations (seeing, hearing, or feeling things that are not really there).

The disciples' belief in the resurrection was based on visionary experiences. According to gospel accounts, following the death of Jesus various people are reported to have seen Him, and accounts of sightings of His luminous figure continued for months after His death.

Aside from Jesus himself, the fact that Christianity came into existence and thrived owes more to the Apostle Paul than anyone else. Some years after the visions of Him by the earliest followers Paul had a profound experience of Him that changed his life. While on the road to Damascus a light from heaven flashed around him that was brighter than the sun. He fell to the ground, heard a voice saying: "Saul, Saul, why do you persecute me? ... I am Jesus," and was subsequently blinded for three days. This experience convinced him that Jesus had in fact been raised from the dead. He drew from his experience the same conclusions that were developing among the original Jesus followers. Jesus had died for the sins of the world. He was raised as the Messiah, the Christ, who would bring judgment and the possibility of salvation in the kingdom of God.

Although it may be easy for skeptics to dismiss biblical accounts as more mythic than real, visions of Jesus have continued to be reported right up to the present. Phillip H. Wiebe, in his book *Visions of Jesus: Direct Encounters from the New Testament to Today* described twenty-eight case studies. Some involve instances in which Jesus is said to have appeared to, that is, been seen in a vision by not just one individual, but to entire groups of people. One took place in the Pentecostal Holiness Church in Oakland, California, in 1959. A woman from the congregation was giving her testimony when she suddenly disappeared and was replaced by a male figure who seemed to obviously be Jesus. He was wearing a glistening white robe and sandals. In His hand were nail marks, and His hands were dripping with oil. He apparently said nothing for several minutes and then disappeared, at which time the woman reappeared. Two hundred people saw and confirmed they had seen this. Remarkably, because very strange things had been happening in the church at the time, everything was being filmed. This occurrence was captured on film and Wiebe himself saw it. Although the film had been lost by the time he wrote his book, he was able to interview five people who had been present. All agreed that they had seen the event (Ehrman, 2014).

THE VISION OF CONSTANTINE

If it had not been for the fourth-century Roman emperor Constantine it is very likely Christianity would have remained a small provincial faith, had it survived at all. Constantine converted to Christianity on the basis of a visionary experience. The story is that in 312 he was engaged in a fierce struggle with his brother-in-law Maxentius to become emperor. Constantine until this time had courted the same gods and goddesses as the other contenders for power in the empire. As he and his army approached Rome, for what was to be the definitive battle, Constantine became consumed by anxiety that all the pagan deities might side with Maxentius.

He could only hope that one of them might look favorably on him and trusted that this would be Sol Invectus, the Unquored Sun. However something quite unexpected happened. According to the accepted but controversial account, on the day before the battle Constantine looked up in the sky and saw something truly remarkable: the figure of a cross and Greek letters spelling out the phrase, "In this sign, conquor." He was then instructed in a dream to inscribe the sign *chi-rho*, signifying Christ, to a battle standard. As the story goes Constantine marched out to face Maxentius with troops carrying shields marked with the cross and following a battle standard that, instead of the golden eagle of pagan Rome, was decorated with the chio-rho sign. Even though his forces were smaller Constantine prevailed, defeating Maxentius, who was killed. As a result of his good fortune in receiving the support of this powerful god Constantine converted to Christianity.

As emperor he resolved to use his new authority to unify the Christian church. He accepted the one and only Christian god and expected his subjects to submit to the sovereignty of one god, one emperor, and one church. Constantine went on to bestow certain favors on Christians, including giving lands to the churches, constructing churches, and giving authority to Christian bishops. Membership in the church grew by leaps and bounds as people clearly saw the advantages of aligning themselves with the new faith. By the end of the third century probably some five to seven percent of the entire population of the Roman empire was

Christian, or three-to-four million people. By the end of the fourth century Christianity had become the religion of half of the empire, perhaps 30 million people (Ehrman, 2004).

VISIONS OF THE VIRGIN MARY

There are numerous accounts of visions of the Virgin Mary in various places even to the present. One occurred in Betania, Venezuela, in 1984. After the Catholic mass a number of people were spending leisurely time near the local waterfall when the Virgin Mary appeared above it. She then came and went, often remaining visible for perhaps five minutes or so, and the last time for half an hour. Psychiatrists, psychologists, doctors, engineers, and lawyers were among those who witnessed this. These visionary appearances continued until 1988. At times up to a thousand people saw Mary, who was bathed in light and accompanied by the scent of roses. Monsignor Pio Bello Ricardo, a Jesuit priest and professor of psychology at the Central University of Caracas, interviewed 490 people who reported they had seen Mary there (Ehrman, 2014).

CATHOLIC SAINTS—CHARISMS

A rich source of material regarding supernormal phenomena, although generally not well known, can be found in accounts of lives of Catholic mystics and saints. The Catholic church recognizes a number of extraordinary phenomena that frequently accompany religious devotion called "charisms." These by themselves are not considered signs of virtue or sanctity, but they are prominent in the lives of those recognized for their great piety. The *New Catholic Encyclopedia* mentions the following:

> Stigmata, the spontaneous appearance of wounds and bleeding that resemble the wounds of Christ.
>
> Inedia, abstinence from all nourishment for great lengths of time.
>
> Visions, the perception of normally invisible objects.
>
> Locutions, interior illuminations by means of words or statements, sometimes accompanied by a vision and seeming to proceed from the object represented.
>
> Reading of hearts, telepathic knowledge of secret thoughts or mood without sensory cues.
>
> *Incendium amoris*, burning sensations in the body without apparent cause. These include interior heat, usually a sensation around the heart, which gradually extends to other parts of the body; intense ardors (when the heat becomes unbearable and cold applications must be used); and material burning that scorches clothing or blisters the skin.
>
> Tears of blood and bloody sweat (*hematidrosis*), the effusion of blood from the eyes, as in weeping, or from pores of the skin.
>
> Exchange of hearts, the appearance of a pronounced ridge of flesh on a finger, representing a ring designating mystical marriage with Christ.
>
> Bilocation, the simultaneous presence of a material body in two distinct places at once.

Agility, the instantaneous movement of a material body from one place to another without passing through the intervening space.

Levitation, elevation of the human body above the ground without visible cause and its suspension in the air without natural support. It may also appear in the form of ecstatic flight or ecstatic walk.

Compenetration of bodies, when one material body appears to pass through another.

Bodily incombustibility, the ability of bodies to withstand the natural laws of combustibility.

Bodily elongation or shrinking.

Mystical aureoles and illuminations, radiance from the body, especially during ecstasy or contemplation, which is considered to be an anticipation of the Glorified Body.

Blood prodigies, bodily incorruptibility, and absence of rigor mortis in human cadavers (Murphy, 1992).

There is certainly more evidence for some of these charisms than others, and some appear clearly impossible.

Very carefully documented descriptions of many of these phenomena can be found in the extensive literature on the canonization of Catholic saints. To become canonized requires a very rigorous examination of the candidate in a process carefully set out by the Catholic church.

In the eighteenth century, under Pope Benedict XIV, the treatise "*De Servorum Dei Beatificatione et Beatorum Canonizations*" was issued, which defined the elements of canonization, clarified the concept of heroic virtue, and established criteria by which to judge the authenticity of miracles. The process is complex, beginning with a thorough investigation of all the particulars of the life and death of the alleged saint that can be ascertained. Every witness is examined under oath in the presence of a trained church lawyer encouraged to raise all the objections he can think of. If the judgment at this point is favorable the case goes for another examination by a higher tribunal. Witnesses are again called to testify to individual facts, but particular stress is also placed on the opinion of those who had dealings with him or her.

Over the last 200 years the rules of evidence have been refined to keep pace with developments in science. Cures that once seemed miraculous can now be considered in light of modern medicine. Psychiatric insights regarding hysteria are applied to the symptoms exhibited by ecstatics. There are criteria by which to distinguish authentic mystical experience from false enthusiasms. Discoveries in psychical research are considered.

The procedure for full canonization takes many years, decades, or even centuries to complete, with numerous hearings and rehearings possible. The first stage is that of "beatification," which involves proof of extraordinary holiness of life and of two miracles. In modern times this rarely occurs within fifty years of the death of the saint. For full canonization proof of two more miracles after beatification is required.

During this long process purported supernormal phenomena are examined in detail by many people who claimed to have observed them, as well as by doctors, physiologists, physicists, and others who might ascertain their authenticity and causes. Any testimony can be called into question by an official called the *Promotor Fidei*, or Devil's Advocate. Because the testimony is presented under oath and the church considers lies or exaggerations to be sins there is considerable pressure upon experts and witnesses to tell the truth. Church canonization records are available dating to the sixteenth century that document accounts of extraordinary functioning occurring at a number of different times and places, providing a rich source of material for analysis unavailable in the orally transmitted legends of other faiths (Murphy, 1992).

STIGMATA

One of the best documented of the charisms, particularly in the lives of the saints, is stigmata. Stigmata are visible marks on the body corresponding to Christ's crucifixion wounds. Most typically they have consisted of bruises, welts, and bleeding wounds on the hands, feet, and side. Some stigmatics have also exhibited apparent abrasions or punctures on the head representing the imprint made by Christ's crown of thorns, crosses on the back or chest, and lacerations representing Christ's scourging.

There is no hard data as to the number of people who have experienced stigmata, but a conservative estimate placed the number at sixty or more by the 1930s, and since then many more have been reported in medical journals and popular magazines [Murphy, p. 484].

The first stigmatic for which we have good evidence is Saint Francis of Assisi. Although his followers withheld news of his stigmata from the public until after his death, once released it caused something of an immediate sensation. Observations of his stigmata were repeatedly confirmed by his closest companions. Saint Francis's confidant, Brother Elias, wrote the following to the Provincial of France soon after the saint's death:

> I announce to you great joy, even a new miracle.... For, a long while before his death, our Father and Brother appeared crucified, bearing in his body the five wounds which are verily the Stigmata of the Christ; for his hands and feet had as it were piercings made by nails fixed in from above and below, which laid open the scars and had the black appearance of nails; while his side appeared to have been lanced, and blood often trickled therefrom (Murphy, 1992).

One of the best known of the recent stigmatics is Padre Pio. He was born Francesco Forgione in 1887, in southeastern Italy, joined the Capuchin order in 1903, and in 1907 was ordained a priest. Four weeks later he developed puncture wounds on his hands, which he showed to the parish priest. When he prayed for their removal they disappeared. Padre Pio entered a monastery in 1916, where he remained for the rest of his life. In 1918 he experienced visions of a celestial person who hurled a spear at him, whereupon he found visible stigmata on his hands, feet, and side. These remained until his death in 1968. His fellow friars learned of these wounds a few days later when they discovered his blood-stained bedding. As word spread about his stigmata Padre Pio became an international celebrity, becoming known not only for his stigmata, but for his vivid personality, sanctity, and reputed healing powers. Padre Pio was subjected to exceptional scrutiny throughout his life, with repeated examinations documented with photographic evidence all attesting that the wounds were authentic and sometimes oozed blood without any external manipulation (Murphy, 1992).

CHAPTER 11

TWO PSYCHICS

MARIA VALTORTA

Maria Valtorta (1897–1961) was an Italian mystic who authored an extraordinary account of the life of Jesus that she apparently received as a direct dictation from Him. Maria, when 23, was badly injured and, at 37, was confined to bed for the remaining 28 years of her life. The morning of April 23, 1943, Good Friday, she reported a voice suddenly speaking to her and asking her to write. With the encouragement of her priest she began writing down everything she received. From then until 1947 Valtorta wrote almost every day, and less frequently until 1951. During these years she produced over 15,000 handwritten pages in 122 notebooks, which were typed on separate pages by her priest and became the basis of a 1956, 5,000-page book *The Poem of the Man God.*

Valtorta wrote with a fountain pen in notebooks resting on her knees. She did not prepare ahead of time, not knowing from one day to another what she would write, and she did not reread anything written to make corrections. At times she did ask that what she had written be read back to her. Valtorta always insisted that the work was not hers, but from beginning to end had a divine origin. Maria said of these writings, "I can affirm that I have had no human source to be able to know what I write, and what, even while writing, I often do not understand." She characterized herself as the "mouthpiece," the secretary or feeble "pen" of the Lord. The writing was often extremely difficult, as she would be required by Jesus to write down immediately what she saw or was told, even when she was in the midst of excruciating physical sufferings.

Since we already possess the essentials of the Gospels, we might wonder what could be the purpose of as vast and voluminous a work requiring the expenditure of so much cost to Voltorta herself. In a dictation Jesus said this:

> Do you know, Maria... what I am doing by showing you the Gospel? I am making a stronger attempt to bring men to Me.... With so many books dealing with Me and which — touch them up, retouch them, change, embellish them—have [nonetheless] become unreal, I want to give those who believe in Me a vision brought back to the truth of My mortal days.... I will no longer confine Myself to words. They tire men and detach them. It is a fault, but it is so. I will have recourse now to Visions also of My Gospel, and I will explain them to make them more attractive and clear (Voltorta, 1986).

The visions give a detailed picture of the life of Jesus, from his birth to the Passion, mentioning close to 700 episodes and offering more elaboration than the Gospels provide.

Her accounts often include detailed conversations. While the Gospel includes a few sentences about the wedding at Cana, her text includes a few pages and narrates the words spoken by the people present. She describes the many journeys of Jesus throughout the Holy Land and His conversations with people, including the apostles. Typically, when describing a scene, she provides details of the background, the colors of the clothing worn by Jesus or the Apostles, the trees, the mountains, and the weather conditions that day. In her prelude to the Sermon on the Mount, while describing the road on which Jesus was walking, she says that it was a clear day and Jesus could see Mount Hermon, but not Lake Merom.

Researcher David J. Webster authored a thirty-one-page examination of Valtorta's detailed descriptions of first century Palestine, comparing them with currently known facts. Nine towns and villages she described were not discovered until after her death. Over 30% of the 255 geographical sites she mentioned were not listed in the 1939 *International Standard Bible Encyclopedia Atlas*. In fact, 62 of these were not even listed in the 184-page *Macmillan Bible Atlas*, published seven years after her death. For a first-century eyewitness to include so many obscure and unknown names would be expected, but these names, that were unknown in the 1940s, are being proven authentic (Webster, 2004).

In her accounts Valtorta identified and recorded several planets and star constellations on certain nights. On one she reported seeing Jupiter, Mars, Venus, and "stars of Orion: of Rigil and Betelgeuse, of Aldebaran, of Perseus, Andromeda and Cassiopeia, and the Pleiades," along with a waning moon in the night sky. Harvard theoretical physicist Lonnie Lee Van Zandt, utilizing astronomical computer programs to conduct a stellar excursion into the distant past, discovered that these alignments were correct and only possible for two days in March 0033. This astronomical scenario does not occur for many decades before and after those two days. Van Zandt pointed out that astrophysicists did not have the capability of making such accurate predictions into the distant past until computers became available in the 1980s. For anyone in the 1940s to be capable of determining these astronomical alignments would be impossible. He wrote that these impossibly exact details "tax the credulity of even the immovable atheist more than the alternative that Jesus showed it to Valtorta" (VanZant, 1994).

EDGAR CAYCE

In the first half of the twentieth century Edgar Cayce attracted widespread popular interest in reincarnation and psychic healing through his readings, and his work remains popular today. His story is fascinating and deserves telling. Cayce was born into a farming family in 1877 in Kentucky and died in 1945. He received an eighth-grade education and left the farm for his first job at a dry goods store. Throughout his life Cayce struggled to find good employment and earn enough to support his family. He was a deeply religious man who, as a member of the Disciples of Christ, taught Sunday school and recruited missionaries. Once for every year of his life he read the Bible. The story goes that throughout his life as a psychic he struggled with whether his psychic abilities and the teachings he received were spiritually legitimate (Sugrue, T, 1997).

When he was 23 Cayce began selling insurance with his father. Soon thereafter he experienced such severe laryngitis that he lost all ability to speak. In an effort to find work that would be less straining on his voice he began an apprenticeship in a photography studio. A traveling stage hypnotist happened to be performing in Hopkinsville, where Cayce was living, and upon hearing about his condition offered to attempt to help him. Cayce agreed, and on stage in front of an audience he was hypnotized. While in trance his voice returned, but then disappeared when he awoke.

Since hypnosis had appeared to be somewhat successful, if only very briefly, Cayce was receptive when a local hypnotist, Al Layne, offered to help. Layne suggested that when in a trance Cayce describe his own condition and a cure. What then transpired was a description of his own difficulty from a first-person plural perspective, using the word "we" instead of "I." According to the reading psychological paralysis was the cause of his voice loss, which could be corrected by increasing blood flow to the voice box. Layne gave the suggestion that this happen. Cayce's face is said to have become flushed with blood and his chest to have turned bright red. After twenty minutes, still in trance, Cayce said that the treatment was over. He was awakened and his voice was normal. In spite of a few minor relapses that were corrected by Layne in the same way Cayce's voice remained normal throughout the rest of his life.

Layne was intrigued by what had occurred, and he asked Cayce to describe his own ailments and suggest a cure. The results were accurate and effective. Layne then encouraged Cayce to offer trance healing to the public. Cayce reluctantly agreed on the condition that the readings be free. With Layne first putting him in trance Cayce began to offer treatments to the townspeople of Hopkinsville. He enjoyed great success, and soon requests for help were pouring in. The person to be treated did not even have to be physically present. Cayce could work just as effectively providing a diagnosis and corrective remedy with only a letter giving the person's name and location. Cayce by then had developed a routine in which he would lie down, enter what appeared to be a light trance, and be given the questions of the person seeking assistance. He then would give the reading, often starting by saying "we have the body." Cayce's wife, Gertrude, generally conducted or guided the readings. Once awakened, Cayce generally claimed to not remember what he had said while delivering a trance reading. He explained the process by saying that the unconscious mind has access to information unavailable to the conscious mind.

Cayce invited those receiving readings to test the suggestions, rather than accept them on faith. Furthermore, the readings should only be considered to the extent that they led to a better life for the recipient. Although Cayce was widely acclaimed for the success of his readings, some were clearly inaccurate. His sons actually wrote a book detailing some of his mistakes, which they believed could be accounted for by such factors as the spiritual motivation of the seeker. Skeptics immediately saw this as simply an excuse to prevent Cayce's paranormal claims from ever being disproven.

Over his lifetime Cayce gave at least 21,000 readings, some 14,000 of which have been preserved. They deal with several themes. Most numerous are readings addressing questions about health, which contain many alternative health concepts and practices. Common prescriptions include poultices, osteopathic adjustments, massage, colonic irrigation, various forms of electric medicine, patent medicines, prayer, and folk medicine. Often there were specific recommendations involving special diets and exercise.

In response to the urging of some of those following his work Cayce began to give readings addressing more esoteric questions. These readings emphasized the reality of reincarnation and karma, which are instruments of a loving God, not blind natural laws. The purpose was to teach spiritual lessons. Between lifetimes our souls may spend time on other planets or their spiritual counterparts and, as astrology asserts, the position of the planets at our birth conveys these influences.

When readings of this nature first appeared Cayce, given his strong Christian beliefs, was deeply troubled. Although the subject of reincarnation was popular at the time, it was not an accepted part of Christian doctrine. Apparently the "we" of the readings, his "trance voice," dialogued with him and his "waking personality" persuaded him to continue with these kinds of readings. From then on his readings increasingly came to deal with esoteric themes.

In terms of the origin and destiny of humanity, the readings indicated that human souls are created with a consciousness, that they are one with God, and that they should find their way back to Him. Some have fallen from this state of awareness. Others led by the "Jesus soul" volunteered to save them. The Earth was created as an arena for spiritual growth. Cayce distinguished between Jesus and Christhood. Jesus was a soul like us who experienced many lifetimes, over which he grew spiritually by making and correcting mistakes. Christhood is a condition that He was the first to manifest through His material life. We should also aspire toward Christhood, looking to Jesus as an elder brother and example.

Our dreams, Cayce believed, can be an avenue through which God speaks to us, and he devoted many readings to dream interpretation. Psychic experiences are natural byproducts of soul growth. However, he did not fully endorse mediumship because entities contacted might not be particularly lofty. What is important is to focus on Christ and His teachings (Sugrue, T, 1997).

Cayce enjoyed great acclaim during his lifetime, although he remained a humble and deeply religious man. His influence has continued to this day, with tens of thousands of Cayce students and Cayce centers in twenty-seven countries. The major organization promoting interest in Cayce, the Association for Research and Enlightenment (ARE), has headquarters in Virginia Beach ("Edgar Cayce," Wikipedia).

CHAPTER 12

HEALING

HEALING THROUGH PRAYER

Healing involving the help of spiritual agencies or powers has a very long history. Native American healing as practiced by the Lakotas and numerous other groups is a modern form of shamanism that is very ancient indeed, with origins in hunter-gatherer groups predating even the rise of agrarian societies. Healing the sick was one of the principle activities of Jesus, and healing through his power (or the Father's) has been practiced by some Christian groups or individuals ever since. During the mid-twentieth century there was a surge of interest in faith healing—healing through prayer—in a number of Protestant denominations. This was not the dramatic and highly emotionally charged healing as practiced by TV evangelists, but a movement backed by sober theological scholarship and led by mainstream Methodists, Lutherans, and Episcopalians. Among the most influential were Agnes Sanford, author of the classic work *The Healing Light*, and John Gaynor Banks who, in 1932, founded the organization now known as the Order of Saint Luke, which is a professional and lay order that dedicates itself to promoting the central role of healing in the Church's ministry.

The movement drew inspiration from a number of gifted individuals who attributed their healing abilities to prayer. Among the finest and most beloved faith healers in modern Christianity were Ambrose and Olga Worrall. Both the Worralls as children exhibited unusual abilities. They knew things about people that they could not explain, and they were able to cure people's pain by touching them. Following their marriage word of their healing abilities spread, and in 1957 they established the New Life Clinic at the Mount Washington Methodist Church in Baltimore, Maryland, where they saw hundreds of people every week. Nurses, physicians, and clergy came regularly to their clinic to study with them. The Worralls' book about their work with the healing power of prayer, *The Gift of Healing*, includes examples of the thousands of grateful testimonials from patients, family members, physicians, and other caretakers. Usually they worked by placing their hands on the heads or ailing portions of people being prayed for, but for those not able to be physically present they simply visualized the person and prayed from a distance. The Worralls never accepted money for their services, which they saw as profiting from the sickness, or trouble, or need of others (Mayer, 2007).

Stories of seemingly miraculous healing accomplished by certain gifted individuals can be found down through the ages all over the world. Whether such healing actually occurs has been the subject of serious study for years. As in other areas of unusual or apparently paranormal phenomena a number of investigative procedures were employed early on, such as controlled observation, testimonials of those claiming to be healed, and the like. However, to rule out such natural explanations of any observed healing effects, such as the influence of the healee's (patient's) belief and expectations, the normal remission of the disease process, and numerous other possibilities has been notoriously difficult.

Claims to any effectiveness of healing at a distance are particularly suspect. As in other areas of paranormal or anomalous phenomena, from an orthodox scientific perspective distant mental healing is impossible. The mind is simply an emergent property of the physical brain, localized within it, and entirely dependent upon its workings. A healer at one location cannot affect the physiology of a patient at another because without some kind of physical or psychological intervention there is no mechanism by which the patient can be influenced.

The Worralls freely acknowledged that they had difficulties understanding their own extraordinary abilities and they supported scientific efforts to study Spiritual healing. Ambrose, a professional aeronautical engineer who worked at Martin Marietta throughout his career, wrote:

> I believe that all areas of human and Spiritual activities should be subjected to the most exacting examination, precisely as I expect the stress calculations on the structure of a new aircraft to be examined down to the most exacting requirements. I believe we should employ, in our research into Spiritual therapy, the latest and most applicable scientific methods to gather data that cannot be obtained by casual observation (Mayer, 2007).

The Worralls made themselves available for study whenever and wherever they could, including labs all over the United States run by medical schools, physicists, biologists, and psychologists. They sent data regarding their healings for study to the Rhine lab at Duke, but unfortunately the early experiments in which they participated often relied on methods that were unsophisticated and procedures that were poorly controlled. Nonetheless, some of the findings were intriguing and helped lay the groundwork for subsequent experimental work.

CHA-LOBO: WIRTH STUDY

In September 2001 the results of an investigation conducted under the auspices of the Department of Obstetrics and Gynecology at Columbia University's College of Physicians and Surgeons was published in the *Journal of Reproductive Medicine* (JRM). The study concluded with the statement: "Our data suggest a benefit of IP (intercessory prayer) on IVF-ET (in vitro fertilization-embryo transfer)." For the flagship journal of Western reproductive medicine to decide that the study's evidence supporting the extraordinary claim that prayer makes a difference was strong enough to warrant its publication was itself extraordinary.

The study was authored by two physicians on staff at Columbia: Kwang Cha, a research scientist from Cha Hospital in Seoul, Korea; and Rogerio Lobo, chair of obstetrics and gynecology, along with Daniel Wirth, a lawyer with a long history of involvement in alternative and spiritual healing. It involved 219 women at Cha General Hospital ages 26 to 46 who received in vitro fertilization treatment over a four-month period. They were randomly assigned to one of two groups: one of which received intercessory prayer— prayer focused on benefiting another—and a group that received no prayer. The people who prayed were in the United States, Canada, and Australia, halfway around the world from the women for whom they prayed. None of the Korean women seeking fertility treatment, nor anyone involved in their care, knew about the study, or that anyone was being prayed for. The prayer subjects were identified by a randomized process involving independent statisticians from Korea and the United States, who transmitted their pictures to prayer groups in the different countries. No one directly involved in the study, including the authors, had information about how this randomization was conducted until the study was completed and researchers had evaluated who had and had not become pregnant. Thus double and triple security measures were imposed to ensure anonymity of the data.

The study's results were remarkable. The women who were prayed for were almost twice as successful in becoming pregnant as those not prayed for (50% versus 26%). The odds of pure chance accounting for this difference were less than 13 out of 10,000, or 0.0013. While the number of eggs retrieved and the in-vitro fertilization rate were comparable for the two groups, the prayed-for group had double the implantation rate of the non-prayed-for group, a statistical probability of 0.0005 (less than five out of 10,000).

The results were so radically counter to the scientific understanding of reality that the authors were initially concerned about even publishing them. They did so because, in good scientific conscience, they could not do otherwise. "It was not even something that was borderline significant," Dr. Lobo told the *New York Times*. "It was highly significant!"

The study was outstanding in several respects. First, the outcome measure was superior to those employed in the large number of studies on the effects of prayer on such highly complex diseases as AIDS, cardiovascular illness, or cancer. While a number of those studies had produced impressive and intriguing positive findings, even the best designed and conducted faced the difficulty of assessing outcomes. A change in a disease condition involves a number of factors, such as need for medication, pain, mental capacity, and longevity. There might be improvement in one variable and not another. Can we say, for example, that a longer but symptom-filled life is a positive outcome for all individuals? Pregnancy as an outcome measure does not run into these difficulties. Either a woman is pregnant or she is not.

Another prominent feature of the study was that because standard informed consent procedures were not required neither the women being studied, nor any of the medical personnel involved, were informed that a study was taking place. This allowed valid testing of the effect of someone else's intention on the subject, rather than that effect mediated through the person's own awareness, which would have been a version of the well-known placebo effect (Mayer, 2007).

CHAPTER 13

REINCARNATION, PAST AND BETWEEN LIVES

REINCARNATION

Most western people associate belief in reincarnation with the Eastern religions of Hinduism and Buddhism. However, its origin dates back thousands of years before these religions originated. It has existed in practically every human society and in almost all of the major religions, even including branches of Judaism, Islam, and Christianity. Plato, in ancient Greece, believed that the soul is immortal, that there are a fixed number of souls, and that they regularly reincarnated. There are also references to reincarnation in classical Roman literature. In its earliest and most primitive forms reincarnation was not connected to any moral teachings. Many societies believed that we have a soul that can pass in and out of our bodies during sleep and, after death, it can be reborn in another person. The Druids, who inhabited the British Isles before the invasion of the Romans, who brought Christianity, believed that the soul is immortal and passes into other bodies at death.

Belief in reincarnation has deep roots in Judaism and occupied a fundamental and mainstream role for thousands of years up to the nineteenth century. Around the time of Jesus the Jewish philosopher Philo wrote that our soul comes from God and that only those few on earth who keep themselves free from attachments to the world of the senses will return to God. All others must be reborn in another body. Belief in reincarnation continues to flourish today in Orthodox and Chasidic communities.

Several of the early Christian church fathers, including Origen, Clement of Alexandria, and St. Jerome, believed in reincarnation. Among some early Christian groups, including the Gnostics and Manicheans, belief in reincarnation was popular until it was declared unacceptable by the Council of Nice in 553. Nevertheless, it did not completely die out among Christians. Several sects in the Middle Ages, collectively called the Cathars, held a view of reincarnation that maintained that at death only those who had received the gift of the holy spirit would be reunited with God. Otherwise the soul fled the dying body to take up whatever residence it could find, which might be either a human or an animal.

Reincarnation plays a central role in the various branches of Hinduism, where it is associated with the concept of karma, which states that the conditions of one's life are determined by the religious and moral character of the previous life. Orthodox Hindus believe that the better one's life is lived the higher the caste he or she will be born into in the next life. This succession of lives continues until one achieves salvation and is released from the cycle of death and rebirth. While the various branches of Buddhism have different beliefs as to whether or not there is a soul, they all believe that some principle or essence does pass at death into another individual (TenDam, 2017).

The Tibetans developed the belief that when the head of a monastery dies his true successor will be an incarnation of him, and can be located by special signs displayed by the child so blessed. This is the case for both the Dalai Lama and the Panchen Lama, second only to the Dalai Lama in the Buddhist hierarchy. When the then Panchen Lama died in 1989 the search for his successor began. The acting head of his monastery began collecting accounts from all over Tibet of unusual male children. Signs and dreams were analyzed and the Dalai Lama, in exile, was sent a short list of the most promising. Six years later he made his selection: Gendun Choeyki Nyima, the young son of a doctor in a remote part of the country. He was recognized as the eleventh Panchen Lamai, the authentic incarnation of his predecessor ("Eleventh Panchen Lama Controversy," Wikipedia).

THEOSOPHY

Reincarnation was first introduced to the west in the nineteenth century through the teachings of theosophy. The theosophical movement owed its existence to Helena Petrovna Blavatsky, who was born in 1831 to an upper class family in the Ukraine. She claimed to have traveled widely for a number of years in search of spiritual illumination, during which she met and was taught by certain advanced spiritual masters. From these teachings she developed what she called theosophy. Although many of her claims in hindsight appeared highly questionable, she attracted a large following.

Theosophy emphasizes the concept of reincarnation. Our spirit came into our current body to learn lessons necessary to evolve toward higher dimensions of spirit or truth. These lessons involve the principle of karma or universal justice. We reap in this current lifetime what we sowed through our activities in our past lifetime. However, karma is not deterministic in the sense of forcing us to carry out any particular activity. Rather, it sets up situations that offer an opportunity to learn particular lessons. If we fail to do so in this current life we will encounter situations in our next life posing the same lessons. Some people evolve more rapidly than others, but eventually everything, including us, evolves toward divinity. In the cosmic scheme of the full evolution of spirit one lifetime is no more than a blink of an eye. Death is not viewed in a negative light, but rather as an initiation, a rite of passage, into the school that is our next life (Steiner, 2024).

BRIDEY MURPHY

One of the most significant events attracting a great deal of interest in reincarnation in the last half of the twentieth century was the publication of Morey Bernstein's *The Search for Bridey Murphy*, which became a bestseller and was made into a film. Bridey was one of the first and most publicized personalities to emerge from the then-fledgling practice of employing hypnosis to explore people's past lives. The book stimulated a great deal of controversy, as well as general interest, and spawned some of the first serious attempts to actually investigate the validity of reported past life experiences. We will take this up in a later section of the book where research into questions of life after death are addressed. The Bridey Murphy case has been dismissed by many people as either fantasy or fabrication, but even if it provides little evidence for reincarnation, it still poses some intriguing questions to which so far no one has produced satisfactory answers (Fenwick, 2001).

Bridey Murphy's incarnation in this life was as an American woman, Virginia Tighe, the wife of Hugh Tighe, an insurance salesman. The couple lived in Pueblo, Colorado, and among their friends was a businessman, Morey Bernstein, who had taken up hypnotism as a hobby. One evening at a party Virginia volunteered to be a subject for Bernstein. He discovered that she was a good hypnotic subject and persuaded her to allow him to try to regress her under hypnosis back even beyond her birth, an experiment he had long wanted to do.

Virginia underwent six regression sessions with Bernstein between November 1952 and October 1953, which both his own wife and Hugh Tighe witnessed. During the first session Bernstein instructed Virginia to go back and back in her mind until she found herself in some other scene, in some other place, in some other time. Then, he said, when he talked to her again she would tell him about it. Suddenly Virginia began to talk in a soft Irish brogue.

Neither Bernstein nor Virginia had ever been to Ireland. And yet, over the subsequent five sessions, Bridey's Irish brogue grew stronger, and the picture of her life in eighteenth-century County Cork became more detailed. Bridey said she was born on December 20, 1798, came from a Protestant family, and was the daughter of a barrister, Duncan Murphy, and his wife, Kathleen. She said that she lived at "the meadows" outside Cork and gave details of her siblings—an older brother, Duncan, and a younger brother who had died in infancy.

Until she was 15 Bridey had gone to a school run by a Mrs. Strayne, whose daughter Alice married Bridey's brother Duncan. Bridey herself married Brian MacCarthy, son of a Roman Catholic barrister John MacCarthy. The couple went through two marriage ceremonies: one in Cork and a second Roman Catholic ceremony, which was kept a secret from Bridey's parents, in Belfast at the home of a priest, Father John Joseph Gorman. The couple had no children and lived in Belfast until Bridey's death at age 66 as a result of a fall in which she broke her hip. She was, in her own words, "ditched" (ie., buried) in Belfast in 1864.

Bridey claimed that while they were living in Belfast, her husband Brian wrote for the *Belfast News Letter* and taught at Queen's University. She mentioned the names of several places in Ireland, including Galway, County Limerick, Antrim, and a place called Baylings Crossing. She also mentioned various shops she had known there, including a food shop called Farr's and a green grocer called John Carrigan. She described the currency used as pounds, tuppences, and sixpences.

Before Bernstein published his book about Bridey his publisher suggested that some independent research should be carried out in Ireland to check out as many details of her story as possible. When this was done many of the general facts she had given about life in Ireland did indeed prove to be correct. But it was impossible to prove the existence of Bridey herself because records of births, deaths, and marriages did not exist until after 1864, the year in which Bridey died.

Subsequently every statement made by Bridey Murphy has been scrutinized, checked, and analyzed both by people who have wanted to demolish her story and those who have wanted to confirm it. Bridey Murphy's is certainly not a watertight case. It is still floating, but there are holes beneath the waterline.

Some of the facts that have been confirmed are more compelling than others. Many of the places she mentioned—Galway, Limerick, and Mourne, for example—are celebrated enough for most people to have known. But Baylings Crossing did not appear on any map, and it was discovered to exist only by chance, but as a crossing point that would not appear on a map. What *did* appear on an 1801 map of Cork was an area just outside the city called Mardike Meadows, which corresponded very well with Bridey's description of living with her parents at "the meadows." There is no trace of a Roman Catholic barrister called John Brian MacCarthy living at that time, though there was a bookkeeper of that name. Neither has any trace been found of a St. Theresa's Church in Belfast at that time, nor of a priest named John Gorman. But there was a green grocer called John Carrigan in Belfast during the period and a William Farr who sold food—and neither of these names are particularly common or obvious choices for someone drawing on a random store of Irish names. And the "tuppence" that Bridey mentioned was a coin only in circulation during her lifetime, between 1797 and 1850.

Bridey's use of colloquial and contemporary Irish language was also shown to be largely correct. During one session she sneezed violently, then opened her eyes and asked for a "linen," the word for a handkerchief. She also said that her mother had made her some "slips," the word used to describe a pinafore at that time. However, mixed with these convincing "Irishisms" were many modern American words and expressions such as "candy" and "downtown." This is not surprising, as it is not unusual for hypnotized subjects to use some of their own current idiomatic language. One would expect a mixture, rather than consistent use of one or the other language.

Many attempts were made to discredit Virginia Tighe and Morey Bernstein when the story first appeared in America. Bernstein's book was serialized in the *Chicago Daily News* and, not surprisingly, many of the attacks originated in other newspapers. The *Chicago American* pointed out that Virginia Tighe had an Irish aunt who had regaled her with tales of Irish life that provided the background to flesh out a fantasy. More damningly, they also claimed to have discovered the "real Bridey," an Irish woman called Bridie Corkell whose maiden name was Murphy, and who had at one time lived on the same street as Virginia and her foster parents in Chicago. Bridie Corkell, the *Chicago American* claimed, had talked to Virginia many times and knew her well. They also claimed that Virginia had been in love with Bridie Corkell's son. The Bridey Murphy story was exploded as apparently all a hoax. Various newspapers around the world published purported "confessions" to this effect by both Bernstein and Tighe, and on June 25, 1956, *Life* magazine, under the headline "Bridey Search Ends At Last," printed a picture of Bridie Corkell surrounded by her grandchildren (Fenwick, 2001).

That was by no means the end of the story. A further flurry of investigative journalism by the *Denver Post* showed that the aunt referred to by the *Chicago American*, Mrs. Marie Burns, although of Scottish-Irish descent, had been born in New York and had spent most of her life in Chicago and that, in any case, Virginia had not met her until she was 18. A woman called Bridie Corkell had indeed lived opposite Virginia (which Virginia readily admitted) and had a son, John, but Virginia denied knowing her well, or ever having been in love with her son. He was seven or eight years older than she was and married by the time Virginia had started to become interested in boys. It was difficult for the *Denver Post* to find out much more about Mrs. Corkell because she refused resolutely to answer any questions, which may have had something to do with the fact that her son, John Corkell, was in fact the editor of the *Chicago American*'s Sunday edition. Virginia's own response to these claims and counterclaims was evident in a lecture she gave in 1976:

> *Life* magazine ... took it upon themselves to write an exposé ... and people were saying, "Oh well, she heard that all from a neighbor." May I say that the woman lived somewhere in the general vicinity of where I lived. I never said one word to that woman! It came out later, but was never printed, that the woman's son was the telegraph editor of the *Chicago Herald American*. Someone found a woman who would say that she was Irish and that her name was Bridey Murphy and that she'd talked to me. It is not true—my hand to God and my three grandchildren and my three children! Also the parish priest of this particular woman would say that her first name was Bridey or Bridget, but would not sign any paper to the effect that her last name was Murphy (Fenwick, 2001, p. 6).

On the face of it, the most likely explanation of the Bridey Murphy story is that she had at some time acquired all of the information she gave, forgotten it, and that these forgotten memories then resurfaced when she was under hypnosis. This phenomenon, known as *cryptomnesia*, is probably the basis for many apparent past life memories. Little of what she says seems to have been so obscure that she could not have acquired the knowledge if she had set out to do so. But no one has produced a truly convincing explanation of where she might have acquired her knowledge of Ireland and Irish life in the nineteenth century, the name Baylings Crossing for instance, or why she should have done so. Books and films are one obvious source, but Virginia, according to Bernstein, had not the slightest interest in books, and certainly not in the kind of books that would have given her the detail needed to produce the Bridey Murphy story.

Neither did she seem either to welcome the publicity her story stimulated or to profit by it. She appeared under a pseudonym in Bernstein's book, and after she was "outed" refused to make money by becoming a public personality. And there has never been any suggestion that she had any kind of special relationship with Bernstein, the hypnotist, and was either consciously or unconsciously trying to please him, or to attract his interest and attention.

There seems to be general agreement that Bernstein acted in good faith. The worst charge that can be leveled against him is, perhaps, that he accepted too readily that what he heard in the hypnotic sessions was evidence of reincarnation. Most people now would probably agree that the story of Bridey Murphy does little to either prove or disprove the idea of reincarnation. But it may well suggest that sometimes, in the hypnotic state, people can apparently access memories that seem to belong to another time, another place, or another person (pp. 1–7).

While cases like that of Bridey are interesting, there is general agreement that the strongest evidence supportive of reincarnation comes from the spontaneous memories of young children. It seems that they would be much less likely than adults to have acquired the information they report from ordinary means. The only way a child could have obtained verifiable, accurate information regarding a deceased person who had been unknown to him or her would be to have been told this by someone older. Some children have related a considerable amount of specific details about the individual they claim to have been in a previous life and have also exhibited behaviors and interests specific to that individual. To be able to deliberately prep a child to exhibit such a performance for an outside investigator seems highly unlikely.

The study of reincarnation through spontaneous past life recollections of children was pioneered by Ian Stevenson (1918–2007). Stevenson was a Canadian biochemist and professor of psychiatry who, until his retirement in 2002, was head of the Division of Perceptual Studies at the University of Virginia. For forty years he traveled extensively to investigate 3,000 childhood cases that suggested to him the possibility of past lives. Although accounts of children's past life experiences seem to be more common in parts of the world where belief in reincarnation is widespread, such as Asia, west Africa, Brazil, and Alaska, Stevenson also located and investigated a number of cases in the United States (Fenwick, 2001).

BETWEEN LIVES—NEWTON

Although other therapists had encountered interlife experiences in their regressions with clients, Michael Newton has done the most work in helping people explore this dimension. As Newton describes himself in his books *Journey of Souls* and *Destiny of Souls*, he is definitely "old school and not a New Ager" who was "stunned" when he "unintentionally opened the gateway to the spirit world with a client."

During the 1980s, working with individuals in a superconscious state during deep hypnosis, he was able to construct a "working model of spirit world structure" and came to realize that engaging in the exploration of this dimension or state could be very therapeutic for them. A major discovery in working with these clients was "that it did not matter if a person was an atheist, deeply religious, or believed in any philosophical persuasion in between—once they were in the proper superconscious state of hypnosis, all were consistent in their reports" (Newton, 2000).

Based on his work with sixty-seven individuals Newton summarized the journey of the soul upon physical death as follows:

> At the moment of death our soul rises out of its host body. If the soul is older and has experience from many former lives, it knows immediately it has been set free and is going home. There are also souls who choose to remain at the scene of their death for a while, perhaps to comfort someone who is grieving or for other reasons. However, most wish to leave at once. In the early stages of their exit, just outside earth's astral plane all souls encounter a "wispy cloudiness" around them that soon becomes clear, enabling them to look off into a vast distance. This is the moment when the average soul sees a ghostly form of energy coming toward her. This figure may be a loving soul mate or two, but more often than not it is her guide. In all his years of research, Newton has never had a single subject who was met by a major religious figure such as Jesus or Buddha. Still, the loving essence of the great teachers from earth is within the personal guides who are assigned to them. By the time souls become reoriented again to the place they call home, their earthliness has changed. They are no longer quite human in the way we think of a human being, with a particular emotional, temperamental and physical makeup. For instance, they don't grieve about their recent

physical death in the way their loved ones will. Right after death, souls suddenly feel different because they are no longer encumbered by a temporary host body with a brain and central nervous system. Some take longer to adjust than others.

Newton tends to think of souls as intelligent light forms of energy. The energy of the soul is able to divide into identical parts, similar to a hologram. It may live parallel lives in other bodies, although this is not common. Because of the dual capability of all souls, part of their light energy always remains behind in the spirit world. Thus, it is possible to see one's mother upon returning from a life, even though she may have died thirty earth years before and reincarnated again.

Souls experience an orientation period with their guides that is a quiet time for counseling, with the opportunity to vent any frustrations about the life just ended. Orientation is intended to be an initial debriefing session with gentle probing by perceptive, caring teacher guides.

The returning energy of some souls, who were contaminated by their physical bodies and became involved with evil acts, is taken to special centers which some clients call "intensive care units." Here their energy is remodeled to make it whole again. Depending on the nature of their transgressions these souls could be rather quickly returned to Earth. They might well choose to serve as the victims of other people's evil acts in the next life. Still, if their actions were prolonged and especially cruel over a number of lives this would denote a serious pattern of wrongful behavior. Such souls could spend a long while in a solitary spiritual existence, possibly over a thousand earth years. A guiding principle in the spirit world is that wrongdoing, intentional or unintentional, on the part of all souls will need to be redressed in some form in a future life. This is not considered punishment or even penance, as much as an opportunity for karmic growth. There is no hell for souls, except perhaps on earth.

Souls belong to groups that range in size between three and twenty-five members, with the average having about fifteen. Reuniting with one's soul group is experienced as a joyous homecoming with friends who greet them with deep love and camaraderie, often involving hugs, laughter, and much humor, which seems to be a hallmark of life in the spirit world. There are times when souls from nearby cluster groups may want to connect with each other. Often this activity involves older souls who have made many friends from other groups with whom they have been associated over hundreds of past lives.

How individuals view their group cluster setting is based on the soul's state of advancement, although memories of a schoolroom atmosphere are always very clear. In the spirit world educational placement depends on the level of soul development. Simply because a soul has been incarnating on Earth since the Stone Age is no guarantee of high attainment. It takes some students longer to get through certain lessons, just as in earthly classrooms. On the other hand, all highly advanced souls are old souls in terms of knowledge and experience.

In *Journey of Souls* Newton broadly classifies souls as beginner, intermediate, and advanced. Generally, the composition of a group of souls is made up of beings at about the same level of advancement, although they have their individual strengths and shortcomings. These attributes give the group balance. Souls assist one another with the cognitive aspects of absorbing information from life experiences, as well as reviewing the way they handled the feelings and emotions of their host bodies directly related to those experiences. Every aspect of a life is dissected, even to the extent of reverse role playing in the group, to bring greater awareness. By the time souls reach the intermediate levels they begin to specialize in those major areas of interest where certain skills have been demonstrated.

In the spirit world no soul is looked down upon as having less value than any other soul. They are all in a process of transformation to something greater than their current state of enlightenment. Each is considered uniquely qualified to make some contribution toward the whole, no matter how hard they are struggling with their lessons.

Individuals have had a multitude of choices in their past and this will continue into the future. In the spirit world one is not forced to reincarnate or participate in group projects. If souls want solitude they can have it. If they do not want to advance in their assignments this too is honored. The prime motivator of souls is moving toward a greater goodness and a conjunction with the Source that created them. They have feelings of humility at having been given the opportunity to incarnate in physical form.

Once or twice between lives a soul visits a group of higher beings who are a step or two above their teacher guides—a council of elders. Members of the council talk to them about their mistakes and what they can do to correct negative behavior in the next life. This is the place where considerations for the right body in the soul's next life begin.

As the time approaches for rebirth the soul goes to a space where a number of bodies are reviewed that might meet its goals. There is a chance to look into the future here and actually test out different bodies before making a choice. Souls voluntarily select less than perfect bodies and difficult lives to address karmic debts, or to work on different aspects of a lesson they have had trouble with in the past. A soul might ask to go to a physical planet other than Earth for a while. When the new assignment is accepted the soul is often sent to a preparation class to remind it of certain signposts and clues in the life to come.

Finally, when the time comes for their return, souls say a temporary goodbye to their friends and are escorted to the space of embarkation for the trip to Earth. Souls join their assigned hosts in the womb of the baby's mother sometime after the third month of pregnancy so they will have a sufficiently evolved brain to work with before term. As part of the fetal state they are still able to think as immortal souls while they get used to brain circuitry and the alter ego of their host. After birth an amnesiac memory block sets in and souls meld their immortal character with the temporary human mind to produce a combination of traits for a new personality (Newton, 2000).

PAST LIVES THERAPY

Dr. Winafred Blake Lucas, in her brief history of what has become the past lives therapy movement, *Regression Therapy: A Handbook for Professionals* (1993), traces its origin to Freud and his innovative idea that making the unconscious conscious would restore choice and bring healing. More directly relevant was the increasing acceptance of Jung's view that human nature has a spiritual aspect and that there are universal psycho-spiritual patterns (archetypes) that underlie personality.

In the 1950s and 1960s British psychiatrist Denys Kelsey, while using hypnosis to regress patients to early childhood, discovered, as had other therapists, that his patients also reported memories of birth and prenatal experiences. Through this work Kelsey came to believe that people must have some element that is capable of functioning and recording events even in the absence of a physical body. Around this time he became associated with and subsequently married Joan Grant, who had authored popular books discussing memories of her own past lives. Kelsey began to include past lives in much of his therapeutic work and, in 1967, became one of the first professional clinicians to describe the therapeutic retrieval of past life memories in a book, co-authored with Grant, called *Many Lifetimes*. The 1975 publication by Raymond Moody of *Life After Life* provided a great stimulus for this work by appearing to suggest that we do not cease to exist because our bodies die. Lucas notes that "this finding, in one breathtaking leap, confirmed the assumptions of regression therapists about the ongoing nature of existence and reinforced the description of the transition after death as it had consistently been reported in regression work" (Lucas, 1993).

Interest in past lives and past lives therapy grew rapidly in the 1970s. Three very influential books by psychologists were published in 1978: *Reliving Past Lives* by Helen Wambach, *Past Lives Therapy* by Morris Netherton, and *You Have Been Here Before* by Edith Fiore. Wambach, primarily a researcher, conducted past life regressions with groups of hypnotized volunteers, after which they completed questionnaires about what they recalled. From 1,088 responses obtained by this method Wambaugh gathered a large amount of material about the lives, customs, and clothing of various time periods. In analyzing her data she found that the details of clothing and shoes worn and other domestic details were surprisingly accurate and not simply the product of fantasy. Netherton developed an approach to past life work that did not involve hypnosis, but rather what he called bridging. On the basis of the success of this method he established a training program for past life therapists, which he subsequently conducted around the world. Fiore, a clinically trained hypnotist like Kelsey, first encountered past life memories in the process of age regression. The exploration of past- life memories by her patients appeared to be so effective in relieving psychological symptoms that she changed the focus of her clinical practice to emphasize past life work.

BRIAN WEISS

Around this same time psychiatrist Brian Weiss discovered past life therapy, which he first described in his 1988 book *Many Lives Many Masters*. His work is particularly important because of his impressive credentials and deserves to be described more fully. Brian Weiss graduated from Columbia University and received his medical degree from the Yale University School of Medicine, where he was also chief resident in psychiatry. He went on to teach at several prestigious university medical schools and published more than forty scientific papers in such fields as psychopharmacology, brain chemistry, and various mental disorders. He describes himself at that time as "left-brained, obsessive compulsive, and completely skeptical of 'unscientific' fields" such as parapsychology. He said he "didn't know anything about the concept of past lives or reincarnation, nor did I want to."

Shortly after he became chairman of the Department of Psychiatry at Mount Sinai Medical Center in Miami Beach, Florida, in 1981, a patient he calls Catherine was referred to him due to suffering from fears, phobias, recurrent nightmares, and paralyzing panic attacks. She had experienced these symptoms for years and they were becoming worse. Catherine had been in conventional psychotherapy for more than a year, but it did not help. Because she had a chronic fear of gagging and choking she would not take medications that Weiss would normally have prescribed. He suggested hypnosis that he believed would help her recall childhood memories and the repressed or forgotten traumas that he thought must be causing her current symptoms. Among other memories she recalled being pushed from a diving board and choking in the water and being frightened by the gas mask placed on her face in a dentist's office. More serious still, she remembered being fondled by her alcoholic father when she was three years old and having his hand held over her mouth to keep her quiet. Weiss was sure that now having this material surface she would get better, but this did not happen. Perhaps, he thought, there were still deeper traumatic memories.

In her next session a week later he inadvertently gave her the open-ended instruction to go back to the time her symptoms arose. Rather than returning to her early childhood, to his amazement Catherine started recalling details from a lifetime some 4,000 years earlier in the Near East. She described herself with a different name, face, and body, and her clothes and everyday items were from that time. She also recalled a number of events leading up to her death when she drowned in a flood as her baby was torn from her arms by the strength of the water. Immediately after this she found herself floating above her body. Catherine also remembered two other lifetimes: one as a Greek woman a few centuries later and another as a Spanish prostitute in the eighteenth century.

Weiss was skeptical, as he had hypnotized hundreds of patients over the years and had never encountered anything like this. He knew that from his experience with her in therapy she was not psychotic, did not hallucinate, did not experience multiple personalities, and was not particularly suggestible. His only explanation was that these apparent memories must have consisted of some kind of fantasy or dreamlike material. Surprisingly Catherine's symptoms began to improve dramatically, which would not happen if that were the case. With more weekly hypnotic sessions, during which she recalled other past lives, her formerly intractable symptoms continued to disappear.

In her fourth or fifth hypnosis session, after reliving a death in an ancient lifetime, Catherine floated above her body and was drawn to a spiritual light that she always encountered in the in-between-lifetimes state. Catherine then, in a husky voice, said that she was being told there are many gods, for God is in each of us. She told Weiss that his father was there, along with his son, who was a small child. His father said Weiss would know him because his name was Avrom and that his daughter was named after him. His death was due to his heart. His son also had a fatal heart defect, dying soon after birth because "his heart was backward like a chicken's." Weiss was shocked. What she said was completely accurate, yet Catherine knew virtually nothing about his family or personal history. His firstborn son only lived twenty-three days, dying of an extremely rare condition in which the pulmonary veins that should bring oxygenated blood back to the heart were incorrectly routed so they entered his heart on the wrong side, as if his heart was backward. His father, who died in 1979, had the Hebrew name Avrom but went by the English name Alvin. Not only could Catherine not have possibly known this very personal and specific information, but there was no place even to look it up.

Weiss was so strongly influenced by his experience with Catherine that he began to radically change his perspective on psychotherapy. Regressing patients to their past lives opened up a rapid method of treating psychiatric symptoms that previously had taken many months or years to alleviate. As of 1992, when he wrote *Through Time Into Healing*, he had regressed hundreds of patients to past lives in individual sessions and many times that number in group workshops. A number were able to eliminate a wide range of chronic lifelong symptoms. Even more important, they gained the knowledge that we do not die when our bodies do; we survive physical death (Weiss, 1988).

ISIS ESTRADA

In her 2024 book *Past Life Therapy Manual and Certification for Therapists* Isis Estrada describes past life therapy (PLT) as a therapeutic technique that uses guided meditations and hypnosis to help clients directly access and reexperience past lives. This enables them to discover the root causes of current problems, release emotional and energetic blockages, and learn valuable lessons that can aid in their spiritual growth.

It is based on the understanding that we are souls who reincarnate in different bodies, times, and places to learn and evolve. Each life that we incarnate leaves an imprint on our soul which is reflected in our mind, body, and spirit. Some of these imprints are positive, such as talents and virtues. Others are negative, such as fears, traumas, guilt, conflicts, and illnesses. These can interfere with our well-being and our development, creating problems in our current life which we cannot always resolve with therapy using only our conscious minds. Past life therapy can help heal these problems by helping us understand their origin and meaning, and to resolve them in a supportive environment.

Estrada emphasizes that PLT is based on a broader and deeper vision of reality than that held in mainstream psychology. This transpersonal paradigm proposes that time is relative and can be circular, that consciousness is the basis of all that exists, and that human experience is multidimensional and transcends the limits of space and time. Past, present, and future coexist simultaneously in the eternal now, potentially allowing us to access any moment in our personal or collective history. Furthermore, we can modify the past or the future from the present.

Past life therapy can be helpful in a number of ways. Most important among these is to heal illnesses, symptoms, or disorders that have their origin in past lives; to resolve conflicts, difficulties, or limitations that arise in our current life; to discover and develop talents, abilities, or virtues that have been cultivated in past lives; to understand and accept the purpose, mission, or life plan that has been chosen before incarnating; and to connect and communicate with the guides, angels, or beings of light that assist us on our spiritual path.

The main technique in past life therapy is hypnotic regression, which consists of guiding the client through their past life memories to explore, understand, and heal the traumas, conflicts, and patterns that may be affecting their current life. Past life regression can be induced through different hypnosis techniques which can be adapted the particular client. Estrada presents past life therapy in a series of steps or exercises to be followed by therapists.

Exercise 1 has as its purpose to prepare the client for past life regression by creating an enabling environment; establishing a therapeutic alliance, generating trust, motivation, and positive expectations; and giving the necessary instructions and guidelines for the process.

Exercise 2 involves choosing a past life regression induction technique agreed on by therapist and client and guiding them into one of their past lives. Once this occurs she asks them to describe to her what they see, what they feel, what they hear, what they smell, what they know, etc. To help them explore and deepen their experience she uses such questions as: Where are you? What are you doing? How old are you? What is your name?

Estrada then accompanies the person throughout the most significant, important, or relevant moments of their past life which have some connection, relationship, or influence with their present life. She helps them to resolve, release, forgive, reconcile, or whatever is necessary, with respect to people or situations that have caused trauma, conflict, guilt, resentment, etc. in their past life or in their current life. Then she assists them to connect and interact with their soul that has lived all their past lives and that has all the information, wisdom, guidance, and love they need for their current life.

Exercise 3 aims to integrate past life regression, helping the person to return to their normal state of consciousness, to remember and assimilate what they have lived and learned, and to apply it to their current life.

Estrada points out that one of the most important and significant moments of PLT is to help the client return to the spaces between their past lives. This involves a whole new dimension of spiritual experience we have not discussed. Estrada points out that the space between lives is a fundamental stage in past life therapy, as it allows us to access the wisdom of our soul, heal the wounds of our past, and plan our future. The return to the space between lives is a transforming experience that opens the doors to a new dimension of our existence (Estrada, 2024).

CHAPTER 14

PSYCHEDELICS AND THE PARANORMAL

One of the oldest, most universal, reliable, and direct ways to access paranormal experiences involves the use of psychedelic substances, although exactly what those might entail for today's users, whether illuminating, mind blowing, confusing, or even terrifying, has to do with the expectations and setting of the experiencer.

HISTORY

Use of psychedelics for healing and visionary purposes dates back thousands of years and has occurred in a great many cultures around the world. Evidence of psychedelic mushroom use has been found in numerous ancient cave paintings dating to 5000 BCE. Stone effigies of mushrooms have been discovered in Central America dating to the first millennium BC.

Before the European conquest mushrooms were a major element in public celebrations and also played a widespread shamanic role in private gatherings. Poets spoke eloquently and repeatedly of the exalted status in which mushrooms were held and were believed to transport one to heaven. This touched an acutely sensitive nerve in the newly arrived Catholic missionaries, eliciting panic, indignation, and fury. Mushroom use for them seemed to strike at the heart of the Christian religion. In short, the church regarded the worship of the sacred mushroom as an idolatry and public mushroom ceremonies were stamped out. Private use continued but was a closely guarded secret.

In the early 1950s psychedelic use began to be popularized in the US and came to the attention of mental health professionals. A huge outpouring of clinical and research activity resulted involving LSD to treat a wide range of mental disorders. In the early 1960s recreational LSD use became popular in counterculture. Because they did not follow the guidelines for safe use of these powerful substances that had been established through hundreds of years in indigenous cultures and were largely followed in clinical practice some began to experience bad trips that, for a few, resulted in visits to hospital emergency rooms. This resulted in an outpouring of media scare stories. In the late 1960s psychedelics were made illegal (Quimby, 2023).

GROF

Without a doubt, the one individual who is most knowledgeable about mushrooms is psychiatrist Stanislav Grof, who for decades has guided patients and people through many hundreds of psychedelic experiences.

Through his work Grof arrived at remarkable insights into the nature of the deep unconscious mind where these experiences reside. They are comprised of three major realms: the psychodynamic, the perinatal, and the transpersonal. Simply put, the psychodynamic realm of the unconscious includes material involving significant events from a person's life experiences, particularly childhood. The perinatal realm of the unconsciousness includes a rich variety of material relating to a person's actual birth, as well as themes of death, rebirth, and spiritual awakening. The transpersonal realm includes material and phenomena that transcend the normal bounds of time and space and involve psychic and spiritual themes.

THE PERINATAL REALM

Grof discovered that if people continue to work in non-ordinary psychedelic states they sooner or later leave the arena of individual history following birth and a new area of unconscious material comes to dominate their experience. Although this area has not yet been recognized by western academic psychiatry, the experiences involved have been systematically studied and held in high esteem by ancient and preindustrial cultures since the dawn of human history. Grof calls this the perinatal realm because most people associate it with biological birth trauma.

While traditional psychology and medicine deny that an infant can record the experience of birth in its memory, people who had no cognitive knowledge of their births were able to relive, with extraordinary detail, facts concerning their births. These involved appropriate physical movements of their arms, legs, and bodies that accurately recreated the process of the particular type of delivery they actually experienced, including breech births. Bruises and swellings appeared on their skin in places where forceps were applied, and they relived their mother's earliest responses to them. Grof was not satisfied to simply note these unusual experiences but was able, time and time again, to objectively confirm details such as these by questioning hospital records or adults who were present at the delivery (Grof, 1993).

Elements of the rich and complex material experienced in the perinatal realm occur in four typical clusters that have deep parallels with the stages of biological birth. Grof named these basic perinatal mattrices (BPMs I–IV).

The first matrix is concerned with our experiences in the womb prior to the onset of delivery. During this time of undisturbed intrauterine life the baby and mother are biologically and emotionally intimately connected. Conditions for the fetus are almost ideal. Many people in nonordinary states of consciousness report their intrauterine experiences in extremely vivid terms. Typically they feel they have entered a sacred or holy superior order of reality, a kind of "oceanic ecstasy." Profound feelings of cosmic unity, serenity, and bliss dominate. Often there is a feeling that one has direct, immediate, and unlimited access to knowledge and wisdom of universal significance. Symbolism "weaves together, in an intimate and logical way, various fetal, oceanic, cosmic, natural paradisean, and celestial elements."

The second perinatal matrix is characterized by experiences of "cosmic engulfment" and "no exit." Life in the womb is terminated, uterine contractions are encountered, but the cervix is still closed. Adults experiencing BPM II feel trapped in a nightmarish world characterized by a dark and ominous atmosphere often involving unbearable emotional physical and emotional torture. The worst, ugliest, and most hopeless aspects of existence dominate experience. There is a realization of a deep link between the agony of birth and that of death which usually leads to a sense of the meaninglessness and absurdity of life and the futility of any effort to change it. Fear of death, fear of never coming back, and fear of going crazy are very common. The dominant symbolism involves images of hell and the underworld, which may include tortures inflicted by demons or experiences of burning, strangling, or being crushed. In Christian literature this matrix is apparent in descriptions of the "dark night of the soul."

The third perinatal matrix is associated with the second clinical stage of childbirth. Uterine contractions continue but the cervix is now dilated, allowing the fetus to be propelled through the birth canal. An enormous struggle for survival occurs involving crushing mechanical pressures and often a high degree of anoxia and suffocation. A broad range of experiences are reported having as the central theme a determined death-rebirth struggle. Clusters of archetypal and other phenomena involve elements of "titanic fight, sadomasochistic experiences, intense sexual arousal, demonic episodes, scatological involvement, and encounter with fire." Religious and mythological symbolism focus on themes of sacrifice, or combine spiritual pursuit and sexuality. There are quite frequently scenes of pre-Columbian sacrificial rituals, visions of crucifixion, experiential connection with deities symbolizing death and rebirth, episodes of phallic worship, temple prostitution, fertility rites, ritual rape, and various aboriginal tribal ceremonies involving rhythmic sensual dancing.

The fourth basic perinatal matrix is related to the actual birth of the child. The extreme build up of anxiety, pressure, pain, and sexual tension associated with being propelled through the birth canal is followed by sudden release. The person experiencing BPM IV in a nonordinary state of consciousness may relive the specific physiological events and the various obstetric interventions employed. On a symbolic level, the final stage of childbirth involves the death-rebirth experience. Often the ego death immediately prior to rebirth evokes such a strong fear of impending catastrophe that the individual desperately attempts to stop the process. The transition from BPM III to BPM IV involves a sense of "total annihilation on all imaginable levels: physical destruction, emotional disaster, intellectual and philosophical defeat, ultimate moral failure, and absolute damnation of transcendental proportions." The experience of ego death appears to involve "an instant merciless destruction of all reference points in the life of the individual" (Grof, 1988).

Once this occurs a person is likely to be suddenly struck by visions of radiant white or golden light, feel the expansion of space, and be filled to overflowing with a sense of liberation, redemption, salvation, and forgiveness. He or she is filled with feelings of overwhelming love for others and a sense of oneness with nature and the universe. Spiritual and mythological symbolism may be drawn from virtually any cultural tradition. The death of the ego may be experienced in connection with a destructive deity or some sacrificial figure, while rebirth commonly involves union with positive deities. The legendary phoenix often appears. Among the most frequent experiences is an identification with the death and resurrection of Jesus Christ.

The areas of spiritual and religious experiences opened by the intense encounter with death appear to be an intrinsic part of the human psyche and are independent of the individual's cultural and religious background and programming. Grof emphasizes that:

> Even positively oriented scientists, hard-core materialists, skeptics and cynics, uncompromising atheists and anti-religious crusaders, such as Marxist philosophers

and politicians, suddenly become interested in the spiritual quest after they confront these levels in themselves.

He states that, in his experience, "everyone who has reached these levels develops convincing insights into the utmost relevance of the spiritual and religious dimensions in the universal scheme of things."

THE TRANSPERSONAL REALM

The transpersonal realm of the unconscious encompasses an extremely broad range of reported material, which in different respects transcends the limits of what we generally accept as possible. To understand the transpersonal realm, Grof observes, we must begin thinking of consciousness in an entirely new way. We need to give up the preconception that consciousness is something "created within the human brain and thus contained in the box represented by the bony structure of our heads," and that it exists only as a result of our individual lives. Transpersonal experiences include:

The experiential identification with anything in the universe, including the consciousness of animals and plants.

Memories from the lives of one's ancestors, past incarnations, and clear anticipation and precognitive flashes of future events.

Certain astral psychic phenomena such as apparitions of and communication with deceased people, spirit guides in animal and human form, various superhuman entities, mythological and legendary beings, fairy tale scenes, blissful and wrathful deities from different cultures, adventures that seem to be happening in universes other than our own, identification with the Creator and sources of cosmic creativity, and the merging with the Absolute.

Spontaneous events, such as stigmata appearing during ecstatic raptures.

Sightings of and encounters with UFOs.

Spiritualistic occurrences, such as activities associated with poltergeists and haunted buildings.

Experiences of ceremonial magic, healing, and hexing (Grof, 1988).

CHAPTER 15

DOWSING

Dowsing, or divining, is known by its practitioners as a craft or art that has been defined as "a way of finding out by accessing information, with directed intent, using a means outside the five recognized senses and culminating in a physical response within the human body" (Brown, 2010).

Today dowsers are employed around the world by countless utility companies, police forces to locate crime scenes and missing persons, authorities in engineering maintenance and road safety, oil and mining companies, and by farmers and owners of factories and golf courses to find water for irrigation. There is also a thriving group of doctors and homoeopaths using dowsing in diagnosis and treatment. Despite its very wide usage, these employers rarely publicize their activities because of the very negative perception of the scientific community that views them as lacking in any scientific basis and among the myriad of other occult superstitions. The American term for water dowsing is in fact "water witching."

Dowsing is an ancient activity dating back thousands of years. The first recorded use of dowsing or divining is thought to be a cave painting in the Sahara dated at about 6000 BC. Writings of early Egyptians, Greeks, and Old Testament Hebrews mention it. Martin Luther, in 1556, denounced dowsing as the work of the devil. By the end of the sixteenth century dowsing was being used extensively and successfully in Germany to detect undiscovered minerals. Queen Elizabeth I introduced German mineral dowsers to England and they very successfully located mineral mines in the north of England, Cornwall, and Wales. By the end of the seventeenth century dowsing was commonly used to locate gold, metal, and water in practically every part of Europe.

Some of the largest dowsing efforts in recent decades have occurred in Russia, where dowsing began to be developed in 1960. By the 1980s dowsing seminars were held across the USSR that were attended by hundreds of professionals from around the world, including individuals with strong scientific backgrounds such as medical doctors, geologists, physicists, and hydroelectric engineers. All this interest culminated in the establishing of training schools with qualifications and certification for dowsers, some at the postgraduate level (Brown, 2010).

One of the world's foremost professional water and oil dowsers, George Applegate, is an engineer and geologist. During the course of over fifty-five years he has established a formidable track record with more than 2,500 successful boreholes (including several finds yielding up to a million gallons a day) with a less than one per cent failure rate.

Today thriving communities and societies of dowsers are flourishing around the globe. One of the largest, the British Society of Dowsers, had only forty-three members attend its first meeting in 1933, but membership has grown to more than 1,600 members, with over eighty members on its professional dowsing register. The American Society of Dowsers, based in Danville, Vermont, has in excess of 3,000 members.

Dowsing is divided into two main classifications. The best known is field dowsing, where the practitioner is in the presence or vicinity of that being sought, for example, on a site determining the location of water, or the presence of electromagnetic fields. The dowsing tool reacts at, or points to, the spot where the physical target can be found (Brown, 2010).

The second classification is remote dowsing, which has two different types: map dowsing and information dowsing. Map dowsing involves using a map, or plan, or diagram as a means of focus to discern information pertaining to that map. In this technique the dowser uses a map of the site and "asks" the dowsing device to respond at the coordinates to what is sought while the dowser moves a finger along the sides of the map. Map dowsing is quite frequently used by experienced dowsers prior to an on site survey, as it can often save time, although it is less accurate (Miller, 2016).

With information dowsing no map is necessary, and the subject or object may be in the form of a concept, idea, or a theory that has no obvious physical presence (Brown, 2010).

There are a myriad of dowsing tools that have been used throughout history, and many are still in use today. The most commonly recognized is the forked stick, also known as the "Y" or "V" rod. It consists of two branches of equal size and of the same length taken from shoots at the top of a tree, cut below the knot so as to form a Y. The two branches should form an angle of between 25 and 50 degrees and the whole rod should be sufficiently pliable to enable the ends of the branches to be bent almost at right angles and strong enough to resist twisting. All of the leaves and excess twigs are removed.

Dowsers hold the two shorter ends of the "Y" in their hands, with the long part of the "Y" pointing forward and the palms facing upward, with slight tension. When over the target the long part of the "Y" will rise or dip or sometimes, in the hands of an experienced dowser, turn in a complete revolution, twisting and distorting the wood.

Another commonly used tool by dowsers is angle or "L" rods. These consist of two separate rods bent into "L" shapes, with one end longer than the other. They are made of thin, sturdy metal, the simplest being a coat hanger cut in two pieces with the handle cut off. Each is held by the shorter end with the hands approximately body width apart. The longer length projects forward, parallel with the ground. The dowser's arms are extended but with the elbows comfortably bent. The rods turn inward or outward over the target rather than dipping or rising, as happens with a forked stick.

Some dowsers like to feel the rods turn in their hands, while others prefer not to have any contact with the rod and enclose each short end in a sheath, the simplest being a cut down soda straw.

Another involves a pendulum, which is a weight attached to a short cord, thread, or chain. The length of the cord is adjusted to suit one's personal preference. The cord is held in the predominant hand between the forefinger and thumb with them pointing downward, so the pendulum is free to swing in any direction—to and fro, or in clockwise or counterclockwise circles.

The "weight" can be made of glass, wood, metal, plastic, various types of crystal, or an article of personal significance, such as a ring or other piece of jewelry. The shape and design of the pendulum is up to the user (Brown, 2010).

In her 2010 book *Dowsing: The Ultimate Guide for the 21st Century*, Brown discusses information dowsing as a practical tool to enhance and enrich everyday life. The fundamentals of dowsing for personal use, she points out, can be learned in a relatively short time.

For information dowsing it is necessary to first establish a "yes" and "no" response. This can be done with either dowsing rods or a pendulum. With the latter, Brown advises the user to hold the pendulum cord between the finger and thumb with an extended length of about four inches. Gently swing the pendulum to and fro, towards oneself and away again, so it gains some momentum. Now, with the momentum going but with one's hand now still, say to the pendulum: "Show me a 'yes' response." Relax and watch what the pendulum does. If it does not respond the first time, try again. Use the same method to find a "no" answer.

Dowsing provides a tool to identify exactly what is potentially health promoting for one's unique body, with all its individual needs shaped by lifestyle, hereditary traits, conditioning, and environment. Brown discusses six factors that underpin optimal health: hydration, sleep, exercise, diet and nutrition, minerals and vitamins, and mental and emotional stress. Brown also identified through dowsing a number of main electromagnetic fields that can disrupt biological functions, whether these are from a man made source or geopathic stress. For each of these factors specific questions can be asked and the pendulum will indicate a "yes" or "no" response. In the case of sleep, the question can be posed: "Taking everything into consideration, how many hours of sleep per night do I require for my best health and well-being—four? six? eight? nine? What is the optimal time for me to go to bed?—six pm? eight pm?"

Brown notes that when one first starts to dowse you may be lucky enough to just pick up dowsing rods or a pendulum and dowse. On the other hand, it may take weeks and weeks of perseverance and tenacity.

The ability of one's mind to focus is key to your dowsing success because the mind is the interface between a field of information and the final outward physical dowsing response. A dowsing tool responds to the questions that are formulated with the mind, and whether they are verbalized out loud or not is immaterial. The ability to focus will be impaired if one is tired, upset, unwell, angry, resentful, or emotionally involved.

Dowsers are often asked when they are looking for something hidden from sight how they distinguish between the many different factors that may be present. If they are looking for an underground water pipe, how do they know they have not identified a gas pipe or an electricity cable? The answer is that they were not looking for those things, they were looking for a water pipe. They had posed a very specific question and directed their intent to identify the water pipe. In the simplest of terms, the dowsing tool must be told what one wants it to do.

Once the ability to focus is learned the next stage is to master complete mental and emotional detachment. A vested interest in the answers to the questions asked interferes with the response obtained. Only a vested interest needs to be in truth. The dowser begins by focusing with clarity and intent on forming an unambiguous, precise question and then must immediately put aside that mental processing and switch to being the observer of the outcome.

It is important to remember that while dowsers hold a dowsing tool in their hands, the actual dowsing instrument is the human body. The human body or human body mind is the receiver or antenna and the dowsing tool simply amplifies that signal.

Brown points out that it is very important that dowers have a good understanding of how the process of dowsing works and can explain this in clear, rational terms. Unfortunately many cannot, and ascribe the process to mysterious, occult, or religious influences. Skeptics pounce on this to discredit the entire dowsing enterprise.

Her theory of dowsing draws on parapsychological research and cutting edge science, including quantum physics. Basic to this is the concept of fields. The magnetic field of a magnet is the region of influence that extends beyond the magnet, that is invisible and yet exerts a force that has the ability to attract and pull towards it magnetic materials such as iron filings. In the same fashion leading thinkers, such as world renowned systems theorist Ervin Laszlo, believe there is a universal field of invisible energy that pervades all that exists and connects everything to everything else. For thousands of years mystics, sages, and philosophers also held this belief, which in the East was called the Akashic Field.

The way this works involves the concept of holograms. Basically, a hologram is a recording of an interference pattern. If that recording is in the form of a photograph it has strange properties. When a normal photograph is cut in half each piece shows half of the scene. When a hologram is cut in half the whole scene can still be seen in each piece. This is because, whereas each point in a photograph only represents light scattered from a single point in the scene, each point of a holographic recording includes information about light scattered from every point in the scene.

Lazlo explains that each of us humans, along with everything else that has ever existed, leave our holographic wave traces in the A (Akashic) field. This has gone on among generations after generations of humans, and the information in these holograms is available to be read out. The holograms generated by individuals become integrated in a kind of super hologram, which is the "encompassing hologram" of a tribal group, a community, or a culture. These collective holograms in turn interface and integrate with the "super-superhologram" of all people, forming the "collective in-formation pool of humankind" (Lazlo, 2007).

Brown points out that if the universe, our brains, our minds, and the embedded information are all holographic, then when dowsing we are not actually receiving instantaneous information from a location or subject hundreds of miles away that is being transmitted like a broadcast from a radio station. Rather, we are connecting to a holographic information field where everything is everywhere at the same time. We are already intrinsically connected to every part of the universe. An exchange of information in the question and answer process takes place when the dowser's brain/mind becomes tuned into or correlates with the quantum hologram that carries the information.

The information discerned by the dowser from either electromagnetic or A-fields is conducted via the body's signaling system, which manifests in the physical body via the neuromuscular system. This then prompts the minute unconscious physical responses that ultimately culminate in the movement of the dowsing tool (Brown, 2010).

We will discuss criticisms that have been leveled about dowsing, as well as psi phenomena, in the book's next section.

CHAPTER 16

CRITICISM OF PSI AND DOWSING

PSI

Much of the criticism of psi research stems from beliefs based in skepticism and scientism. Skepticism has to do with an attitude of doubt, a way of approaching a particular claim of knowledge with questions as to how certain, or accurate, or complete that knowledge really is. From the days of classical Greek and Roman philosophers to our contemporary world, skeptics have challenged accepted views in metaphysics, science, morals, and religion. Certainly there are things that are accepted as true that, in fact, may not be. Being a skeptic in relation to them is rational and sensible. Skeptics enjoy a high status role in intellectual circles. A skeptic is a smart person who does not just accept unquestioningly whatever is claimed to be true but investigates the evidence that supports that claim. To do so requires that the skeptic has real expertise in that area; that is, they are well grounded in the way research in that field is done and what has been discovered and verified through the scientific process.

The proper understanding and functioning of skepticism is greatly confused, though, by the existence and activities of numerous pseudoskeptics, people who claim to be skeptics but who are really adherents to and advocates of some other belief system that, they believe, already has all the necessary truth. Such pseudoskeptics call themselves skeptics because of the high prestige of that term.

In addition to the pseudoskeptics, consciousness researcher Charles Tart believes that one of the main obstacles in the pursuit of knowledge about our human existence and the reality in which we live is scientism, "a materialistic and arrogantly expressed philosophy of life that pretends to be the same as essential science but isn't." The term *scientism* is typically used to criticize a totalizing view of science that presumes science is capable of describing all reality and knowledge, or is the only true way to acquire knowledge about reality and the nature of things. Scientism is frequently used as a synonym for scientific imperialism, an attitude toward knowledge in which the beliefs and methods of science are assumed to be superior to and to take precedence over those of all other disciplines ("Scientism," *New World Encyclopedia*).

By posing as true science rather than a "limited belief system" scientism creates dangerous confusion. If someone tells us that his religion is the only truth and, according to it we are crazy, we could easily discount this because we would view the person as a fanatic. If someone is identified as a scientist and tells us our spiritual beliefs are quaint and old fashioned superstitions that long ago were shown to be false and that we should give them up to adjust to reality that would be much more difficult to discount (Tart, 2009).

From its outset psi research was and continues to be attacked in subtle and not so subtle ways, often by those holding pseudoskeptical and scientistic views. Some criticism has been biased and naïve, and some well-deserved. From the perspective of fundamentalist Christianity, psi type phenomena often involve "dark side" elements, spirits and demons, and "unhealthy" influences that it believes are best left alone. If, on the other hand, these are legitimate God-oriented spiritual phenomena then attempting to reduce them to the kinds of natural things that science can and should study diminishes them and their creator. From the perspective of science these phenomena are at best imaginative, or the result of fuzzy thinking, and to dignify them with the trappings of science diminishes all of science and feeds the kind of sloppy antiscientific bias many scientists believe our contemporary culture is prone to. Orthodox psychology does not look favorably on psychical research. Historically many leaders in the field worked hard to align themselves with science and often took an even more critical approach to supposed anomalies than their peers in the hard sciences. For the branch of the psi field that first attracted many of the early investigators—life after death—psychologists continued to point to one supposed bottom line fact: the brain produces consciousness. In recent years they believe studies of brain imaging and the full weight of cognitive science reinforces this fact. Whatever it is, if anything legitimate at all, that investigations of mediums, children's past lives memories, and near death experiences (NDEs) tell us, it is not that our personal consciousness survives the death of the body and brain. That is just not possible. End of story.

Early on, as we have seen, questionable and downright fraudulent activities of mediums attempting to cash in on the hugely popular interest in spiritualism were more often the rule than the exception. One of the main reasons to take psi investigation into the laboratory was to exercise better control and ensure more reliable data. Much of the more recent research in real life settings has been able to achieve at least the degree of objectivity characteristic in other types of field studies. However, such areas as near death studies involve reports of people describing their subjective experiences. We have no direct way to peer into their minds to see if what they say occurred really did, and if it did, precisely when. Unfortunately controversies continue to crop up that add fuel to the arguments of the skeptics.

Given the considerable public interest in psychic phenomena, I would not be surprised that someone who has reviewed the research presented here might wonder, "Why haven't I ever been exposed to this?" In *The Conscious Universe* Radin provides an excellent discussion as to why parapsychology or psychical research has encountered difficulties in making its findings known outside its own dedicated group.

Two main dynamics are at play. For many people the term parapsychology brings to mind an array of supposed unexplained, strange, and often spooky phenomena. Movies and cable television capitalize on our fascination with the paranormal to feature stories in which dramatic and often threatening things occur. Sometimes credulous investigators or ghostbuster types go around looking into these things. Although the phenomena often featured are quite dramatic, they do resemble in some ways unexplained things that actually happen in people's lives. Many people are likely to take these fictional stories as more or less real and are ready to believe in the existence of all kinds of strange things that may have little reality. The credulous true believers pose one type of threat to serious work in parapsychology. Supposed well-informed media commentators are quick to tell us we should hesitate to take these, and in fact any beliefs in psychic phenomena at face value.

Their hesitancy is supported by the other major impediment for psi researchers, the extreme or pseudoskeptics. Because of many people's gullibility a small number of very vocal skeptics have expressed alarm that the general public is being misled into accepting what they view as essentially nonsense. They see as the culprits those researchers whose investigations have produced findings supportive of the reality of psi. It is interesting in this regard that these skeptics do not vocally attack those scientists working in such fields as robotics because of fictionalized accounts of intelligent machines taking over the world or mainstream religion for things going on in such formerly popular television programs as *Touched by an Angel* or *Charmed*, which would also seem to be encouraging a belief in "nonsense."

The general public just does not typically get exposed to serious work in parapsychology. Instead, even those television programs that do present real paranormal phenomena often have a panel of experts that inevitably includes a vocal skeptic who can describe why the phenomena are not real and argue that those so-called experts who believe otherwise are naïve. The implication clearly is that the skeptic represents the voice of reason with whom the show's producers want to be associated. They would not want to alienate him and have him contact their large corporate sponsors.

The common stereotypes about psi research that get generated in this and many other ways, Radin emphasizes, are "overly simplistic at best and, in many cases, just plain wrong." As an example he quotes philosopher Paul Churchland, who in his 1984 book *Matter and Consciousness: A Contemporary Introduction to the Philosophy of Mind* made the statement:

> Despite the endless pronouncements and anecdotes in the popular press, and despite a steady trickle of serious research on such things, there is no significant or trustworthy evidence that such phenomena even exist. The wide gap between popular conviction on this matter, and the actual evidence, is something that itself calls for research. For there is not a single parapsychological effect that can be repeatedly or reliably produced in any laboratory suitably equipped to perform and control the experiment. Not one (Radin, 1997, p. 207).

As Radin points out this is just plain wrong. As he says, and as we have seen, a number of psi effects revealed in scientific studies have been replicated dozens to hundreds of times in laboratories around the world.

A few of those individuals Radin labels as extreme skeptics publicly label parapsychology as a pseudoscience, which implies fraud or incompetence on the part of the researchers. He quotes skeptical British psychologist David Marks, who in a commentary in the prominent journal *Nature*, March 1986, wrote:

> Parascience has all the qualities of a magical system while wearing the mantle of Science. Until any significant discoveries are made, science can justifiably ignore it, but it is important to say why: parascience is a pseudo-scientific system of untested beliefs steeped in illusion, error and fraud (in Radin, 1997, p. 208).

These opinions published in influential journals, Radin asserts, have made many funding agencies reluctant to sponsor parapsychological studies because they fear being associated with what conventional wisdom has declared a "pseudo science."

He points out that the same kind of vigorous debating that occurs in the other branches of science also occurs in the professional society of scientists and scholars interested in psi phenomena, the Parapsychological Association. However, the extreme critics that manage to make their voices heard do not come from that organization. In fact, the vast majority of this small group of armchair quarterbacks have not contributed any original research related to the field. They appear to operate from the assumption that if psi cannot exist then why should they bother to spend the time and money to study it? They then "use every rhetorical trick in the book" to convince us that they are correct and that any evidence to the contrary is somehow flawed.

The struggles of parapsychology for recognition also relate, Radin says, to a heavily distorted portrayal of these studies in the media and in college textbooks. He describes the 1985 work of psychologist Irvin Child, then at Yale University, who reviewed several academic books about psi research, including those authored by British psychologist Mark Hansel, psychologist James Alcock, and psychologists Leonard Zusne and Warren H. Jones. Child discovered one flawed description of the research the authors described after another, leading to his conclusion that these books contained "nearly incredible falsification of the facts about the experiments" (Radin, 1999).

Perhaps even more disturbing is the treatment of psi research in college introductory psychology textbooks, because they contain all the detail that most students will ever know about the field. Radin refers to the efforts of psychologist Miguel Roig and his colleagues who, in 1991, published a detailed analysis of the treatment of parapsychology in these textbooks.

Of the sixty-four textbooks they surveyed published between 1980 and 1989 one-third did not even mention the topic, although college students find it fascinating. Forty-three included some mention of parapsychology, but much of the coverage reflected a lack of familiarity with the field and displayed an unacceptable reliance on secondary sources, most of which were written by nonparapsychologist critics. Reflecting these sources, thirty-five of the forty-three mentioned lack of replication as the most serious problem, with poor experimental designs and fraud being the second and third most serious problems with the research. The textbooks typically concluded with a wait-and-see stance toward psychic phenomena (Radin, 1991).

Textbooks often rely on information published by the Committee for Skeptical Inquiry. Their intention, when it was started in 1976, was to submit a burgeoning number of psychic phenomena claims to scientific investigation. From its beginning it appears to have been dominated by anti-paranormal crusaders who were not particularly committed to the evenhanded investigation of paranormal claims (Schmicker, 2000).

The fact that a few extreme skeptics continue to loudly proclaim that after more than 130 years psychical research has not conclusively demonstrated the existence of any paranormal phenomena is indeed sad. That otherwise well-informed people take what they say without question is a serious obstacle for the advance of science and our understanding of who we are in the grand scheme of things.

One of the biggest obstacles for psychical research due to the various criticisms leveled against it is its lack of financial support. While large numbers of people believe in psi as real, they do not offer adequate dollars to fund the effort to help understand how it operates. It is illuminating to compare two specific scientific endeavors: the search to investigate subatomic phenomena and the question as to whether the Higgs Boson particle is real, and if so can it help unify the four elementary physical forces; and the search to discover if psi is real and, if so, whether it can help explain the experiences of deep connections and meanings that seem to go beyond our everyday lives.

In 2000 nine billion dollars was spent to develop the Large Hadron Collider (LHC) with the goal of answering the first question (Randall, 2011).

Gary Swartz provides an insider's look at his research into questions involving mediums and spirit. He talks about working on a shoestring budget. One very important piece of equipment costing $2,500 he characterizes as being "relatively affordable." Securing financial support was an ongoing challenge. Swartz mentions meeting with numerous potential donors over the years, with some giving "seminal" contributions. What these were in dollars and cents he does not say, but he is quite impressed when one person offered a $20,000 gift (Schwartz, 2011).

In 2012 scientists announced that the Higgs Boson had been discovered. Lawrence Krauss, in a piece in the *New York Times*, wrote that this capped "one of the most remarkable intellectual adventures in human history." (I certainly would be more impressed by a *New York Times* headline calling any one of the discoveries in psychic or spiritual research "one of the most remarkable intellectual adventures in human history" than the headline announcing the discovery of one esoteric subatomic particle not even visible to the human eye.)

One of the major criticisms that has been leveled against psychical research throughout its 130-year history is its lack of a scientifically accepted explanatory theoretical model. Without such an underpinning the critics have said that psi can be viewed as something supported only as a belief, allowing it to remain pretty much ignored by science on the par with astrology. In fact, several such theories have been put forward that are discussed by Chris Carter in his 2012 book *Science and Psychic Phenomena*. Space here does not permit discussing these, but we did look at a theory of dowsing offered by Elizabeth Miller.

DOWSING

Despite the large amount of published literature attesting to the usefulness of dowsing for finding a very wide range of things and businesses and organizations investing large amounts of money in this endeavor, the science community has continued to criticize it. They do recognize that successful results from dowsing have been widely reported, however, they believe these can be explained within a scientific framework. Several views have been put forward.

One is that the dowsing tool is simply responding to the random movements of the person holding the rods. When water dowsing seems to work, it most often does so in areas where there is so much groundwater close to the surface that any location will yield a productive well. A widely held view in the science community involves ideomotor phenomenon, a psychological response where a subject makes motions unconsciously. Another involves the expectancy effect. When someone (a dowser) expects a given result that expectation unconsciously affects the outcome or report of the expected result.

Most damning, according to the skeptics, involves the results of scientific tests that have failed to find positive results. Associate Professor of Physics at West Texas A&M University

Christopher S. Baird points out that various controlled scientific studies over the last hundred years have repeatedly found that water dowsing does not work (Baird, 2024). Professor of Psychology at the University of London Chris French has noted that "dowsing does not work when it is tested under properly controlled conditions that rule out the use of other cues to indicate target location." Science writer Peter Daempfle asserts that when dowsing is subjected to scientific testing it fails. The Wikipedia article on dowsing maintains that "the scientific evidence shows that dowsing is no more effective than random chance. It is therefore regarded as a pseudoscience."

Brown herself readily acknowledges that dowsing does not typically respond well to official testing. It is perfectly possible to obtain accurate results in the field when and where there is a genuine need, but frequently dowsing fails abjectly when tested under controlled conditions.

Several factors, she says, contribute to dowsing's poor performance under scrutiny. The first is loss of focus. Being tested in a television studio is the antithesis of a relaxed and calm setting. Even the most focused individual can have their concentration undermined by the movement of a camera or when a film crew appears. From her years of dowsing experience, as well as a previous career filming more than 200 television commercials, she finds it extremely challenging to dowse as television cameras scrutinize her every move. This scrutiny unconsciously puts the dowser's body on alert. Dowsing requires the flow of energy through a relaxed and happy body.

The negative impact of disrupted focus on dowsing is on display in a film on YouTube featuring Clive Thompson, ex-president of the British Society of Dowsers. He was challenged to prove dowsing does indeed work by the stage magician and professional debunker James Randi. For years Randi has made a living from the exposure of alleged charlatans, frauds, and tricksters.

Randi put up one million dollars for anyone who can show "under proper observing conditions, evidence of any paranormal, supernatural or occult power or event." Dowsing he claimed fits into this category. His online newsletter called it "a medieval notion, a crackpot idea, and a phenomenon that has zero evidence to support it."

Psychologist and parapsychologist Michael E. Thalbourne pointed out Randi had "a reputation among parapsychologists as an unduly vociferous and occasionally irrational skeptic possessed of an unfortunate tendency to distort the truth so as to obtain favorable publicity for himself and his crusade against psi" ("Science versus Showmanship: A History of the Randi Hoax" the *Journal of the American Society of Psychical Research* in 1995).

Brown interviewed Thompson about his testing experience. Prior to filming he was kept waiting alone for over two hours in a tiny, cramped room. He was shown the studio set up and then returned to his room. When he was invited back out to film he found everything was set up in a completely different way. Surprised, confused, and disorientated, with little information and no support, he felt unable to concentrate and, in his own words, "not in a fit condition" to dowse. His dowsing performance suffered and he was only able to locate the object of the search on the third attempt. Randi proclaimed that this was no better than what would be expected by chance.

Another factor contributing to a dowser's poor testing performance may well involve the fear of failure. Having to perform under testing, fear of failure, and the emotional need to prove something one believes in disturbs the relaxed and happy physical, mental, and emotional state that is absolutely essential to dowsing.

There is, Brown notes, a third factor that is detrimental to testing dowsing under controlled conditions: the potentially negative input from the instigators, organizers, or witnesses involved in the testing. This may not be conscious or deliberate, as in the case of Randi's tests, but nevertheless influences the dowers. Another clip on YouTube features a series of dowsing tests administered by Chris French. A group of volunteer dowsers is put through scientifically designed double-blind tests to identify the location of a single plastic bottle of water from five plastic bottles filled with sand. They systematically failed, resulting in palpable shock. French, when interviewed by Brown, confirmed that the final results were exactly chance level. This was what he had expected to find under controlled conditions.

Despite the perspective offered by Brown, the fact of the matter is that the poor results of testing under controlled laboratory conditions is plenty enough support for skeptics to maintain that dowsing can't actually work because the science says it doesn't.

CONCLUDING REMARKS

The wide range of paranormal phenomena we have discussed that science tries to tell us are not real, but that many have personally experienced in their lives, holds great importance in many respects. They tell us that they are part of the overall structure of reality; they are an aspect of what is. Good science has as a basic goal to strive to better understand what that reality entails. The fact that most scientists do not recognize paranormal research as legitimate speaks to a lack of their vision, not science itself.

Because of the strong stance of most scientists that the paranormal phenomena we have discussed are not real because they do not play by the same rules governing the physical universe, people are left with questions about their own psychic experiences and what they may say about their rationality, and even basic sanity. Hopefully our discussion has laid these concerns to rest.

PSI

Accepting that psi phenomena are indeed real raises some challenging questions. When it comes to the study of psychic phenomena we can group them into two main types: strong psi and weak psi. Most people have some degree of weak psi ability. Spouses often tune in to their partner's thoughts. However, the psi phenomena that show up in laboratory studies, usually with nonrelated subjects, often are so weak as to be only detectable with large numbers of subjects participating in large numbers of trials. Statistically these studies show that in comparison to chance, given enough data astoundingly high rates of success can be demonstrated. But we are not talking about anything remotely resembling the psychic powers exhibited by fictional television characters.

Outside the lab, the relatively rare appearance of these same phenomena can seem much more robust, since some few individuals do have much greater strong psi ability. The whole topic of mind over matter (psychokinesis, or PK) is particularly challenging and presents troubling moral and legal issues, as well as serious threats to the whole scientific enterprise. If it is something more than a very small and rare force as observed in the laboratory, as suggested by accounts of Ted Owens and Jack Houck's bent spoons, then there are quite profound implications.

What if, for a scientific experiment, the results appearing on computer printouts were actually unintentionally caused by experimenter PK? Suppose this were to happen even once in physics research, such as the multi-billion dollar successful search for the Higgs Boson particle? If the results were revealed to have been the product of PK shock waves would have been sent through the physics community. Perhaps mercifully we would never know. If PK can happen in the lab, how might scientists protect their work against it? What if people with strong PK abilities are actually able to directly influence the minds and behavior of unsuspecting victims? Our legal structure does not recognize this possibility.

Most people who heard about Owens disregarded his claims as being ridiculous and labeled him as a crank, or worse. Yet I suspect the willingness to disregard Owens for this reason offered a convenient rationale to avoid the implications if he were to be taken seriously. I recall a line from Jack Nicholson's character, Colonel Jessep, in the movie *A Few Good Men*. When asked about potentially suspect military activities Jessep snapped, "You want the truth? You can't handle the truth!" Can we handle what might be the truth here? Are we willing to look even if the likelihood of strong PK seems remote?

Precognition or foreknowledge is just as troublesome as mind over matter. Most basically it violates the commonsense assumption that time flows strictly in one direction from the past, to the present, to the future. If precognition is in fact real its effects on our daily lives could be seriously disruptive. In the world of business, one could use precognition to do a kind of super insider trading. Any one of us with strong precognition could pick a winning lottery ticket. Precognition poses a number of murky philosophical questions, most notably the issue of free will. If we have foreknowledge about something then it would seem a course of events involving it is fixed, or predetermined. If we see the future are we locked into acting out the preview? And if not, and we do act to change the future that we have glimpsed, then could it really be the future since it did not actually happen? There is abundant anecdotal evidence, as well as at least one study from the 1950s that we looked at that suggests sometimes people are able to use premonitions of some future tragedy to avoid that situation.

As with the other classical types of ESP, telepathy, and clairvoyance, the possibility of strong abilities also poses serious difficulties. As a diplomat or business person it certainly would be advantageous to know what those I am dealing with are thinking. It would not be so nice if they could read my mind as well. It is hard to imagine how we could interact with others if our minds were completely transparent. As a military commander it would be hugely advantageous to clairvoyantly see into enemy research facilities, but again, not for them to see into mine.

As long as we confine our investigations of ESP and PK to laboratory conditions during which observed effects are very small and at the same time laugh off reports of strong psi in the real world as impossible we have been able to keep the psi genie in the bottle. Can we afford to continue to do so?

Recall in our discussion of the history of psychical research that in the second decade of the twentieth century there was an abrupt change of direction, with efforts shifting from investigations of life after death issues and mediums to laboratory based study of ESP and PK. Although ninety years of very good research have demonstrated to the unbiased and knowledgeable observer that these phenomena exist, this fact has not moved the staunch opposition of the science community. It is too easy to disregard the data that shows up only statistically as very small variations from chance. It has frequently been said that unusual claims require unusual evidence, certainly when those claims violate established scientific laws. And because science is viewed by the public as the final arbiter regarding what is really real then this work does not appear in college textbooks and does not attract public research dollars.

There are a few things we could do to further paranormal research. If sufficient funding were available we could establish a team to review the sensationalized and likely untrue reports of the behavior of psychics or psi phenomena in the popular media displayed at the checkout line of grocery stores. Even if only one account in fifty at first glance seems to have any substance we could send an investigator to take a closer look. From this a few genuine appearing accounts could then be identified and formally investigated.

Recall that in remote viewing research one of the most talented viewers, Joe McMoneagle, was initially discovered on the basis of a profile of individuals who might be good remote viewing subjects put together by the military. He was flown to California, and after passing preliminary remote viewing experiments with flying colors began an eighteen-year career as a remote viewer in a secret Army project that came to be called Star Gate. An advertisement could be placed in newspapers asking for self-identified psychics to respond. Screening assessments could be constructed for different forms of psi, then they could be administered to the more promising respondents. These individuals could then be formally investigated.

A number of paranormal events are regularly televised. Sunday morning channel surfing will turn up religious services featuring charismatic preachers laying on hands to bring about seeming instantaneous cures among the faithful. It seems possible to locate believers who would be willing to demonstrate their preacher's power. They could be carefully screened as to their medical condition before going forward in a service to be healed. Following this, they could again be screened to note any changes. If changes are observed these might well be attributed to the power of belief, and not something paranormal. Even so, the finding would be highly significant.

More direct action could be taken to influence college textbook publishers to provide accurate information about psychical research. Perhaps a petition drive might work calling for this, say in introductory psychology texts. There are online organizations that provide assistance with this. Membership lists of those belonging to organizations featuring psychical research could be consulted and members encouraged to sign such a petition. Petitions could also be sent to college and university administrators asking that they establish relevant courses in psychical research. Student organizations might also support this effort.

Among the many accounts of unusual phenomena we have discussed, none comes close to the things Ted Owens supposedly did in terms of appearing flat out impossible. If Mishlove still has the materials in his files that he drew on in writing *PK Man* it would seem imperative that an impartial individual or team take another careful look. This is not because Mishlove should be suspected of playing loose with the facts, but because the whole account is simply too important to be allowed to fade from memory with no further commentary.

SPIRITS

People around the world, for many thousands of years, have been involved with spirits for religious purposes and to seek their assistance. A major kind of assistance has been for health related difficulties. In modern times medicine has replaced spirits, and health care has evolved into a vast number of specialties in both physical and mental health areas. In terms of the latter, currently nearly one in five American adults will have a diagnosable mental health condition in any given year. Over half with a mental illness receive no treatment.

People experiencing mental health difficulties who do seek treatment have two options: medication and psychotherapy. Roughly speaking, they seem to be equal in terms of effectiveness, and this the research tells us is not outstanding, perhaps 70%. Medication shows more immediate results in improving symptoms, but in the long term psychotherapy works better because it can teach more effective ways for people to manage their lives; that is, improve their mental health.

To work psychotherapy requires time and a number of sessions with a therapist. Psychologist Paul Clemont, who carefully tracked measures to determine the effectiveness of his psychotherapy for forty-five years, found that approximately 82% of his patients completed therapy within twenty-five sessions and the mean number of sessions per patient was 18.82. He characterized the majority of his practice as consisting of what the literature identifies as "short term therapy" (Clemont, 2013).

In our discussion of spirits and help achieved from them we encountered a number of practices. Some occurred within a religious context, such as Lakota Sioux medicine, and some did not require that the help seeker have any particular belief system other than hope it might work, such as releasement therapy.

In terms of the latter, a comparison between it and conventional psychotherapy is illuminating. With releasement therapy the client's problem is typically resolved in one session, not twenty, although it is important to note that, for the most part, in reports of releasement therapy only successes are mentioned. In conventional psychotherapy, even the form called brief therapy, one-session cures rarely occur.

Traditional healers working with spirit assistance, such as shamans, do not see the need to prove their effectiveness. If they did not help people no one would seek them out. Releasement therapists who help people by ridding them of negative attaching spirits are able to attract clients because what they do works. The very large numbers of people with mental health difficulties do not pursue this form of therapy. Most have probably not heard of it. As we have discussed many times, science says spirits, positive or negative, are not real. Any form of help involving them, if it appears to work, must do so for other reasons.

In an attempt to help remove the stigma associated with spirit related healing and make it more visible and available, research studies of its effectiveness could be conducted along the lines of those done with psychotherapy. Clermont asked his patients to complete scales rating the effectiveness of their therapy in resolving or improving the problem that was dealt with. The same could be done with such approaches as releasement therapy.

OTHER PARANORMAL PHENOMENA

There is a breathtaking abundance of information available to us if we remove the shackles of the scientific materialist perspective. This information may come to us spontaneously or be deliberately sought. In terms of the latter, use of psychedelics is one of the most effective and well-documented approaches. Although recently there has been a resumption of psychedelic research it has focused on therapeutics, not on gaining information about ourselves and our broader reality.

Today we live in a seriously challenged world, whether we think of "world" as the physical planet Earth or as a collective term for the society, politics, and culture of those of us modern people who live on it. Historically, when challenges have arisen, our creative juices have been stirred and we have undertaken efforts on many fronts to meet them. Currently there seems to be a sense among large numbers of people in this country that the challenges are beyond our individual capacities to resolve and perhaps beyond the collective capacity of our government as well. Every day we see this playing out in our lives in obvious and not so obvious ways, in an increase in mistrust of our leaders, anger and conflict in our interactions with one another, and underlying anxiety rooted in a sense that we are losing control of our lives. The institutions and values that have sustained us throughout our history as a nation appear to be crumbling. We badly need the insights available from what are unfortunately viewed as paranormal sources.

BIBLIOGRAPHY

"A Course in Miracles." https://en.wikipedia.org/wiki/A_Course_in_Miracles.

Alexander, E. Proof of Heaven. New York: Simon & Schuster, 2013.

Allen Kardec. https://en.Wikipedia.org/wiki/Allan_Kardec.

Allitt, P. "The Second Great Awakening." Lecture 8 American Religious History. Chantilly, VA: The Teaching Company, 2001.

Almeder, R. Death and Personal Survival. Lanham MD: Rowman and Littlefield, 1992.

An Introduction to Maria Voltorta and her Epic Narrative The Poem of the Man-God. http://www.valtorta-maria.com/Pages/003_Valepic.htm.

Armstrong, K. A History of God. New York: Balantine Books, 2011.

Baird, C. The Top 50 Science Questions with Surprising Answers, Faradays Flame: Los Angeles, CA , 2024.

Baldwin, W. Healing Lost Souls: Releasing Unwanted Spirits from Your Energy Body. Newburyport, MA: Hampton Roads Publishing. Kindle Edition, 2023.

"Baptism for the Dead." Wikipedia. https://en.Wikipedia.org/wiki/Baptism_for_the_dead.

Bass, D. Christianity After Religion: The End of the Church and the Birth of a New Spiritual Awakening. New York: Harper Collins, 2012.

Beischel, J. Investigating Mediums. Tucson, AZ: The Windbridge Institute, LLC, 2015.

Blum, D. Ghost Hunters. New York: the Penguin Group, 2006.

Borg, M. Jesus: A New Vision. New York: HarperCollins e-books, 2009.

Botkin, A. Induced After Death Communications. Charlottesville, VA: Hampton Roads Publishing, 2005.

Braude, S. Immortal Remains. Lanham MD: Rowman and Littlefield, 2004.

Brown, E. Dowsing: The Ultimate Guide for the 21st Century. Hay House: Carlsbad, CA, 2010.

Brown, J. E. The Sacred Pipe: Black Elk's Account of the Seven Rites of the Oglala Sioux. Norman, OK: University of Oklahoma Press, 1989.

Clemont, P. "Practice-Based Evidence: 45 Years of Psychotherapy's Effectiveness in a Private Practice" American Journal of Psychotherapy, Volume 67, Number 1, 2013.

Cook, P. Deliverance From Evil Spirits. Online Books Redbag.com. http://www.readbag.com/porn-free-pdf-deliverance-course, 2015.

Crabtree, A. Therapy for Possession, in Regression Therapy, vol II, Deep Forrest Press: Palo Alto, CA, 1993.

Cumeo, M. *American Exorcism: Expelling Demons in the Land of Plenty.* New York: Broadway Books, 2002.

Deloria, V. Jr. God is Red. Westminster MD: Penguin Adult HC/TR, 1973.

Dossey, L. Power of Premonitions. New York: Dutton, 2009.

"Eban Alexander." Wikipedia. https://en.Wikipedia.org/wiki/Eben_Alexander_(author).

"Edgar Cayce." Wikipedia. http://en.Wikipedia.org/wiki/Edgar_Cayce.

Ehrman, B. "Christianity and the Conquest of Empire." Lecture 24 From Jesus to Constantine, Chantilly, VA: The Teaching Company, 2004.

Ehrman. B. *How Jesus Became God.* New York: HarperCollins, 2014.

"Eleventh Panchen Lama Controversy." Wikipedia. https://en.Wikipedia.org/wiki/11th_Panchen_Lama_controversy.

Eliade M. *The Myth of the Eternal Return.* Princeton: Princeton University Press, 2005.

Fenwick, P. & E. *Past Lives.* New York: Berkley Publishing Group, 2001.

Fenwick, P. *The Art of Dying.* New York: Bloomsbury Academic, 2008.

Fenwick, P. "Science and Spirituality," IANDS Research Articles. Accessed 2015. http://iands.org/research/nde-research/important-research-articles/42-dr-peter-fenwick-md-science-and-spirituality.html?showall=&start=6.

Fiore, E. The Unquiet Dead. New York: Ballantine Books, 1995.

Fontana, D. Is There an Afterlife? Ropley Hants, UK: Deershot Lodge, 2005.

Gallup, G. Adventures in Immortality. Ashland, OH: McGraw Hill, 1982.

Gallup. "Belief in the Paranormal." Accessed 2005. http://www.gallup.com/topic/all_gallup_headlines.aspx.

Grof, S. Adventure of Self-Discovery. Albany, New York: State University of New York Press, 1988.

Grof, S. Holotropic Mind. San Francisco: Harper, 1993.

Guggenheim, W. and J. Guggenheim. Hello From Heaven. New York: Bantam, 1997.

Hanegraaff, W. New Age Religion and Western Culture. New York: State University of New York Press, 1998.

Harner, M. Cave and Cosmos. Berkley CA: North Atlantic Books, 2013.

Harner, M. The Way of the Shaman. New York: HarperOne, 1990

IANDS. "Distressing Near-Death Experiences." http//www.iands.org/distressing.html.

Illes. J. *Encyclopedia of Spirits: The Ultimate Guide to the Magic of Fairies, Genies, Demons, Ghosts, Gods & Goddesses.* New York: HarperOne, 2010.

"In search of the real Panchen Lama." Accesed 2010. SMH, http://www.phayul.com/news/article.aspx?id=27669.

Ireland-Frey, L. "Clinical Depossession." *in Regression Therapy*, vol II. Crest Park: Deep Forrest Press, 1993.

James, W. *Varieties of Religious Experience.* New York: Longmans, Green, 1916.

Johnson, L. "What Is Religion," Lecture II, Early Christianity: The Experience of the Divine, Chantilly, VA: The Teaching Company, 2002.

Johnson, L. "Glossolalia and the Embarrassments of Experience." Lecture XV Early Christianity: The Experience of the Divine, Chantilly, VA: The Teaching Company, 2002.

Johnson, LT. "Mystical Traditions: Judaism, Christianity, and Islam." Lectures 4–13. Chantilly, VA: The Teaching Company, 2008.

Kardec, A. *The Spirits' Book: Revised Edition. (*3rd ed.). Spiritist Educational Society: Thousand Oaks, CA, (August 29, 2019).

Keating, R. *The Ultimate Guide to Shamanism*. Beverly, MA: Fair Winds Press, 2021.

Keen, M. "The Ultimate Psychic Challenge—A Challenge to James Randi." Letter by Montague Keen to Assistant Producer of "Living with the Dead." http://www.survivalafterdeath.info/articles/keen/randi.htm.

Kelly, Edward & Emily. Irreducible Mind. Lanham MD: Rowman and Littlefield, 2006.

Klimo, J. Channeling. Berkley, CA: North Atlantic Books, 1998.

Koestler, The Invisible Writing. Boston: Beacon, 1954.

Lame Deer, J. F. Lame Deer Seeker of Visions. New York: Simon & Schuster, 1972.

Layton, J. "How Exorcism Works." http://science.howstuffworks.com/science-vs-myth/afterlife/exorcism.htm.

Lazlo, E. Science and the Akashic Field: An Integral Theory of Everything. Rochester, VT: Inner Traditions, 2007.

Leonard, T. J. Talking to the Other Side Lincoln NE: iUniverse, 2015.

Long, J. & B. Bernstein. Dutch NDE Study Attracts Worldwide Attention. Accessed 2015. http://iands.org/research/nde-research/important-research-articles/464-dutch-nde-study-attracts-worldwide-attention.html.

Lucas, W. Regression Therapy: A Handbook for Professionals. Crest Park, CA: Deep Forrest Press, 1993.

Lumbley, S. "Exorcism: Ancient Art or Hocus Pocus?" Accessed 2006. http://www.religionnewsblog.com/14664/exorcism-ancient-art-or-hocus-pocus.

MacNutt, F. Deliverance from Evil Spirits: A Practical Manual. Baker Publishing Group, 2009.

Magic: "Supernatural phenomenon." (last updated 2016) In Encyclopedia Britannica Online. https://www.britannica.com/topic/magic-supernatural-phenomenon.

Mayer, E. Extraordinary Knowing. New York: Bantam, 2007.

McClenon, J., M. Roig, Matthew D. Smith, G. Ferrier."The Coverage of Parapsychology in Introductory Psychology Textbooks:1990–2002," The Journal of Parapsychology Spring 2003.

Meek, G. *After We Die What Then?* London: Ariel Press, 1998.

Mcgaa, E. *Mother Earth Spirituality: Native American Paths to Healing Ourselves.* San Francisco: HarperOne, 2011.

Melton, J. "Pentacostalism," Encyclopaedia Britannica.

Miller, A. "Dowsing: a review.—Network." https://explore.scimednet.org/wp-content/uploads/2016/05/article1-4.pdf.

Mishlove, J. "Thinking Allowed." interview with Nancy Tramont.

Mishlove, J. "Introduction." *The Human Personality and Its Survival of Bodily Death.* Charlottesville, VA: Hampton Roads Publishing, 2001.

Mishlov, J. *The PK Man: A True Story of Mind Over Matter.* Charlottesville, VA: Hampton Roads Publishing, 2000.

Mohatt, G. & Eagle Elk, J. The Price of a Gift. Lincoln: University of Nebraska Press, 2000.

Moody, R. Life After Life. New York: HarperCollins, 2001.

Moore, D. "Three in Four Americans Believe in Paranormal." Gallup News Service. ://www.gallup.com/poll/16915/Radin, D., 2005.

Murphy, M. The Future of the Body. New York: G.P .Putnam's Sons, 1992.

Newton , M. *Destiny of Souls.* St. Paul MN: Llewellyn Publications, 2000.

Newton, M. Journey of Souls. St. Paul MN: Llewellyn Publications, 2010.

Osis, K. and E. Haraldsson. At The Hour Of Death. New York: Avon, 1977.

"Out-of-Body Experience." Wikipedia. https://en.Wikipedia.org/wiki/Out-of-body_experience.

Olson, Bob. "Answers About the Afterlife." http://www.answersabouttheafterlife.com/.

Paranormal America 2018 Chapman University Survey of American Fearsblogs.chapman.edu/wilkinson/2018/10/16/paranormal-america-2018/).

Parnia, S. and J. Young. Erasing Death. San Francisco, CA: HarperOne, 2013.

Passer, M. and Smith, R. Psychology: Science of Mind and Behavior. Ashland, OH: McGraw Hill Education, 2013.

Prabhavananda & Manchester 1957 in Kelly E. Irreducible Mind. Lanham MD: Rowman and Littlefield, 2006.

Quimby, S. Psychedelics: A Full Story: Yesterday, Today, and Tomorrow. New York: Austin Macauley, 2023.

Radin, D. The Conscious Universe. San Francisco: HarperOne, 1997.

Radin, D. Entangled Minds. New York: Simon & Schuster, 2009.

Randall, L. Knocking on Heaven's Door. Alexandria, MN: Echo Press, 2011.

RavenWolf To Ride a Silver Broomstick. St. Paul MN: Llewellyn Publications, 2012.

"Reincarnation." Wikipedia. https://en.Wikipedia.org/wiki/Reincarnation.

"Religion Facts, Christianity on the Afterlife." http://www.religionfacts.com/christianity/afterlife.

Research Scales Used to Classify an NDE : the Greyson Scale, Horizon Research Foundation Near Death Experiences Series, Article 14.

Ring, K. *Mindsight.* Bloomington, IN: iUniverse, 2008.

Ritchie, G. Return From Tomorrow. Ada, M : Revell-Baker Publishing Group, 1996.

Roberts, J. Adventures in Consciousness: An Introduction to Aspect Psychology. Needham, MA: Moment Point Press, 2005.

Roberts, J. The Seth Material. New York: New Awareness Network, Inc., 2011.

Robinson, B. "Demonic Possession, Demonic Oppression, & Exorcism." Accessed January 20, 2014. Religious Tolerance.orghttp://www.religioustolerance.org/chr_exor9.

Robinson, B.A. Purgatory, Ontario Consultants on Religious Tolerance. Accessed 2008. http://www.religioustolerance.org/purgatory.htm.

Robinson, J. *Honest to God.* London: SCM Press, 2011.

Rommer, B. *Blessings in Disguise.* St. Paul MN: Llewellyn Publications, 2000.

Ruiz, T. "The World of Witches." Lecture XXI, The Terror of History, Course Guidebook, Chantilly, VA: The Teaching Company, 2002.

Russell, B. 1935/1974 in Kelly E. *Irreducible Mind.* Lanham MD: Rowman and Littlefield, 2006.

"Salem witch trials." Wikipedia. http://en.Wikipedia.org/wiki/Salem_witch_trials.

Schmicker, M. *Best Evidence.* Lincoln, NE: Writers Club Press, 2000.

Schucman, H. *A Course in Miracles Volume II Two Workbook for Students.* Temecula, CA: Foundation for Inner Peace, 2007/

Schwartz, G. *The Sacred Promise.* New York: Atria Books, 2011.

Schwartz, G. *The Afterlife Experiments: Breakthrough Scientific Evidence of Life After Death.* New York: Atria Books, 2002.

"Shakers." (last updated Jan 2017.) Wikipedia. http:/en.Wikipedia.org/wiki/Shakers].

Smith, S. "Preface." *The Human Personality and Its Survival of Bodily Death.* Charlottesville, VA: Hampton Roads Publishing, 2001.

Soloman, S. quoted in "Death Denial," Marc Parry, M. Accessed June 22, 2015. *The Chronicle of Higher Education.* http://www.chronicle.com/article/Mortal-Motivation/230303.

Solomon, S., Greenberg, J. and Pyszczynsk, T. *The Worm at the Core: On the Role of Death in Life.* New York: Random House, 2015.

"Spiritism." Wikipedia https://en.wikipedia.org/wiki/Spiritism.

"Spiritualism." Wikipedia. https://en.Wikipedia.org/wiki/Spiritualism.

Stevens, J. Storming Heaven. New York: Grove Press, 1987.

Stevenson, I., Pasricha, S. & N. McClean-Rice. "A Case of the Possession Type in India with Evidence of Paranormal Knowledge." Journal of Scientific Exploration 3, pp. 89–109, 1989.

Stevenson, I. *Twenty Cases Suggestive of Reincarnation.* Charlottesville, VA: University of Virginia Press, 1980.

Steiner, R. *Theosophy: An introduction to the supersensible knowledge of the world and the destination of man.* E- Bookarama, 2024.

Storm, H. *Lessons Learned.* Archway Publishing Bloomington, IN, 2014.

Storm, H. *My descent into death and the message of love which brought me back.* East Sussex: Temple Lodge Publishing, 2001.

Sugrue, T. *Story of Edgar Cayce: There Is a River.* Virginia Beach, VA: A.R.E. Press, 1997.

Tarnas, R. *The Passion of the Western Mind.* New York: Crown Publishers, Inc., 1991.

Tart, C. *The End of Materialism.* Oakland CA: New Harbinger Publications. 2009.

Tart, C. *States of Consciousness.* New York: Backinprint, 2001.

TenDam, H. *Exploring Reincarnation: The Classic Guide to the Evidence for Past-life Experiences,* [[company]] 2017.

The Complete Bible; An American Translation. Chicago: University of Chicago Press, 1948.

"The Fox Sisters and the Rap on Spiritualism." A *Smithsonian Magazine* special report. https://www.smithsonianmag.com/history/the-fox-sisters-and-the-rap-on-spiritualism-99663697/.

"The Process of Beatification & Canonization." https://www.ewtn.com/johnpaul2/cause/process.asp.

Tucker, J. *Return to Life: Extraordinary Cases of Children Who Remember Past Lives.* New York: St. Martins Press, 2013.

Turner, A. The History of Hell. San Diego: Harcourt Brace, 1993.

Underhill, 1911 in Kelly E. Irreducible Mind. Lanham MD: Rowman and Littlefield. 2006.

Unger, C. *Fall of the House of Bush.* New York: Charles Scribner's Sons, 2012.

Valtorta, *The Poem of the Man God.* Centro Edittoriale Valtortiano, 1986.

VanZant, L. L. "Astronomical Dating of "The Poem of the Man-God." Accessed 1994. Lafayette, IN, https://engineering.purdue.edu/~zak/Van_Zandt.pdf].

"Vedas" Wikipedia. https://en.Wikipedia.org/wiki/Vedas.

Wasson, RG. "Seeking the Magic Mushroom." Originally published Life Magazine 1957, The Psychedelic Library. http://psychedelic-library.org/lifep2.htm.

Webster, D. "Maria Valtorta Was an Eye-Witness to the First Century Ministry of Our Lord Jesus! Her Numerous Strikingly Accurate Descriptions of First Century Palestine Prove it." Accessed 2004. http://www.saveourchurch.org/descriptionspoem.pdf].

Weiss, B. Healing Through Time. New York: Touchtone, 2012.

Whitton, J. "Gaining Wisdom in the Life between Life," Regression Therapy: A Handbook for Professionals. vol II. Crest Park, CA: Deep Forrest Press, 1993.

Wiebe, P. Visions of Jesus: Direct Encounters from the New Testament to Today. Abilene, TX: Leafwood Publishers, 1998.

"Wicca." Wikipedia. https://en.Wikipedia.org/wiki/Wicca.

Wilkinson, T. (2007). The Vatican's Exorcists. New York: Grand Central Publishing, 2007.

Williams, K. "People Have Near-Death Experiences While Brain Dead." Accessed 2014. Near Death Experiences and the Afterlife. http://www.near-death.com/science/evidence/people-have-ndes-while-brain-dead.html.

"Witchcraft." Catholic Encyclopedia. http://www.catholic.org/encyclopedia/view.php?id=12422.

Youngblood, E. "Where Did They Hide the Bodies? The Population Problem," The Journal of Regression Therapy. Volume 13, Number 1, 1999.

SCOTT QUIMBY, after attending the University of Vermont with a major in English and religion and working as a social worker and high school teacher, earned a PhD in counseling and psychology from Purdue University. Following graduation, he taught four years at Sinte Gleska University on the Rosebud Sioux Reservation, where he worked closely with local Lakota medicine men. For the next sixteen years he taught a wide range of mental health courses at Northern Kentucky University. The next phase of his career involved work for twenty years as a clinical psychologist in Ohio juvenile and adult prisons. Since retiring Scott has published five books: Help for a Troubled Time, Alternative Resources for Our Challenged World, Psychedelics: A Full Story, Going Home, and Investigating the Unexplained. Scott has been interested in paranormal experiences and human possibilities for fifty years. He lives with his wife, Sally, in northeastern Tennessee.